Journal of the Australian Catholic Historical Society

Volume 41 2020

Journal of the Australian Catholic Historical Society

Volume 41 2020

Era of Growth: The Late Nineteenth Century

Saint Mary's Church, Mudgee, Built 1876

Adelaide
2020

General Correspondence, including membership applications and renewals, and Journal submissions should be addressed to

The Secretary
ACHS
PO Box A621
Sydney South, NSW, 1235
Enquiries may also be directed to:
secretaryachs@gmail.com
http://australiancatholichistoricalsociety.com.au/

Editor: James Franklin
Editorial control and subscriptions remain with the Australian Catholic Historical Society

ISBN: 978-1-922582-20-1 soft
978-1-922582-21-8 hard
978-1-922582-22-5 epub
978-1-922582-23-2 pdf

JACHS ISSN: 0084-7259

Cover image:
Saint Mary's Church, Mudgee, NSW, Photo, G Lupp 2011
See article starting on page 45

Published by:

An imprint of the ATF Press Publishing
Group owned by ATF (Australia) Ltd.
PO Box 234
Brompton, SA 5007
Australia
ABN 90 116 359 963
www.atfpress.com
Making a lasting impact

Journal of the Australian Catholic Historical Society, Volume 41/2020

Contents

Journal of the Australian Catholic Historical Society, Volume 41/2020

Bicentenary of our First Official Priests: Fr Philip Conolly and Fr John Joseph Therry

*Edmund Campion**

For Tony Baine

On the third of May 1820, the ship *Janus* sailed into Sydney Harbour with two Irish priests as passengers, Fr Philip Conolly, aged thirty-four, a Maynooth College man, and Fr John Joseph Therry, aged thirty. They were our first official priests. Fr Therry's story is well-known: he said he would stay here for four years and in fact he remained for forty-four years, dying in 1864 as pastor of Balmain in Sydney. By then, Balmain was a settled parish such as we knew until just the other day: daily Mass, weekly confessions and Sunday night devotions.

Fr Conolly's story is somewhat different. When he died, nineteen years after arriving here, he had been suspended *a divinis*, that is barred by the Bishop from saying Mass, preaching, celebrating the sacraments and struck off the government's list of chaplains and so without a settled income. Therry was by his bedside to give him the last rites and then to bury him, putting on his gravestone the psalmists's doleful lament, 'My days have declined like a shadow and I am withered like grass.' (Ps 101:12)

The two priests began together in Sydney and after ten months Conolly sailed to Hobart, where his initial Mass drew nine worshippers. He stayed with Edward Curr, a Catholic storekeeper who would become a nabob, accorded a long entry in the *Australian Dictionary of Biography*. The Lieutenant-Governor gave Conolly five acres on the edge of town to build a church and presbytery. Within six months he had raised nearly 100 pounds, so he built a house with a lean-to chapel attached to it.

* Edmund Campion is a Sydney priest who taught church history at the Catholic Institute of Sydney. He is the author of *Australian Catholics* and other books.

In Ireland, Fr Conolly had circulated an appeal for prayerbooks, catechisms, vestments, altar requisites and books 'for the use of the poor convicts'. His biographer, the late Fr Terry Southerwood,[1] claims that Conolly baptized more than 650 persons in Van Diemen's Land (VDL); however a visitor in 1833 found the ramshackle lean-to chapel a mess, its altar cloths filthy, the sacred vessels black and three of Edward Curr's children unbaptized. The chapel seemed a symbol of pastoral failure. And the promised church remained unbuilt.

On the other hand, Fr Southerwood says that Conolly's main work was counselling the convicts: in two years he stood on the scaffold praying with 34 men sentenced to execution, an unnerving experience. One of these was Alexander Pearce. With another convict, Pearce had escaped from Macquarie Harbour; then, feeling hungry, he had attacked his companion with an axe, striking him four times, and afterwards sliced a fillet from his thigh, which he roasted for dinner.[2]

Conolly also acted as a pastor to captured members of the Brady gang of bushrangers who maintained a reign of terror in the colony for two years. When Matthew Brady was captured, he was found to have a multitude of admirers, who sent him flowers, fruit and sweets in gaol. They petitioned the government for a reprieve and applauded Brady on the scaffold.

Patrick Dunn was a friend of Brady's and a notorious drunkard. The police may have fitted him up on a criminal charge because he wouldn't pay them bribes, so he became a folk hero to many Catholics. Dunn went to his death wearing a white alb made by Mrs Curr, with a black cross on its front, and he mounted the scaffold with a crucifix in his hands saying the rosary. Catholics took up a collection to buy an expensive coffin for him and packed out his funeral in Conolly's chapel.

1. WT Southerwood: *Lonely Shepherd in Van Diemen's Isle* (George Town, Tasmania: Stella Maris Books, 1988). This book, in minuscule type, is best read with a magnifying glass. Fr Southerwood's chapter on Conolly's landholdings is a masterpiece of historical research. See also his articles in *Australasian Catholic Record* 1977, 1983, 1984, 1985. He corrects earlier writers on Conolly, such as Cardinal Moran, Archbishop Ullathorne and HN Birt OSB. Fr Southerwood was parish priest of Launceston in Hobart diocese. One of his ancestors had been a marine on the First Fleet.
2. Asked what was said from the scaffold, Conolly wrote his report in Gaelic, a mystery language to government men, who thought it might be Hebrew.

Fr Conolly did not approve: he thought executions should be deterrents against crime, not gateways to glory. His sympathies lay with the lonely settlers who were targeted by the Brady gang.

Ninety per cent of Irish convicts had been sent to New South Wales but the ten per cent who went to VDL kept Conolly busy. Some of the women had committed crimes in Ireland in order to join their husbands in the antipodes. Once here, they often re-offended, prostitution, vagrancy and drunkenness being common crimes. Half the women in the House of Correction were Catholics who did the washing for government institutions and spun wool and horsehair.

With a parish the size of Ireland, Conolly soon realized that he needed priests to help him. The trouble was, he did not seem to get on with other priests. The first of these was Fr Therry, whose relations with the government were frequently strained, leading to his being put off the government payroll for twelve years . . . sacked as chaplain. In this, Conolly sided with the government and sought Therry's recall. In letters to Bishop Poynter of London, he denigrated his brother priest, saying he was imprudent, vain, unlettered, conceited, affected and—worse!—money-hungry. Therry ignored such complaints, secure in his people's affections.

Then there was a Carmelite priest, Fr Samuel Coote, who arrived in May 1824, with government approval but without church faculties from the Bishop of Mauritius, in whose diocese VDL then was. He brought with him a case of church plate and vestments, but lacking church faculties he could not be gazetted as a chaplain. Acting as Vicar-General, Conolly allowed him to say Sunday Mass and catechise the children *pro tempore.* In the meantime, Conolly bad-mouthed Coote to the Bishop, saying he was 'very illiterate' and 'a man of no manners' who 'blundered through' the Mass. The Bishop supported his Vicar-General and recalled Coote, who had travelled through the countryside gaining signatures to a petition against Conolly. The government supported Conolly too. By this time, the Carmelite had got a bad name as a receiver of stolen goods and a tavern-singer with 'the lowest class of convicts', as Conolly said. Coote escaped to Sydney and thence to Mauritius, where he passes out of our history.

Eleven years later another religious order man turned up in Hobart. This was John Bede Polding OSB, the newly appointed bishop for New Holland, on his way to take up his appointment in Sydney. Bishop Polding was dissatisfied with Conolly's ministry and so he left behind in VDL a young Benedictine monk, James Ambrose Cotham, to augment the work.[3] Conolly and Cotham did not get on. One reason may be the secular priest's disdain for religious priests. Another reason may be that Cotham lent a friendly ear to the complaints of Conolly's enemies. Within a year this tension would explode.

Conolly's closest friend in VDL was the Anglican priest, Robert Knopwood, a Cambridge man and a landholder, who was 24 years older than the Irishman. For the last 35 years of his life, Knopwood kept a diary, a valuable historical source. Conolly is named in it 588 times, an index of their friendship. They formed a habit of having Sunday dinner together, sometimes sleeping overnight in each other's homes. And, as friends will, they often drank together. Knopwood's biographer says 'his liquor bills provide plenty of evidence of his conviviality'.[4]

Before Bishop Polding's arrival a lay committee, calling itself 'The Friends of the Roman Catholic Religion' was set up to get rid of Fr Conolly. These activists were, you might say, an unusual church committee: a forger, a shoplifter, a swindler, a street brawler, a convicted libeller . . . They filled Fr Cotham's ear with their complaints and before long he was writing a long report to the Bishop detailing the Irish priest's failings, which may be summarized as sloth, drunkenness and, *mirabile dictu*, satanism[5]. The young monk threatened the Bishop that if he did not intervene he, Cotham, would leave VDL.

Apart from the young monk's allegations, there was a question about the chapel land—did it belong to Conolly or to the Church? Strangely, there were no government documents to answer this question; it depended on people's memories, which changed over

3. In 2019 a biography of Cotham was published in England, Joanna Vials, *The Indomitable Mr Cotham: Missioner, Convict Chaplain and Monk* (Leominster: Gracewing, 2019). See Dr Colin Fowler's review in *Journal of the Australian Catholic Historical Society*, 2019.
4. Today a waterfront pub in Hobart is called 'The Bobby Knopwood'.
5. 12 March 1836. Cotham to Polding, 'Entre nous, I really sometimes have taken him to have dealings with his Satanic Majesty; nay, really one night when he was *inebriatus*, I thought by what he said, his countenance, and the figure he cut, that he was the devil incarnate.': HN Birt, *Benedictine Pioneers in Australia* (London: Herbert and Daniel, 1911), Volume I, 104.

time and, in any case, were contradictory. Fr Conolly insisted that the land, which he had improved, was his and some government officials supported him; others disagreed.

Thus when Bishop Polding came down to Hobart with his Vicar-General, WB Ullathorne, a fellow monk, he required Conolly to give an account of his administration and to answer charges about his lifestyle. Ullathorne sent a report of this encounter to Rome, saying that the priest had answered the Bishop 'insolently'; to which the Bishop had responded by stripping him of his priestly faculties—*suspensio a divinis.*[6] Which means, as I have said, that he could no longer say Mass, nor preach, nor celebrate any sacrament. On his part Conolly sued Bishop Polding for libel, but that was unsuccessful. In the Catholic community their pioneer priest was now a pariah.

So he remained for the last three years of his life. Polding had the good sense to send the other pioneer priest, Fr Therry, as Vicar-General to VDL to charm Conolly back, which he did.

And thus Conolly died, fortified by the last rites, on 3 August 1839, aged fifty three, a few months after his friend Bobby Knopwood.

6. The sentencing read over Fr Conolly in a packed chapel will interest students of history: 'Whereas you, the Rev. Philip Conolly have contumaciously persisted in refusing to us, your ecclesiastical superior, an account of the property of the Church in your holding or possession, as in obedience and duty you are bound to render; and whereas you have contumaciously refused to place in our hands a sum equal in amount to the collections made in the chapel, or otherwise obtained from the faithful for religious purposes and not yet carried into effect; and whereas having refused to render the same account and to give into our hands the said monies, you have also contumaciously disobeyed our requisition on your obedience that you should testify to the correctness and completeness of the account rendered and of the monies given in; and whereas in answer to a charge affecting your moral and sacerdotal character, and to which we directed your attention—you returned an insolent reply as regards us your superior, insolent and highly disrespectful as regards the charge; vague, irrelevant and unsatisfactory—a charge of harshness and cruelty towards certain individuals;—as regards the period within which the said answer was required to be delivered, knowingly and purposely deferred beyond the time by us specified; and whereas in your communications to us of the 23rd and 25th inst. you have advanced propositions false and subversive of ecclesiastical discipline and destructive of all order and subordination in the Church of God; now we, having given Canonical admonition and being invested by the Supreme Head of the Church with full authority for the same, do suspend and hereby declare you, Rev. Philip Conolly to be suspended from the exercise of all sacerdotal functions, no authority, save that of the Holy See and our own, can absolve you.'

Therry sang his Requiem while all Hobart stood still; and Therry buried him, putting that apt quotation from the psalmist on his gravestone, 'My days have declined like a shadow and I am withered like grass' (Ps 101:12).
May he rest in peace.

'Firebrand Friar'–Patrick Fidelis Kavanagh OSF (1838–1918)

*Colin Fowler**

Patrick Kavanagh was born in Wexford in 1838. After initial studies at St Peter's College, the Ferns diocesan seminary, he joined the Franciscan Order in 1849, receiving the brown habit and the name 'Fidelis' at the novitiate friary, Madonna del Piano in Capranica, sixty kilometres north of Rome. From there he proceeded to the convent of St. Isidore in Rome for his ecclesiastical studies.[1] He was ordained in 1865 and the following year returned to Ireland, where he served in counties Kerry and Cork.

Rev PF Kavanagh, from the title page of *A Popular History of the Insurrection of 1798* (Veech Library)

He came to the attention of the public when he published a history of the 1798 rebellion as it was fought in his home county of Wexford. The small book, 120 pages,

* Colin Fowler was parish priest of Pyrmont. His *150 Years on Pyrmont Peninsula: The Catholic Community of Saint Bede 1867–2017*, edited by Daire was reviewed in *JACHS* 37/2, and his *At Sea with Bishop John Bede Polding: the Journals of Lewis Harding—1835 & 1846* was reviewed in *JACHS* 40/2019'

1. The Irish Franciscans founded a range of colleges on the continent during the 17th Century: St Anthony's in Louvain in 1607, St Isidore's in Rome in 1625, the College of the Immaculate Conception in Prague in 1629, the Friary of the Annunciation in Wielun in Poland in 1645, a residence in Paris in 1653 and the friary at Capranica in 1656.

was published in Dublin with no date indication, though the year 1870 has been suggested.[2] Kavanagh had family connections with the rebels—Father Michael Murphy, whose role in the rebellion was highlighted in the book, was a grand-uncle on his mother's side, and his paternal grandfather was supportive of the rebels. An expanded version of the book, 304 pages, was published in 1874 with the title: *A Popular History of the Insurrection of 1798: Derived from every available written record and reliable tradition.*[3]

In the preface Kavanagh claimed originality for his contribution to the history of '98:

> Before he ever read a work on the subject of which he treats, he had acquired no small amount of information from those who were best calculated to impart it—the actors in the struggle. Born in the centre of the district where the contest was most fiercely waged, many of those who took part therein were his own near relatives, and from their lips he learned much of what he now narrates.[4]

Printed on the title page was the opening verse of Thomas Davis' 'A Song for the Irish Militia', but without recognition of the source:

> The Tribune's tongue and Poet's pen
> Must sow the seed in slavish men;
> *But t'is the soldier's sword alone*
> *Can reap the harvest when 'tis grown.*[5]

2. See Anna Kinsella, '1798 Claimed for Catholics: Father Kavanagh, Fenians and the Centenary Celebrations', in Daire Keogh and Nicholas Furlong editors, *Mighty Wave: the 1798 Rebellion in Wexford* (Dublin: Four Courts Press, 1998), 172, n. 6.
3. Patrick Kavanagh, *A Popular History of the Insurrection of 1798: Derived from every available written record and reliable tradition* (Dublin: McGlashan & Gill, 1874).
4. Kavanagh, *Popular History,* v.
5. Thomas Davis (1814–1845) was an Irish writer and the chief organiser of the Young Ireland movement. He graduated in Law at Trinity College, and received an Arts degree in 1836, and was called to the Irish Bar in 1838. In September 1842, he established The Nation newspaper, in which his songs and poems were published. He was the author of the famous Irish rebel song 'A Nation Once Again'.

In contrast to Davis' assertion of the essential role of physical force in the struggle for Irish independence, Kavanagh concluded his preface with an expression of hope for independence achieved without bloodshed: 'In conclusion, it may not be amiss to express a hope that our onward journey towards long-lost liberty may be made by peaceful paths—that when the crown of an independent nation is placed upon the brow of Erin, no stain of blood may be seen upon its golden round.'[6]

Commentators have described Kavanagh's purpose as giving to the '98 Rising a distinctly Catholic character and a blatantly religious dimension:

> Kavanagh's *Popular History of the Insurrection of 1798* was first published in the aftermath of the failed Fenian rising of 1867, and quickly became the popularly accepted account of 1798. For the firebrand friar, the Rising was a struggle for 'Faith and Fatherland', the response of a Catholic people to a reign of terror by Orange oppressors. Kavanagh claimed his work was based on the recollections of survivors of the Rising, and his family connections ensured his credibility . . . Kavanagh was dismissive of the leadership role played by Protestant United Irishmen in Co Wexford.[7]

It has been asserted that the influence of Kavanagh's book in its many editions 'led to one of the biggest myths of the 1798 Rising—that the Catholic Church was responsible for and supported the Rising in Wexford.'[8]

The official Catholic attitude to the United Irishmen of 1798 and to their Fenian successors was a rejection of oath-taking in these secret societies. Cardinal Paul Cullen, archbishop of Dublin and Papal Legate, was a fierce advocate of this policy. Following the failed Fenian rising of March 1867, Cullen and the Irish bishops successfully

6. Kavanagh, *Popular History*, vi.
7. Patrick Comerford, '1798: the lost leaders', *Irish Times*, 10 January, 1998. In the expanded centennial edition, an acknowledgement of the role of Ulster Protestants is found 'buried in a footnote' (Guy Beiner, *Forgetful Remembrance: Social Forgetting and Vernacular Historiography of a Rebellion in Ulster* [Oxford: Oxford University Press, 2018], 269).
8. Aengus Snodaigh, 'Remembering the past: a reluctant rebel', *An Phoblecht*, 2 July 1998.

petitioned the Pope to condemn the Society.[9] Kavanagh adapted his strong nationalist sentiments to the policy:

> Kavanagh, fearing that such harsh condemnation might alienate the people from the clergy, chose this time to publish his history of the Wexford Rebellion . . . He remained in a difficult position, having to publicly denounce the Fenians, while personally sympathising with their separatist aspirations. Kavanagh's answer was to distance the excellent character of the men who join secret societies from the societies themselves.[10]

It was this friar who, in April 1879, wrote from Cork to his Provincial in Dublin, belatedly offering himself for the new Irish Franciscan mission in Sydney:

> Dear Father Provincial.
> Supposing that a great many would offer themselves for the Australian Mission, I did not at first send in my name; in the absence of others I now do so—and request you to propose me as a candidate for the Mission.
> Hoping to hear from you as soon as convenient,
> I remain, dear Father Provincial, Yours P. F. Kavanagh O.S.F.[11]

Not having received a reply, he wrote again in October: 'I am anxious to know what decision has been come to concerning my offer to

9. 'As it may be doubted by many whether the society of Fenians is included and denounced among the societies condemned in the Pontifical Constitutions, our most Holy Father Pius IX, having first taken the opinions of the eminent cardinals, the inquisitors-general appointed to guard against heretical perversity in the universal Christian republic, lest the hearts of the faithful, particularly the simple, should be perverted, to the imminent danger of their souls, and adhering to the decrees of the congregation of the General Inquisition issued in like circumstances, especially the decree of 5 July 1865, has decreed and declared that the American or Irish society called Fenian is comprised among the societies forbidden and condemned in the Constitutions of the Supreme Pontiff, and in particular by that lately issued by his Holiness, dated 29 October 1869 . . .' (Roman Inquisition, *Apostolicae Sedis Moderationi,* 12 January 1870).
10. See Kinsella, '1798 Claimed for Catholics', 141.
11. Franciscan Provincial Archives, Waverley, NSW, Kavanagh File. Later sources, including Kavanagh's reminiscences, specified health reasons for his transfer to Australia.

join the Australian Mission.'[12] His offer was accepted; he and two confreres set sail on the iron-barque steamship *Cuzco* from Plymouth on 6 March 1880, arriving in Sydney on 22 April.[13]

Eleven months earlier, on 15 May 1879, two Irish Franciscans, Fathers James Hanrahan and Martin Holohan, had arrived in Australia on the *Cuzco*, and were assigned by Archbishop Vaughan to the care of the extensive Waverley mission, which comprised the whole area along the east coast of Sydney from Port Jackson to Botany Bay. The Dublin *Freeman's Journal* had reported on the departure of the missionaries:

> On Monday morning two members of the Irish Franciscan Province—the V.RR. James P. Hanrahan and Martin A. Holohan—left the North-wall [Dublin] for Plymouth, where they will go on board the steamship Cuzco, bound for New South Wales. At the urgent request of the illustrious Archbishop of Sydney, the Most Rev. Roger Bede Vaughan, D.D., the Irish Franciscans have undertaken the charge of the important mission of Waverley, situated in the suburbs of Sydney.[14]

Patrick Fidelis Kavanagh's arrival in Australia was highly anticipated by Sydney's Catholic newspaper. In March and April 1880 it cited articles from the *Cork Examiner* and *Dublin Irishman*, which expressed much regret at the departure of 'this good and patriotic priest': 'With the priestly virtues which Father Kavanagh possesses in a high degree

---

12. Francisico Provincial Archives.
13. The *Cuzco* was an Orient Line iron screw *steamship with* barque rigging, built in Glasgow 1871. Its voyages to Australia alternated between *routes via Suez or via the Cape of Good Hope. The Franciscan voyages in 1879 and 1880 were both via Cape Town.*
14. Reprinted in Sydney's *Freeman's Journal* (18 July, 1885): 15.
    Franciscan Peter O'Farrell, who ministered in Australia from 1854 to 1874 and died in Ireland in 1875, had left £3,700 towards the establishment of the Irish Franciscans in Sydney (*Freeman's Journal*, 11 March 1893).
    Archbishop Vaughan had negotiated with the Rome-based Minister-General for the sending of a Franciscan community. After the arrival of Hanrahan and Holohan, he wrote to Rome noting that two friars did not constitute a community, and asking that three more be despatched quickly [*presto*] (Vaughan to Minister-General, 6 June 1879 [Sydney Archdiocesan Archives, wallet: Vaughan's correspondence re Franciscans, 1875–1883]).

are combined rare literary attainments.'[15] The concluding words of the farewell address of the Mayor of Cork were quoted: 'Your history of an eventful period, giving the true story of a patriotic struggle, your pamphlets and lectures, pointing out duties of Irishmen, make us regard you as the true type of Priest and Patriot.[16]

Also aware of his Irish patriotism was Sydney's English Archbishop, as later recounted by Kavanagh:

> In the beginning of the year 1880 I left Cork for the Australian mission. Doctor Vaughan was then Archbishop of Sydney, and my first visit was paid to him. He received me with great kindness, and during our conversation said: 'I have heard that you are an Irish rebel, but do not think worse of you for that, for if I were an Irishman, I might be a rebel too'.[17]

In Sydney he dedicated himself to participation in the pastoral ministry of the Waverley friars, while taking every opportunity to advocate for the cause of Irish independence. In 1883 he was very involved in the visit to Sydney of the Redmond brothers, John and William, delegates of the Irish National League.[18] During their visit the controversial brothers were denied access to the largest venues in the city, and had to make do with smaller church buildings. At the Darlinghurst parish hall in September, William delivered a lecture on the Coercion Act. Kavanagh was appointed to move the vote of thanks:

> I rise with great pleasure to give expression to the thanks of this assemblage to Mr. Redmond for his very able and interesting lecture in which he so clearly shows the injustice of the treatment to which himself and so many others engaged in late agitation in Ireland were subjected. Untried and unconvicted of any offence whatever against the law of the land, hundreds of the trusted leaders of the people were subjected to indignities and severities which would be harsh if inflicted even upon the veriest criminals. It is needless to say that we his countrymen deeply sympathize with him for his sufferings, and honour him for his unflinching courage and sterling patriotism.

15. *Cork Examiner*, 3 January 1880 (quoted in *Freeman's Journal* (20 March 1880): 14).
16. *Freeman's Journal* (20 March 1880): 14.
17. PF Kavanagh, 'People I have met', *Freeman's Journal* (8 April 1899): 22.
18. John Redmond (1856–1918); William Redmond (1861–1917).

He proceeded to claim personal bonds with the Redmonds:

> It gives me double pleasure to move this vote of thanks as I too am a Wexford man, and was well acquainted with Mr. Redmond's family, whose name is honoured in their native country. Mr. Redmond is no unworthy scion of a family of ancient lineage. Sprung from that valiant Norman race whose honour was bright as their flashing swords, the proudest of that knightly warrior race need not blush to recognize as a worthy inheritor of their valour and patriotism the true gentleman and genuine patriot who has addressed us tonight in eloquent vindication of his cause, and I may say of our cause as that of our brethren at home.

He concluded with a prayerful expression of commitment to the cause: 'The cause of Ireland is the cause of truth and justice, and as such must finally triumph. Heaven send that triumph soon, such peaceful triumph as best befits a noble peace-loving, Christian nation. I have great pleasure in moving the vote of thanks.[19]

At his farewell address in November 1883, John Redmond, finally given access to the premier venue of the Gaiety Theatre in Sydney, paid homage to 'Father Kavanagh, a Wexford man, and who, I am proud to say, is here by my side this evening (applause)', and to his 'valuable work' on the Wexford rising, 'to which I am largely indebted'.[20] Redmond was not entirely indebted to Kavanagh's work, for he diverged significantly from his 'faith and fatherland' interpretation of 1798: 'Father Murphy, valorized in Kavanagh's account, received mention only once in Redmond's lecture, as the last name in a list of leaders of the rising.'[21]

In February 1885, Father Kavanagh was farewelled at a Waverley gathering prior to his return to Ireland. He expressed his appreciation of the many words of praise spoken during the evening:

> You speak of my devotion -to 'Holy Church' and 'Mother country'. Such devotion, I am happy to believe, I only share in

19. *Freeman's Journal* (15 September 1883): 10.
20. *Freeman's Journal* (8 December 1883): 17.
21. Malcolm Campbell, 'John Redmond and the Irish National League in Australia and New Zealand, 1883', *History*, 86 (2001): 361. See also Dermot Meleady, *Redmond, the Parnellite* (Cork: Cork University Press, 2008), 76–77.

> common with the great majority of my fellow-countrymen, at home and abroad, in whose hearts an ardent love of country and an unswerving attachment to religious faith are, and ever have been, inseparably united. You are kind enough to mention in terms of praise my few and feeble literary efforts in the cause of nationality and religion. I am truly gratified to learn that what I have written has met with your approval, whose minds are as intelligent and cultured as your hearts are true and kind. Of such praise I may feel justly proud. Accept, my dear friends, my sincere thanks for all your kindness.[22]

He sailed on the mail-steamer *City of Sydney*, heading across the Pacific to San Francisco via Auckland and Honolulu. He would keep in touch with Australia as the *Freeman's* Irish correspondent. His first letter was published in October, soon after his arrival in Ireland:

> By the last mail we received a letter from the Rev. P. F. Kavanagh, O.S.F., late of the Waverley and Woollahra mission, who returned to the old country some time back. The rev. gentleman is settled down in the Franciscan Convent, Carrick-on-Suir, Waterford, and is quite happy. He says he left Australia with regret, and had he not loved another country more, he would never have quitted this 'bright and sunny land'.[23]

After several letters on the political situation in Ireland, there began in May 1886 a series headlined 'FROM SYDNEY TO SAN FRANCISCO'. These articles were extracts from Kavanagh's ship-board diary, 'written expressly for the Sydney *Freeman*, and dedicated to my Australian friends'. The series, comprising ten chapters, concluded in August 1886.[24]

The friar turned to poetry in the 1890s; many of his poems were published in the *Freeman's Journal* during these years: 'A FRANCISCAN POET—Sydney people who cherish a recollection of the Rev. P. F. Kavanagh, O.S.F., will be interested in the following extracts from "The Poets of Ireland" just issued.'[25] A poem published

22. *Freeman's Journal* (28 February 1885): 15.
23. *Freeman's Journal* (24 October 1885): 17
24. *Freeman's Journal* (28 August 1886): 17
25. *Freeman's Journal* (5 November 1892): 7

in April 1896 was the first expression of what would become a major preoccupation of Kavanagh into the twentieth century—support for the Boers during the Second Boer War, 1899 to 1902. The poem was entitled, 'The Jameson Ride, a priest's parody' with the following chorus

O, long life and success to the straight-shooting Boers,
And may their fame never die while this world endures.
May all British marauders still shake in their shoes
When their rifles ring out o'er their veldts and karoos.[26]

The poem concluded with a 'Moral' for Ireland:

'O could we but shoot like the brave Boer men,
The freedom long lost might be ours once again.

The Jameson Raid was a botched attack against the Transvaal, which eventually led to the outbreak of war in 1899. In January 1896, the newly appointed Poet Laureate. Alfred Austin, had published a poem in the *Times* beginning:

When men of our own blood pray us
To ride to their kinsfolk's aid,
Not Heaven itself shall stay us
From the rescue they call a raid.

The Laureate's poem met with much ridicule and many parodies, including that of Kavanagh. The *Freeman's Journal* quoted from the *London Daily News*:

> Mr. Alfred Austin's poem on Jameson's filibustering ride (says a London paper, Jan. 13) has simply pulverized and scattered to the wind whatever reputation he possessed as a poet. . . . Dr. Jameson has not deserved altogether well of his country in his last exploit, but he certainly has merited nothing so bad as this. When his case comes before the proper tribunal, his judges ought to remember, as a plea in mitigation, that he has already been the victim of Mr. Austin's verse.[27]

---

26. *Freeman's Journal* (4 April 1896): 19, veldt—a rolling plain; karoo—elevated plateau.
27. *Freeman's Journal* (29 February 1896): 7.

In November 1897, the *Freeman* announced the forthcoming centennial edition of Kavanagh's history of 1798, noting that this would be the seventh edition of the book:

> The author, who writes from the Franciscan Friary, Liberty-street, Cork, Ireland, explains that the new edition is already in the press, and will be ready for sale before the end of the year. It will be of course the Centenary Edition, and printed on good paper, with cloth binding, and copiously illustrated. The price fixed—half-a-crown—is very moderate. Guy and Co., of Patrick-street, Cork City, are the publishers. Father Kavanagh' s work is admitted to be the best written on this exciting period of Irish history, and its popularity is proved by the fact that the six editions already published were all quickly bought up. We learn in connection with the new edition that the author, besides revising the original work, has added much valuable information, and has brought his book up-to-date in every respect. To those who know Father Kavanagh it should be unnecessary to say that he is bringing out the Centenary Edition, not to make money, but to serve the National cause. The price at which the book is to be sold will leave little if any margin for profit to the author or publisher. There should be a large sale in Australia, and particularly in New South Wales.[28]

The volume, of 344 pages, was bound in green and gold, and was dedicated by the author 'to all Irishmen at home and abroad who love their native land'. Throughout the centennial year of 1798 the *Freeman* carried news of Kavanagh's involvement in Irish commemorations of the Rising.

In December, Sydney's second Catholic newspaper, *The Catholic Press*, founded in 1895, was alone in reporting a speech in which Kavanagh touched on a theme, for which he would become notorious during the Boer War—Irishmen in the British Army: 'Rev. P. F. Kavanagh, the eloquent Irish priest, recently delivered a powerful speech on the subject "Our Faults and Our Dangers", at Schull, County Cork. The flower of the British Army is, as well known,

28. *Freeman's Journal* (20 November 1897): 2.
Only two Australian libraries hold copies of the book—Macquarie University Library and the Catholic Institute's Veech Library, whose librarian has provided Kavanagh's photograph from the book.

largely composed of Irishmen, and Father Kavanagh arraigned his countrymen for assisting Great Britain in her unjust wars.' He cited the example of the British campaign in the Sudan, which had climaxed in the victory at Omdurman in August 1898: 'Only the other day I read of a Royal Irish regiment that helped England to win a glorious victory in the Soudan. A glorious victory, indeed; no, but a most inglorious massacre of brave men who were defending their native land with a heroic but unavailing valor.'[29]

In the week leading up to the Boers' declaration of war on 11 October 1899, the Dublin *Freeman's Journal* reported that Kavanagh, 'the brilliant historian of the Irish insurrection one hundred years ago', had denounced Irishmen who were 'marching under the standard of the Great Pirate, the oppressor of weak nations, to devastate the lands and trample upon the liberties of the brave Boers'.[30] On the following Sunday, Irish recruits were condemned on large green posters plastered throughout Dublin: 'Enlisting in the English Army is Treason to Ireland.'[31] Kavanagh's green posters and handbills were still being distributed in the New Year. In February 1900, an Irish Unionist member of the Imperial Parliament[32] asked the Attorney-General for Ireland whether he was aware of 'a green handbill circulated in Dublin addressed to Irish Roman Catholics, and headed "England's Robber War," in which it is stated, on the authority of the Rev Father Kavanagh, that every man who engages in such war, if he dies in it, must suffer the loss of his soul'; he asked what was being done about the offence. The Unionist Attorney-General replied: 'The police have been instructed to seize and destroy the circulars when found. The matter is being carefully watched, but up to the present the Government have not considered it necessary to take further action.'[33] William Redmond, interjected: 'Is it not perfectly notorious

29. *Catholic Press*, (24 December 1898), 3. The Royal Irish Regiment was garrisoned in Clonmel, County Tipperary and was made the county regiment of Tipperary, Kilkenny, Waterford and Wexford; most of its recruits were local Irish Catholics.

30. *Freeman's Journal* (Dublin) (3 October 1899).

31. See Donal P McCracken, *Forgotten Protest: Ireland and the Anglo-Boer War* (Belfast: Ulster Historical Foundation, 2003), 45.

32. William Johnston (1829–1902) Independent Member for Belfast South (1886–1902).

33. John Atkinson, Baron Atkinson, (1844—1932): elected a Conservative MP for North Londonderry in 1895; upon his election, he was appointed Attorney-General for Ireland, an office he held for the next ten years.

in Dublin that the circular was got out by the Orange party?' This was received with laughter and cheers by his fellow Irish Parliamentary Party members.[34]

In February 1900 a Kavanagh letter appeared in Sydney's *Freeman's Journal* questioning the decision to send Australian troops to engage in the war: 'What came over the generous heart of Australia to unsheath her virgin sword to smite these struggling freemen whose cause is so undeniably just? Would Australians permit England to rule them to-day? No true Australian would entertain the idea for a moment.'[35]

In April 1900, following British losses in the Boer War during December 1899, a Royal Visit of the eighty-year-old Queen Victoria to Ireland was arranged in order to promote Irish recruitment. Kavanagh, as President of the Limerick Young Ireland Society, received an invitation from the local High-Sheriff to attend a meeting to organise an address of welcome for the Queen. In reply Kavanagh took the opportunity to give full rein to his attitude to the visit and to the war; the Melbourne Catholic newspaper, *The Advocate*, published the letter in full on its front page:

> Dear Sir,—I have just received a circular in which you, as High Sheriff of Limerick, request a meeting of all those who wish to present an address of welcome to her Majesty the Queen on the occasion of her approaching visit to Ireland. The fact that I am an Irish Nationalist would be sufficient to deter me from attending the proposed meeting, but there are other reasons why no Irishman, whatever may be his political opinions, should take part in it. I will give these reasons.
>
> During her Majesty's long reign, she has never earned the gratitude of the Irish people by an act of kindness towards them, and has never, even in words, shown any sympathy with them in their sufferings, which have been so manifold and grievous. During forty years she has never visited the country, and never manifested any interest in its fortunes. She, in fine, has not done or said anything to merit our gratitude, and it would be hypocrisy on our part, to pretend that she has. During her reign she has indeed, signed some forty Coercion Acts, but surely we cannot be expected to be grateful for that.

34. Commons Sitting of Thursday, 15 February 1900 (House of Commons Hansard).
35. *Freeman's Journal* (24 February 1900): 6

> Our respect for the blameless character of the aged Queen in private life cannot blind us to the fact that she is the head of a State which has in the past cruelly oppressed, and in the present oppresses our native land. The visit of her Majesty at this particular time was very ill-advised. Its chief, if not sole, motive is but too apparent—that of furthering the enlistment of Irishmen in the British army, but if England thinks the doubtful honour of a visit from the Queen will help fill the ranks of her oft-defeated and much-depleted army engaged in the present unjust war with fresh recruits, she will find herself deceived. Irishmen have been lately learning what, they seem to have been long strangely ignorant of—that Christian men should fight only in defence of their own country, and never in an unjust war.
>
> As the Queen's visit is in the minds of most people intimately connected with the war at present being waged in South Africa, and as the majority of those who attend the proposed meeting will probably consist of persons who profess to draw their code of morality from the sacred source of the Bible, I would direct their attention to this precept of Decalogue therein contained, 'Thou shalt not kill', which command forbids unjust war which is but homicide on a large scale.
>
> I trust that when Ireland becomes in fact what she is by right, an independent nation, her people will receive with due honour any respectable Royal personage who may choose to visit their land.
>
> I remain, dear sir, yours truly, P. F. Kavanagh.[36]

Throughout the years leading to the First World War, Kavanagh was regularly called upon to speak at dedications of memorials to Irish patriots. In 1904, during another Royal Visit, he spoke at the dedication of a memorial at Baltinglass, County Wicklow, to Michael Dwyer (1772—1825) and Sam McAllister, who in February 1799 gave his life during an ambush so that Dwyer could escape. Dwyer, known as the Wicklow Chief, was deported to New South Wales as an unsentenced exile in 1805. He died in 1825. Seventy-three years later, during Sydney's celebration of the '98 centenary, his remains were reinterred together with those of his wife in Waverley cemetery.

36. *The Advocate* (19 May 1900): 1

A monument to the Rebellion and its many martyrs, Catholic and Protestant, was raised over their graves; it is said to be the world's largest memorial to the 1798 Rising.[37]

Towards the end of his speech in Baltinglass, Kavanagh adverted to Edward VII's presence in Dublin:

> What a contrast between this great and enthusiastic assemblage of Irishmen who have come here to honour the memory of these brave patriots and the bellowing slaves and genteel dastards who in other parts of Ireland have gathered to fawn, with feigned and sycophantic loyalty upon an English King [Edward VII], who, whatever may be his personal good qualities, is the representative of the unjust and cruel power which has inflicted unparalleled misery upon our country. What generous mind can view without contempt these poor abject, self-abasing slaves, who are not ashamed of 'this dance, in their chains, this shout in their slavery that saddens the skies.' God bless Wicklow and. her freedom-loving sons, and may the spirit which animated the breast of Michael Dwyer and of McAllister never depart from the men of their race. May the freedom for which these great-souled patriots fought with such heroic valour, yet be won, and joy once more revisit the long-sorrowing heart of our 'Dark Rosaleen' (Cheers).[38]

In November 1906, the *Freeman* presented a 'character sketch' of Father Kavanagh. The article sought to locate his position on the scale of Irish nationalism: 'In politics Father Kavanagh is considered an extreme Nationalist, but he is not an irreconcilable. He recognises the changed situation in Ireland and her brightening prospects by means of constitutional agitation.' Those prospects were the moves towards Home Rule, culminating in the royal assent to 'The Government of Ireland Act' in September 1914.

At the onset of war in 1914, because Home Rule had been formally passed into legislation, though suspended for the duration

---

37. See Colin Fowler, *150 Years on Pyrmont Peninsula: The Catholic community of Saint Bede, 1867–2017* (Adelaide: ATF Press 2017), 253–259.
38. *Freeman's Journal*, (25 June 1904): 8, 'bellowing slaves and genteel dastards': in his *Gaol Journal* entry for 27 May 1848, John Mitchell wrote: 'Dublin City, with its bay and pleasant villas—city of bellowing slaves, villas of genteel dastards—lies now behind us.'

of the conflict, Kavanagh wrote in support of John Redmond's call for Irishmen to enlist. He explained what could have been seen as a dramatic reversal from his opposition to enlistment during the Boer War:

> 'When Ireland was denied her right to freedom and was treated as a slave, I raised my humble voice before a crowded audience to condemn the enlistment of Irishmen in the British army or navy, and I would do the same today were the circumstances similar. But if I did so now I should be deserving of the contempt and reprobation of my fellow countrymen.'[39]

His voice was not heard regarding the Easter Rising in May 1916. However, it was later asserted that 'when the late Mr. J. Redmond defined Ireland's attitude in the war he [Kavanagh] endorsed it in a letter to the Press, but subsequent events [1916?] made him bitterly regret his action.'[40]

Patrick Fidelis Kavanagh died in 1918 at the age of 80. The old 'firebrand friar' collapsed after having left his sick-bed in the Wexford friary to vote in the crucial election of 18 December 1918; he was found in a kneeling position in his room. The election resulted in the Sinn Fein party winning a resounding majority of the Irish seats in the Westminster Parliament. The elected members refused to take their places in London and instead chose to sit in Dublin as the parliament of the Irish Republic.[41]

---

39. *Southern Star* (31 October 1914).
40. *W. A. Record* (1 March 1919): 16.
41. John Redmond died in March 1918; in June 1917 his brother Willie was killed in action in France.

Journal of the Australian Catholic Historical Society, Volume 41/2020

Fr Julian, Southport and the Kennedy/Ransom Family–their story

*Tess Ransom**

What I have decided to write on Fr Julian Tenison Woods will be in two parts, the first part being fact and taken from historical notes we have on him and the second part is how, after much reflection, I imagine he would have been as he worked in Southport and surrounds.

Part 1

Tucked away in the southern-most tip of our Island State is the sea-side town of Southport. It was here that my grand-parents, Margaret and Henry Ransom, in the 1860s, settled and brought up their family, two boys and one girl. The youngest boy, Timothy Maurice, was my father. At this time Southport was mainly known for its timber industry at which most people worked, cutting the huge trees with nothing but axes. Some historians give the population at the time as approximately 500.

In 1855, as a young man, Julian Woods came to Hobart. Two years later he was ordained a priest in Adelaide on 4 January 1857. As well as Priest, Julian was also a scientist, geologist, writer, poet, musician, artist, and popular lecturer. But most of all he was a gifted missioner and it was this strong sense of mission that led him to Southport when he returned to work in Tasmania from 1874 to 1876. Southport was a far-flung and distant part of the island, being 97 kilometres south of Hobart. There were no made or mapped roads and the only means of transport was by horseback, so the journey from Hobart to Southport would have taken several days.

* Sister Tess Ransom, a Sister of St Joseph in Hobart, grew up in the family home where Father Julian Tenison Woods stayed with her grandparents during missions in Tasmania. She shares her memories and impressions.

Life, certainly, was not easy in those far off days as Fr Julian wrote to his friend, William Archer, from Honeywood (now Geeveston). '*I have just returned from a most difficult and I may say dangerous trip to Southport: over mere bridle tracks, slippery and steep through the mountains. It rained too, and my horse fell, hurting my left hand, both unpleasant addenda. But it was a most interesting journey to me and will make the material for some good papers.*'[1]

At Southport Fr Julian stayed with my grandparents. While there he wrote several prayers and hymns, many of which we still have today. Julian has been described as possessing '*profound, though romantic convictions, based on a child-like piety*'[2] with '*great simplicity, courtesy and kindness of manner.*'[3] It is in that light that we should read his writings today.

Julian loved our Island State, referring to it as 'St Joseph's Island',[4] but he was worried about the plight of our forests. In his paper on the Tasmanian Forests: their Botany and Economical value he wrote: '*The only way to prevent the wholesale destruction of timber will be by proclaiming reserves or State forests . . . or the forests of Tasmania, peerless and priceless as they once were, will soon be things of the past.*'[5] I believe that Julian was one of the first clergy to preach publicly on the care of the environment in Tasmania.

In this small, and often neglected part of our Island, Julian worked tirelessly to extend the Kingdom. From Southport he visited other outlying country townships that today are only ghost towns, but in his time many people lived there and people were very important to Julian. On his visits to other places nearby, such as Lune River,[6] he would have come across the quartz quarry, a place of great interest for him.

---

1. Woods to William Archer, 22 January 1876, in edited by A Player, *The Archer Letters* (North Goulburn: Sisters of St Joseph, 1983, reprinted 2016).
2. DH Borchardt, 'Tenison-Woods, Julian Edmund (1832–1889)', *Australian Dictionary of Biography*, http://adb.anu.edu.au/biography/tenison-woods-julian-edmund-4700/text7787, published first in hardcopy 1976.
3. A Liversidge, 'Anniversary address' and bibliography, *Proceedings of the Royal Society of New South Wales*, 24 (1890).
4. JE Tenison Woods to Sr Francis McCarthy, August 1887, in Josephine Brady, 'St Joseph's Island', Julian Tenison Woods and the Tasmanian Sisters of St Joseph, (New Town, Tasmania, ATF Press, 2012), xix.
5. *Mercury*, (Wednesday 26 June 1878): 3 http://nla.gov.au/nla.news-article8964746.
6. Lune River is nine kilometres from Southport.

My mother sometimes spoke to me of Fr Julian, remembering what she had been told by my grandmother. I do not recall much of what she told me for I was only a very small child. Also, I did not know at that time I would become a Sister of Saint Joseph. How I regret now that I did not pay more attention to what she was telling me, and how I would love to go back to those days, gain more information and know better the real Julian!

At home we had a studio photo of Julian and when I entered the Novitiate my mother gave it to me. As a good novice, I handed it in and do not know what happened to it, though I would dearly love to have it today, knowing that Julian had given it to my grandparents.

Julian had great trust in the Providence of God and knew of God's loving care of him. He stood open-handed before God and had total trust that God would be with him in all he did.

The Church at Southport was blessed and opened by Bishop D Murphy on 23 February 1876. Fr Julian preached at this celebration of the aptly named church of Our Lady Star of the Sea. The view from the church steps was breath-taking and took in, across the water, Bruny Island and beyond. My great-grandfather, ex-convict John Kennedy, in family documents is recorded as being at the forefront of having the Church built. Undoubtedly, Julian encouraged him in this. The beautiful little church, where my family and I had worshipped, was burnt down in a bush fire in 1950. My younger brother had seen the fire coming and was able to save anything that was moveable. These he took to our home.

Here, in the very house where Julian had stayed, history repeated itself, and once again Mass continued to be celebrated each month. I have a feeling that Julian would be pleased.[7]

Part 2

I often muse on how Julian must have enjoyed Southport, for there was everything on which his creative and reflective spirit could dwell.

---

7. There was at least one other Tasmanian Sister of St Joseph with whose family Father Woods stayed while he preached in the area—Sr Stanislaus Fitzpatrick (1860–1931) from Cygnet.
   Mercury (Saturday 4 December 1875): 2 (5) http://nla.gov.au/nla.news-article8941545 accessed online 4 October 2020.
   Mercury (Wednesday 15 December 1875): 2 (5) http://nla.gov.au/nla.news-article8941746 accessed online 4 October 2020.

I see Julian walking the snow-white sandy beach, chatting to the children at play there and sometimes helping them to build their sandcastles. Did he talk to them of the beauty of God's creation that surrounded them?

Did he know the cold of a Southport winter, when the puddle-holes froze over and stayed that way for days?

Was he compensated for this by the comfort of a warm bed, a homely kitchen, a kettle always on the boil and good country food?

And I wonder if Julian, in his wanderings and travels, found the native orchids and Aboriginal middens that we knew existed not far from our home?

Was his heart stirred with each new sight and sound and did he find delight in the glory of the sunset, its many-hued colours, and then darkness as it slipped into the night? On clear nights there would have been the inspiration of the stars and moon as he surely pondered the destiny to which he was called.

Did he enjoy the tiny sand-pipers that nested high on the beach, and the majestic sea eagles, with a wing-span of three metres, that flew across the bay; the large Pacific gulls as they floated on the thermals; the forty-spotted pardalotes whose homes were in the cliffs along from the beach; the gannets that dropped like stones from the sky when they saw a fish in the water below; the rock pools that contained many and varied species and where we as children fossicked, as I believe Julian also did; the shells, kelp and seaweeds that were dragged from the depths of the sea and dumped on the beach as the heavy seas pounded in across the bay from the Great Southern Ocean? He would certainly have shown much interest in all these things for his mind was always active and full of imagination.

And there was the small brackish creek that flowed across the beach into the bay and was filled with plankton and many other small creatures. As children we had enjoyed all these things as I am sure Julian did. Was it from such things, so small and seemingly insignificant, that Julian was able to turn his reflective and fertile mind and write so tellingly for future generations?

I am so grateful that I was born at Southport into the Ransom/Kennedy family, the family that knew Julian and was able to offer him hospitality and friendship. I thank God for the influence he had on my grandparents, for all that they learned from him and which they passed on to their grandchildren. I am also grateful to God that I was called to the congregation that Julian and Mary co-founded, and that has been my life for so many years

Southport is now only a small holiday retreat with a few resident locals, and many shack owners who frequent this lovely little town in holiday time.

The influence of Julian's ministry is very much alive in the Sisters of Saint Joseph today.

Journal of the Australian Catholic Historical Society, Volume 41/2020

Breadalbane, Ben Hall, and the Spurious Case Against Thomas Lodge

*James McDonald**

Ben Hall

Many people assisted the bushranger, Ben Hall, in the mid 1860s. Most of them, willingly. When Hall's gang held up a stage-coach at Breadalbane, a village halfway between Goulburn and Gunning, and brought their captives back to the Breadalbane Hotel, which was owned by Thomas Lodge, the Goulburn police were sure that the publican and many of his patrons were complicit in Hall's crimes. Although Thomas Lodge was acquitted of a subsequent charge of receiving a stolen saddle, it continues to be stated that the avuncular publican was prominent in Hall's network of 'bush telegraphs' at Breadalbane. But the facts do not support this conclusion. While gossip would convict him, the evidence does not. Lodge was caught up in extreme events and scapegoated by a nervous colonial hierarchy intent on quashing the bushrangers at whatever cost. His accusers were only too willing to assume guilt. Lodge was a leader in a predominantly Catholic community overshadowed by Protestant 'squire', James Chisholm. This article revisits the case against him and attempts to form a better understanding of Breadalbane-Goulburn politics, sectarian tensions,

* James McDonald is an ex-Classicist who has recently edited the first volume of Douglas Kelly's posthumous Commentary on Xenophon's *Hellenika* (Hakkert, Amsterdam). He has also published widely on the early history of Canberra and its surrounding districts. This article builds on research included in J. McDonald, *Three Henry Currans* (Canberra: Sorley Boy, 2018), 445–77.

and the broader context which led to this man being so erroneously portrayed as a bushranger's patsy in literature and film down to this day.[1]

Origin and Influences

Thomas Lodge certainly had the background of someone we might expect to be sympathetic to Hall's gang and, as an innkeeper, he was vulnerable to their depredations. It has been speculated that he saw cooperation as a deliberate ploy to avoid financial losses.[2]

Lodge's uncle, James, had been convicted of 'frame-breaking' (Luddism) and as such had shown himself willing to fight against a distanced authority for the conditions of the lower orders. This uncle was transported to Australia in 1817 on the eve of the Pentrich Rebellion.[3] When he saw the tremendous opportunities in the Antipodes, James Lodge encouraged his brother, Henry, to join him. Henry and Rebecca Lodge had lost ten of their children to the disease and toxicity of the Bradford industrial slums. Only Thomas (a ten-year-old at the time) and his baby sister had survived by the time their parents decided to emigrate in 1842.[4]

But origins can be deceiving. The Lodges in Australia tried their best to integrate and win the trust of their 'masters' in order to build a sort of life barely imaginable in the Old World. They became active

1. Early examples of works that portray Lodge as aiding and abetting criminals include: RT Wyatt, *The History of Goulburn, NSW* (Goulburn: Municipality of Goulburn, 1941), 103; F Clune, *Ben Hall* (originally released as *Wild Colonial Boys*) (London: Arkon, 1970), 453. The most recent representation is Matthew Holmes' 2016 film *The Legend of Ben Hall*. The closest thing I can find to an account willing to entertain Lodge's version of events (albeit fleetingly) is E. F. Penzig, *Ben Hall: the Definitive Illustrated History* (Katoomba: Tranter Enterprises, 1996), 329–33.
2. For Example ML Croke, *Hotels, Inns and Shanties of the Upper Lachlan Shire* (Goulburn: privately published, 2012), 162; JL Tracey, *Upper Lachlan Shire Community Heritage Study 2007–2008* (Sydney: Heritage Council of NSW, 2010), 65. Some of the sloppy claims made in these two publications are repeated almost verbatim.
3. Transportation register of the *Lord Eldon*, 30 September 1817; Certificate of Freedom for James Lodge, 14 March 1831 (31/145).
4. Passenger list of the *Earl of Durham*, 11 July 1842 and assisted passage records for Henry and Rebecca Lodge and children.

contributors to their new community. Henry and Rebecca ran a small farm at largely-Catholic Menangle for nineteen years. Henry was interviewed by Caroline Chisholm at Camden when she was building her case to encourage emigration to Australia. He is reported as being an enthusiastic supporter of the New World, seeking Chisholm's assistance to get an orphaned niece out to the colony and saying in his written statement to her that the 'country is a deal better than England for any labouring man'.[5] Even his Luddite brother had embraced the new society and signed two congratulatory letters published to honour a local magistrate and a military officer.[6] In Breadalbane, we will see a similar pattern of integration with the next generation of Lodges.

The First Hotel (1853–1858)

Thomas Lodge married Mary Anne Lee in 1853 at Campbelltown. With assistance from his parents, he took over the lease of a Breadalbane inn on the Great South Road called the Red House, but more colloquially known as Yabber Joe's.[7]

Things began well. The young Lodges benefited from a steady stream of travellers making their way south to the goldfields, or on the route home, generally, with emptier pockets. Gold was even discovered at Breadalbane itself, which must have also increased

5. Quoted in C Chisholm, *Emigration and Transportation Relatively Considered; in a Letter Dedicated by Permission to Earl Grey* (London: 1847), 34–35. First noted by J Booth in her unpublished diploma thesis, 'Lodge Family News: the Good and the Bad', Sydney, 1998, 25–6. I am grateful to her for sharing this with me, as her research and painstaking review of the sources has been critical in developing an understanding of the early and late years of the family.
6. Namely, Campbelltown magistrate and grazier, William Howe, and Captain Thomas Meyrick of the 39th Regiment of Foot. See *Sydney Gazette and NSW Advertiser*, 19 February 1831, 2; *Sydney Herald*, (2 July 1832): 2; *Australian*, (6 July 1832): 4.
7. *Sydney Morning Herald* (hereafter *SMH*), (5 December 1848): 3; *Goulburn Herald and County of Argyle Advertiser* (hereafter *GHCAA*), (16 December 1848): 3; *GHCAA* (23 December 1848): 2; *GHCAA* (3 February 1849): 2 (*cf* 3) [February 1849], 3); *SMH* (4 April 1851): 2. The editor of the *Macquarie Dictionary* (Susan Butler) kindly informed me that 'yabber' is derived from local Pidgin and the first recorded usage meaning 'chatter' comes in 1841; that is well before 'Yabber Joe' Fletcher ran the Red House, suggesting that Fletcher was either a talker, or, if the moniker is ironic, laconic.

Thomas Lodge (c 1885)
The woman is believed to be his wife, Mary (Lodge family collection)

patronage while a local mini-rush unfolded.[8] The Red House was used as a changing post by coaches for horse teams. Travellers took advantage of the hiatus in their journey to purchase fresh scones and other refreshments. Thomas bred horses and was appointed superintendent and/or judge at local race meetings and he and Mary catered at large community events attended by up to 300 people.[9] The hotel sold newspapers and general supplies and was also used by visiting professionals, such as dentists.[10] In an 1855 account of a visiting German touring musician, Hermann Lau, the inn is described as being a centre for local music, with Thomas a keen exponent of the fiddle. The two men bonded and Lau worked at the hotel in March and April in a number of roles: shooting game for the table, serving at the bar, washing carriages and babysitting. Lau even said that he had been included in the family's 1855 Easter celebration and used roots he collected locally to dye some festive eggs.[11]

The Red House was also used as one of the early venues in the district for Catholic Mass before St Brigid's was built in 1865. The family hosted a luncheon for Bishop Polding in 1858, in which fifty locals turned out to meet the renowned cleric.[12] Thomas donated

8. *GHCAA* (21 June 1856): 4.
9. *SMH* (26 March 1856): 3 (reprinted in *Bell's Life in Sydney and Sporting Reviewer* [hereafter *Bell's*], 29 March 1856, 1); *Bell's*, 24 May 1856, 2; *GHCAA* (3 July 1858): 2.
10. For example *GHCAA* (29 September 1855): 2.
11. For Lau in Breadalbane, see H Lau, *Vier Jahre in Australien* (Hamburg: 1860), 51–9. *Cf* J Fletcher, *Hermann Lau and His Sojourns (1854–1859) in Sydney, Goulburn, Braidwood, Araluen, Moruya and Shoalhaven* (Sydney: 1991), 9–10; Booth, 'Lodge Family News', 40. Also note *The Goulburn Herald* (hereafter *GH*), (22 July 1863): 2, in which Lodge is acquitted of a charge of allowing music and dancing at his premises on a Sunday.
12. *The Freeman's Journal* (hereafter *FJ*), 13 (March 1858), 3; *Empire* (hereafter *Emp*), 13 March 1858, 5. This visit by the Archbishop would have been a major local event (*cf* KL Brown, *Where Once the Wagons Met: An Introduction to Some Inns*

to the Gunning Catholic Church and Mary served as the district's midwife and nurse.[13]

The Lodge family was not only a critical part of the community, but on good terms with the local police. In December 1854 a bushfire threatened the hotel. With the help of Constables M'Connell and Brennan, they beat the conflagration. However, as we will learn, the relationship with the Protestant Goulburn-based constabulary was an altogether different matter.[14]

The Second Hotel (1858–1865)

Buoyed by a solid start, the Lodges looked to build their own hotel. As tenants they had been vulnerable to the vagaries of their lease. Hence, in 1856 they purchased land and built a twelve-room stone hotel, which has survived today as the homestead now known as Sweetwood Lea.[15] As part of a possible broader plan to extend the family's interests

---

and Innkeepers of Early Gunning from Breadalbane to the Gap on the Old South Road: 1830–1899 (Gunning: Gunning and District Historical Society, 2017), 17). Polding needs no introduction, but for an overview of his life, see *Australian Dictionary of Biography,* edited by B Nairn and D Pike (hereafter *ADB*) (Melbourne University Press, Melbourne, 1967) volume 2, 340–7; B Maher, *Planting the Celtic Cross: Foundation of the Catholic Archdiocese of Canberra and Goulburn* (Canberra: privately published, 1997), *passim*. For the other activities, see *Bell's*, 24 May 1856, 2.

13. M O'Connor, *A Sketch of the Rise and Progress of the Yass Mission from Its Foundation, 1838, to the Present Time* (North Sydney: Library of Australian History, 1861, 1984 facsimile), 34; *cf* M Hannan, *Where Were They and What Were They Doing in 1872: A Story of the Hannan, Kelleher, Madigan, Greenwood, Watson, Hynes and Hallam Families in the Colony of New South Wales* (Wagga Wagga: Triple-D Books, 2007), 17–18.
14. *Emp* (3 January 1855): 3; *FJ* (6 January 1855), 9. The Corporal Brennan in these reports (Melbourne: Melbourne University Press, 1967), is Martin Brennan, who wrote *Reminiscences of the Gold Fields and Elsewhere in New South Wales: Covering a Period of Forty-eight Years' Service as an Officer of Police* (Sydney: William Brooks, 1907). Unfortunately no reference is made to his time at Breadalbane in his manuscript.
15. *Emp* (9 October 1856): 3; *GHCAA* (19 December 1857): 2; *GHCAA* (3 July 1858): 2. For the block, see Bennett's 'Plan of 99 portions of land at the Third Bredalbane (*sic*) Plain, Mutmutbilly, Dairy Flats *etc*. County of Argyle. 1856' (NLA 230000804); *cf*, the 1939 Mutmutbilly Parish Map (block 13 = Lot 34), which still has original 1856 purchasers marked. For a history of Sweetwood Lea, see Hannan, *Where Were They and What Were They Doing in 1872*, 17–20.

in the local hotel industry, Thomas' parents, Henry and Rebecca, sold up their small leasehold at Menangle and bought the ailing John Barleycorn on the western edge of Goulburn, which they renovated.[16]

Local squatter James Chisholm junior was not happy that his tenant was setting up in direct competition close by.[17] Nevertheless, in October 1856, Thomas and Mary Lodge risked all and purchased their own 268-acre block (£402 total cost) at Breadalbane.[18] The new tenant of the Red House soon clashed with Lodge over the contract for the district's postal services, but the local residents lobbied for Lodge, and it was he who was eventually made postmaster at Breadalbane in 1860 at £12 per annum (with Mary actually undertaking the daily duties).[19]

Lodge's Breadalbane Hotel, c. 1870 (image courtesy of Shlomi Bonet). *The faint individuals on the right may be Hannan family members*

16. *GH* (5 July 1862), 3 (*NB*: this masthead was used by the *GHCAA* in the 1860–1864 period). For the licensees and history of the John Barleycorn, see I. Wood, *The Hotel Licensees of Goulburn, 1.7.1848–31.12.1900: A Collection of Facts*, privately published, Melba, 2005, entry 25.
17. For the Chisholm family's interests and influence in the Goulburn district, see Wyatt, *History of Goulburn*, 1941, 33, 44, 115, 121–2, 159–60, 178, 221.
18. *Emp*, (9 October 1856), 3; *GHCAA* (19 December 1857): 2; *GHCAA* (3 July 1858): 2.
19. NAA, SP 32/1 (item 433412), Breadalbane (Mutt Billy) Post Office file (box 99). Note the references to the postal function in Lodge's letter to Cowper, 27 February 1865. *Cf* G Weatherstone, *Parkesbourne: a Journey Into the Past* (Goulburn: Argyle Press, 1986), 35; Hannan *Where Were They and What Were They Doing in 1872*, 18 (although both incorrectly identify the postmaster as James Lodge). Also see Brown, *Where Once the Wagons Met*, 17. Finally, note that Mary Lodge also served as the postmistress at Mandurama when she and Thomas were there in the late 1870s until her death in 1899 (T Treasure, *Mandurama and Its Neighbours* [Mandurama: Mandurama School of Arts Committee, 1992], 44, 132).

The new inn was named the Breadalbane Hotel.[20] The opening on 1 July 1858 was a significant event, with the enthusiasm of the locals depleting all stocks of champagne. It was a bold venture by a couple so young, but it is one which evinces their deep commitment to the local community and strong hopes for a long Breadalbane future. Other families were also putting down roots in the area and the inn quickly became a nucleus. The construction of the railway in the 1860s also increased custom. The 170-year-old towering bunya pine (*araucaria bidwillii*) that today towers beside the old hotel is a testament to their dreams, no matter how quickly they were to dissipate after the catastrophic events of February 1865.

The Bushrangers and their Impact

Bushrangers were certainly active in the area during the 1860s. In February 1863 two masked men ransacked the hotel, seizing cash and jewellery valued at £50, including Thomas' own engraved watch.[21] They also stole a bay mare, for which Lodge posted a reward of £2 with another £5 upon conviction.[22] According to a local family, later that same year, the Lodges were again targeted by bushrangers. Thomas gave a handful of gold sovereigns to Mary, who concealed them quickly in a hollow candlestick that she held while the bandits searched the premises. According to this story, the disappointed bushrangers felt obliged to pay for their own drinks and bemoaned how poorly the Lodges were faring as hoteliers.[23]

As mentioned, pundits have repeated the claim over the years that the Lodges' hotel became a 'robbers' roost' and Lodge a 'bush telegraph' of the Clarke Brothers, Frank Gardiner, and Ben Hall.[24]

---

20. *GHCAA* (16 April 1859): 2. Although some publications erroneously claim it was called the Breadalbane Inn. This commonly repeated error possibly began with WS Gilbert and LW Wilson, *Rural Inns of the Goulburn District (1830–1900): Signs, Locations, Dates, Licensees, History Notes* (Goulburn: privately published, 1989), 10–11.
21. *New South Wales Police Gazette* (25 February, 1863): 56. But note that he is misreported as J Lodge.
22. *GH* (7 March 1863): 3.
23. D England to J Booth, April 1990, as reported in 'Lodge Family News', 1998, 44.
24. For example, see SJ Tazewell, *Grand Goulburn, First Inland City of Australia: a Random History* (Goulburn: Council of the City of Goulburn, 1991), 252; Croke,

There is no firm evidence of this. First, the Clarkes were not active in the area until *after* the Lodges had left, which serves to show how ill-informed much of this speculation has been. Second, Gardiner is not confirmed to have visited Breadalbane at all. However, Hall and his gang were active in Breadalbane and two episodes at the end of their career involve the Breadalbane Hotel, but the alleged connection of Lodge to the gang rests precariously on a repudiated statement made by a convicted teenage felon.[25] In any case, the resulting charge was not that Lodge was assisting the bushrangers; rather, that he had simply bought a saddle, which had been stolen by Gilbert and sold on to him at full price by the boy. Moreover, the jury considered the allegation to be false and acquitted Lodge. This failed charge has been exaggerated over the years to the point that many writers have simply accepted it as fact, when his peers had resoundingly rejected the notion of complicity and the testimony of Lodge's compromised accuser. To understand why, let us examine the events.

In November 1864, Hall, Gilbert, and Dunne held up the Yass Mail. After ransacking the mailbags and luggage, they ordered the driver on to Lodge's. It is highly likely that it was young Catholic journalist, Henry Curran, who wrote up the account of this robbery in the *Goulburn Herald and Chronicle* and that he used his future brother-in-law, Lodge, as his main informant.[26] The passage relevant to the Breadalbane Hotel states:

Hotels, Inns and Shanties of the Upper Lachlan Shire, 162–3; Tracey, *Upper Lachlan Shire Community Heritage Study*, 65; Brown, *Where Once the Wagons Met*, 17. All take a contrary view to the court that acquitted him, but none explain how this conclusion was reached.

25. There was a robbery at Chisholm's in late October (*Emp* [1 November 1864]: 5, reprinted widely); a hold-up of the Yass Mail in November (*Goulburn Herald and Chronicle* [hereafter *GHC*] (12 November 1864): 3, reprinted widely); a second attempt on the Yass Mail in January 1865 (*SMH*, (26 January 1865): 8 [account by Frederick Castle/s, also reprinted widely]); and an unconfirmed sighting (*SMH* [14 February 1865]: 4).

26. For Curran, his career and connection to Lodge, see J. McDonald 'Henry Curran, Bushrangers, and a Boorowa Dream', *Journal of the Australian Catholic Historical Society* 38 (2017): 20–33; *Three Henry Currans*, 67–83. Finally, note that the bushrangers paying for their own drinks is an element in the local story about the 1863 incident, discussed above. The story may be a jumble of elements from different incidents.

> *They [Hall's gang] then ordered the mailmen to drive to Lodge's public-house and accompanied him there, where they had something to drink, and treated Mr. Dawson [a magistrate travelling on the coach], the coachman, and some six or seven roadmakers who were present, throwing down a pound-note and refusing the change.*[27]

It is possible that in writing up this incident, Curran inadvertently played a part in his fiancé's brother's downfall. Perhaps his candid article backfired in that the police were made to look inept and their adversary, Ben Hall, was glamorised as a 'gentleman' shouting lunch for his captives. The truth of the matter, of course, is that this episode is a common one and the gang bailed up numerous coaches and inns over the years and generally (but not always) ignored the poorer captives, sometimes humouring them and, as in this instance, even showed courtesy to a wealthier victim. There was no implication of the publican doing anything other than what the armed criminals demanded. Yet it probably enraged the Goulburn Police, who may have seen collusion where there was none. Nevertheless, it has to be admitted that the Breadalbane Hotel at this time had a poor reputation in Goulburn, despite its popularity with locals and travellers. Lodge's inn is described by police in late 1864 as a 'resort of disorderly characters' and Thomas himself as a 'habitual drunkard'.[28] It may be polemic, or it may be true. But it was only with great effort and the taking of a temperance pledge that Lodge was able to retain his licence.

The Police Raid on the Breadalbane Hotel, 23 February 1865

After a tip-off from police informer, Daniel Supple, a party of troopers was convened in Goulburn by Augustus Huthwaite, Deputy Police Magistrate. It contained Huthwaite himself, Supple, the enigmatic Detective James Pye—who had assisted in the capture of Frank Gardiner—and Troopers Gall, Gracey, Greer, Parker and Wiles. There was not a Catholic or local among them[29] and it was only Huthwaite

---

27. *GHC* (12 November 1864): 3.
28. *Goulburn Herald* (hereafter *GH*), (4 May 1864): 2–3.
29. Editions of the *NSW Police Gazette* and registers of *NSW Police Employment* for the period show that all troopers and Huthwaite were Protestant, with two of them (Gall and Greer) specified as Presbyterian. Zouch was Anglican.

who had any familiarity with life on the Breadalbane Plains, albeit as an absentee 'squire' of his wife's Wollogorang estate near Collector.

It is thought that Huthwaite's party was headed for Breadalbane, acting on specific information from Supple, that Hall, Gilbert and Dunn were likely to rendezvous at the farm of Thomas Byrne in Mutbilly on 23 February.[30] On the way, it was suggested that the police party should stop first at Lodge's inn, as an informant claimed that their movements were likely to be observed by 'bush telegraphs'.[31] In any case, Lodge's inn was the closest hotel to Byrne's farm and it would have made the most logical point for the troopers to muster. This they did. They apprehended everyone at the inn and hid their horses nearby at the Lodge family's former hotel, Red House (now operated by John Hilton), while not permitting anyone to leave the premises. They suspected a man named Sullivan—who is most probably, John Sullivan, Breadalbane carrier and a neighbour of the Byrne family—as a 'bush telegraph'.[32] They also joined up with their informer, seventeen-year-old Thomas Jones, who had known Gilbert for several years and had been an accomplice of the gang. He had already been charged with receiving stolen goods himself and was now in the employ of the police. It is fair to assume that he was hoping to ameliorate the case against himself through cooperation. This, of

30. For Lawler, see *GHC*, (2 September 1865): 4.

31. Police suspicions of 'bush telegraphs' are reported in a flawed report (*SMH*, [14 February 1865]: 4), which says that a police guard of the Yass Mail stopped at Lodge's where they thought that there may have been agents of the bushrangers posted. The report also says that, at one stage, there had been no other hotels on the road between Murrumburrah and Fish River, which is a huge area (120 km or so) in which there had been scores of hotels operating since the 1830s. In any case, the Breadalbane Hotel was opened by Lodge in 1858, when there were also Hilton's Red House and Keeffe's Harp of Erin nearby. The police information and/or the local knowledge of this account seems fundamentally flawed. While police did seem to detain 'two young men supposed to be bush telegraphs' at Lodges (*The Tumut and Adelong Time*, [2 March 1865]: 2), no charges were ever laid, or formal arrests made of any of these suspected informants. Of course, the police were losing any attempts to win over local support with their heavy-handed tactics and must have, out of frustration, assumed a much greater level of complicity than there actually was. Nevertheless, later writers have taken this one-sided information derived from erroneous accounts as 'fact' (for example Clune, *Ben Hall*, 453).

32. For John Sullivan, see Hannan, *Where Were They and What Were They Doing in 1872*, 182. Sullivan's and Byrne's contiguous properties are clearly marked on the Mutmutbilly Parish maps.

course, is the youth who accused Lodge of knowingly buying a saddle stolen by Gilbert; that is the charge mentioned above.[33]

As we will see, in a letter dated a few days later (transcribed in full below), Lodge complained to Charles Cowper, the Colonial Secretary, that he, his family, and guests were treated poorly by the police during the raid and that the troopers had been drunk and abusive. He said that he had received no satisfaction when he immediately raised his complaint with the Goulburn Superintendent of Police, Captain Henry Zouch. It is strange that, with about twenty adult witnesses available, the complaint was never tested.[34] Zouch and his masters ignored it, which suggests that either there was something to hide, or the complaint was so doubtful it could be ignored.

Letter from Thomas Lodge to Colonial Secretary Charles Cowper

27 February 1865

Sir—It becomes my painful duty after making a report to the Superintendent of Police here, which received little or no attention, to address you, upon what I consider an overstepping the boundary of their duty by some members of the Goulburn Police Force.

33. According to NSW birth, marriage, and death registers, this is Thomas William Jones, born 1848, Mummel (near Goulburn), the son of William Jones (1809–1862) and Susan Ritchie (1830–1910). He married Anna Maria Smith on 12 July 1876 at Goulburn and returned to Lost River (near Crookwell). His father resided in Clinton Street directly across from Henry Lodge's inn, John Barleycorn, where he died in 1862 (*GH* [8 November 1862], 3). Thomas Jones says in the trial that he knew the Lodge family. There may have been 'bad blood' between the families motivating the son's actions; if not, there certainly would have been after the son's actions against Thomas Lodge as a paid police informer. Jones was eighteen at the time of his trial, but seventeen in early 1865. He said that he had known Gilbert for about seven years.

34. The estimated number of people detained is first reported in *Illustrated Sydney News* (hereafter *ISN*), (16 March 1865): 2. Although this late composite article is seriously flawed, this particular detail may be roughly right. There were the members of the Lodge family (6), servants (2–4?), post office clients (2?), patrons (6–12?) and teachers (2); that is, up to twenty six people detained in a single room of the hotel. The rooms of the building are all relatively small, except the guests' lounge, which could accommodate twenty six people without too much discomfort for several hours. I am in the debt of current owner, Shlomi Bonet, for showing me through the old inn.

On Thursday the 23rd instant a policeman, not at all in uniform and beastly drunk, rode up to my house and threatened "I'll shoot you if you don't give me some information about the bushrangers". He left, returned afterwards and begged my pardon – a proof of overstepping the boundary of his duty. He remained at my place from this hour (about 3 P.M.) untill [sic] 8 o'clock, when he joined a party of Police which arrived under the command of Mr. Huthwaite, P.M. and Detective Pie [sic]. This party rode up, dismounted, rushed into the house, snatched the candle off the counter and when my wife remonstrated, threatened to handcuff her. They ordered my servants and some persons who had called in for letters (this being the P. Office), myself and family and the teachers into a room, refusing to allow us to make tea and not permitting us to provide such for travellers which was called for.

They attempted by persuasion and threat to induce my hostler to say He saw the bushrangers dancing in my Hotel, and afterwards told one they would hold me responsible for his safe custody. About half past nine o'clock all but two policemen left the place who were left in charge, one of whom previously assaulted my child with his carbine.

When this party arrived I was engaged in making the mail for despatch to Goulburn the following morning. On hearing the noise I came out, when I was asked if I was Lodge, ordered into the room as before stated, during which time my house was ransacked including the Post Office, the letters for transmission defaced with ink.

On Saturday night Detective Pie and two policemen (not in uniform) arrived at my place and without any warning, in brigand style, presented arms through doors and windows, calling out to those inside "I'll shoot the first one that moves".

Now, Sir, I make a statement which I am in a position to prove, namely, the whole of this body or party of police were drunk or labouring very much under the effects of strong liquor and as a proof, one of them lost his revolver which was picked up by a child 7-years-old and Detective Pie dropped his carbine the following morning (24th) out of his hand and rode about four hundred yards before he discovered his loss.

I am Sir Your

Most Obet.

Humble Servt.

Thos. Jas. Lodge

In the early morning the police released everyone at Lodge's inn, except for Sullivan, whom they took with them, it is said, to ensure that the gang was not warned.[35] It is also possible that Sullivan—if I have identified him correctly—lived next to Byrne and had been co-opted as a guide for their moonlight march. It took the troopers almost four hours to travel just three km to Byrne's farm, which is extremely slow progress, even at that hour of the night. It has been alleged that the party was either incompetent or—as Lodge claims—drunk, to have taken so long in their peregrination.[36] Alternatively, it is possible that Sullivan deliberately waylaid them to buy time for his friend and neighbour. But if this were the case, then this line of logic would also beg the question—if the inn were indeed full of accomplices—why one of the locals had not already slipped out to warn Hall. The strongest explanation, therefore, is that they were inebriated, as alleged by Lodge in his letter to Cowper, which is almost universally ignored by the pundits.[37]

There are two completely different accounts of the ensuing gunfight at Byrne's barn. The police said that the party arrived just after dawn and expected to apprehend the gang in the family's small homestead. However, Hall, Gilbert, and Dunn were sleeping off the effects of the night's gin separately in the barn and the police party inadvertently surprised them as they passed its open door. A brief shoot-out followed. Hall seems to have been wounded in the arm by Huthwaite. Wiles was shot in the hand by Gilbert. Somehow, the outnumbered bushrangers managed to escape barefoot through a cornfield in between armed police, leaving behind their horses, some weapons and supplies. This is the scene so vividly portrayed in the recent film on Hall by Matthew Holmes. Hall and his gang subsequently hid for a while at Purcell's farm. In the meantime, Huthwaite's party arrested Thomas Byrne and his two sons on charges of harbouring bushrangers, as well as Purcell (later dropped). The police then retired to the Red House to await reinforcements. Two days later, the gang's stash of cash and other goods were found by Zouch in the bush close to Byrne's.[38]

35. *SMH* (8 July 1865): 5–6.

36. R Bayley, 'The Battle at Byrne's Barn', *Goulburn and District Historical Society Newsletter*, 2009, *passim*.

37. Penzig (*Ben Hall*, 333–4) is a rare exception.

38. See DJ Shiel, *Ben Hall, Bushranger* (St Lucia: University of Queensland Press, 1983), 199–200.

The Byrne family, however, claimed a very different version of events in their trial.[39] It was their story that the jurors believed when the Byrnes were acquitted in July1865.

Lodge's own account of what happened at his hotel on the preceding evening is significant evidence in that it is a detailed first-hand account to have survived concerning the police raid on the Breadalbane Hotel separate to the testimony at the trial, badly epitomised in the press four months later. Yet it certainly has a ring of indignation and looks overly defensive—as indeed does the reported police testimony—but there were many witnesses available to test the accuracy of Lodge's complaint in relation to the events of 23 February. Why then did the authorities bury it? Perhaps they hoped to divert attention from themselves through the charge against Lodge and thought that the complaint would simply disappear. If so, they were correct.

The hostility of the Goulburn party to the locals at Breadalbane stands in stark contrast to the positive relationship generally enjoyed with the *local* police, who had helped them fight bushfires in 1854. I am inclined to the view that Lodge's letter of complaint to the Colonial Secretary, while likely to be exaggerated, was embarrassing for the police. Such a complaint of mistreatment, even if partially true, must have had the effect of the authorities closing ranks against the complainant. It would have been easy for them to pressure young Jones to concoct further charges against Lodge (as demonstrated in his testimony). They must have known how little chance the charge had of standing up in court, but this would not have mattered, as any charge would have had the effect of distracting attention from themselves.

Before forwarding Lodge's letter to Cowper, the Inspector General, John McLerie (the colony's top police officer), annotated it with the remark: 'The writer of this letter has been committed for trial for receiving property stolen by Ben Hall's gang.' The annotation sums up what he thought about Lodge's complaint and it is no wonder that Cowper ignored it. McLerie was a prominent Freemason and on a mission to quell bushranging. He probably had a dim view of the growing Catholic enclave at Breadalbane and its confident publican.[40]

39. *Cf SMH* (8 July 1865): 5.
40. H King in *ADB*, volume 5, 188–9.

He may have presumed that this was an area which needed to be pressured in order to flush out Hall and his associates. He was not going to blink. It is also possible that Curran's article—reprinted widely throughout the colonies—may have embarrassed him and Lodge's letter was too controversial to allow himself to believe the allegations of misconduct.[41]

Attached to Lodge's letter of complaint in the Colonial secretary's file is Huthwaite's fourteen page report of the search for Hall and the gunfight at Byrnes' farm. In it is a very brief section on the police raid of the Breadalbane Hotel.

> I received certain information which confirmed my previous opinion [i.e. that the gang was headed to Byrne's farm] and determined me to bail up Lodges Public House, there being four telegraphs there watching and my party had been seen by a person known to me to be friendly to Hall's gang and who was a head [sic] of me on the road going there (to Lodges). I therefore pushed on, arrived at Lodges before him, surrounded the house, and accompanied by Det Pye proceeded to search and examine the parties there. I found at the house four at least notorious telegraphs one of whom, Walsh, I caught going off on his hands and knees in the dark beside a very suspicious circumstance in a bedroom (which will appear in evidence in a forthcoming prosecution for harbouring). At about eleven I left two men on guard at Lodges with orders to let no one leave the house until released by me—and took all the horses to Hiltons to feed—I was here joined by Trooper Wiles and the lad Jones the approver. Saddled up and started at ½ past 2 a.m. I released the people at Lodges with a caution except one Sullivan alias Grant, whom knowing that if I let him go he would be at Byrnse' [sic] before me. I kept under the pretence of making him shew the road and keeping the side of the ranges when within ½ a mile of the house dismounted and left the horses in charge of Trooper Parker, with the lad Jones to assist him, and proceeded on foot to the house.

41. It is tempting to speculate that Curran's article also angered the newspaper's co-owner, John Chisholm, and might explain why Curran switched his employ to the *Goulburn Evening Penny Post.*

The two versions are so contradictory that their differences cannot be attributed to any natural anomalies that might be expected in separately recalled accounts of the same event. We must conclude that one (or both) of the informants is lying. I suspect that Huthwaite is being less honest than Lodge. If the complaint had been investigated and the witnesses interviewed, the matter could have been resolved. The two juries, several months later, believed the account of the people of Breadalbane over that of the Goulburn Police.

Comparison of the Accounts of Lodge and Huthwaite

Even without Huthwaite's repudiation, Cowper would have been unlikely to have taken Lodge's complaint seriously. At Goulburn, he relied on the patronage of none other than the Chisholm brothers, whose connection to the district began with their father, James senior, a member of the NSW Corps. Second son, John, was a co-owner of the *Goulburn Chronicle*. He had been a key supporter of Cowper in the 1856 election. In the 1860s, the patriarch of this family was the eldest brother, James Chisholm junior who, in effect, was the 'squire' of Breadalbane. He was also a member of the NSW Legislative Council (1851–1856, 1865–1888) and in Cowper's faction. James Chisholm had been annoyed by Lodge's high bid in the land purchases of 1856 and resentment may have simmered.[42] The success of the new Breadalbane Hotel would also have been unwelcome as it eclipsed the Red House leased on Chisholm's land, a few stone throws away. It would be surprising if Cowper had not consulted the Chisholms in the matter of the 1865 court action against Lodge and we could hardly expect a glowing endorsement from the brothers under these circumstances.

In any case, even if I have overstated the likelihood of prejudice against Lodge and his fellow Breadalbanites, his complaint about drunken police at his hotel who had mistreated his family and guests (including the local teachers), was ignored. Lodge must also have known that by submitting his complaint, there would be little hope

42. *Emp* (9 October 1856): 3; *cf GHCAA*, (19 December 1857): 2. For the political connection between the Cowper and Chisholm families, see P Moore in *ADB*, volume 3, 479–80. For the career of the elder Charles Cowper, see JM Ward in *ADB*, volume 3, 475–9.

Lodge	*Huthwaite*
A lone drunken policeman bails up the hotel threatening to shoot the inhabitants unless they provide information about the bushrangers. He leaves, but returns at 3:00pm, remaining until 8:00pm.	No police arrive until the late evening.
Huthwaite's party (also drunk) arrive at 8:00pm and take control of the hotel, search it and lock everyone up, including servants, guests, children and the two teachers; refusing tea for those apprehended in a single room.	At an unstated time the police party arrive, but before a 'bush telegraph' gets there to warn them.
Police ransack the hotel and post office and deface the mail with ink.	Huthwaite and Pye search the hotel, finding four 'notorious telegraphs' including Walsh hiding in a bedroom.
Police interrogate the hostler alleging that the bushrangers were seen dancing in the hotel. One of Lodge's children is assaulted by a trooper with a carbine. One of Lodge's children finds a policeman's pistol and returns it to him.	
All but two police leave at 9:30pm	At 11:00pm two police are left to guard Lodge's while Huthwaite and the rest take the horses to the Red House, where they are also joined by Trooper Wiles and the young informant, Jones.
The remaining police leave in the early morning for Byrne's farm. Pye drops his rifle as he rides off but returns and retrieves it from one of Lodge's children.	Huthwaite and the others return to Lodges at 2:30 am, release the guests and ride to Byrne's farm, taking Sullivan/Grant with them under pretence as a guide

of renewing his publican's licence given that his choice of presiding magistrates to approve the renewal were likely to be Zouch or one of the two Chisholm brothers.[43] His investment in acreage and a twelve room stone inn at Breadalbane was well in excess of £500, some of it, no doubt, borrowed from his father, who had himself over-invested in the refurbishment of the John Barleycorn.[44] Both Lodge families now stood on the brink of financial ruin. Yet Thomas, it would appear, was a man prepared to risk all on a matter of principle.

It is well known how the Colonial authorities were increasingly anxious to bring Hall's gang to justice and brought in extreme steps to do so. Outlawry was certainly a Draconian measure, albeit ultimately effective. This is the context in which we should consider the question of the veracity of the charges laid against Lodge. At the very least, I

43. For the magistrates, see Wyatt, *History of Goulburn*, 1941, 178.
44. *GHCAA* (3 July 1858): 2; *GHC* (16 September 1865): 4.

suspect collusion between Huthwaite and his troopers at Goulburn as they scrambled to cover up their poor behaviour at the Breadalbane Hotel on the night of 23 February. At the Byrne men's trial, Huthwaite and Pye, offer unsolicited statements that they had been sober, as if to pre-empt the counter-charge. I am agnostic, however, about the extent of involvement of the embarrassed Zouch and even less suspicious about McLerie and Cowper. We can understand the attitude that they must have had towards the complainant and how they would have trusted their officers on the ground and what they said, but even if we exonerate these men from suspicion of the deliberate abuse of power in suppressing Lodge's complaint with a false charge, their prejudices and political circumstances would have left them with little option but to trust their Goulburn colleagues and to see only wickedness in Lodge and his largely Catholic and lower-order neighbours. Zouch was a brave officer and efficient in the administration of his duty, but he was Anglican and had little in common with the people of Breadalbane.[45]

The Trial, 7 July 1865

It is not clear why Lodge's trial for accepting stolen goods did not proceed at Goulburn in March 1865.[46] Perhaps the authorities were concerned about support for Lodge in that city, where more people were familiar with the circumstances and where his family had run a popular tavern and his brother-in-law was a prominent journalist and a Catholic leader in Goulburn.[47] Or perhaps they were just being careful and recognised that there was a conflict of interest with the involvement of the local magistrates, Huthwaite and the Chisholm

45. See SC West, 'The Role of the "Bush" in 1860s Bushranging', *Journal of the Royal Australian Historical Society*, 91/2 (2005), 133–47. This is a superior and insightful discussion of bushranging at this time. See, in particular, 136, concerning the frustrations felt by police at this time in securing cooperation at a local level and the impact of sectarian and social divisions.
46. *GHC* (1 March 1865): 2; *GHC* (8 March 1865): 2.
47. Curran was also an active member of the Goulburn Literary Society. It is interesting to note that he read a paper at one of its meetings titled 'The Best Means to Be Adopted for the Suppression of Bushranging in New South Wales' (delivered 29 April 1867; see *GHC* [1 May 1867]: 2]). No doubt, it was a means of suggesting to his fellow townsmen that there were better ways than the heavy-handed tactics of McLerie and Huthwaite.

brothers. In any case, the trial became a high-profile matter brought before the Supreme Court in Sydney, despite the insignificance of the felony itself. The Crown appointed Peter Faucett, arguably, its most senior prosecutor.[48] Lodge may have used his church connections—for he certainly had no money to pay for a sophisticated defence—as he secured the services of the colony's most preeminent Catholic barrister, William Dalley, a friend of Polding, as well as leading Sydney counsel, the Jamaican-born, Robert Isaacs.[49] Fortunately for Lodge, the matter was heard before Justice Alfred Cheeke, who was a man unlikely to be swayed by sectarian or political considerations.[50]

Lodge's trial was reported in the *Sydney Morning Herald* (8 July 1865, 5–6). The report shows that the case brought against him was weak. In his summation, Justice Cheeke advised the jury to be wary of an *unsupported* account by a young felon such as Jones. Even so, they must have needed little guidance to question Jones' testimony themselves. If, on the other hand, the jury did actually think that Lodge was a confidant of the bushrangers, they must have wondered why he would have been so dim-witted to have bought a saddle from a third party at full price. No one would pay full price for stolen goods. It simply does not make sense. It could also be asked that, if Lodge were indeed a bushranger's accomplice, why would he have used an intermediary. It is not surprising that the jury only needed a 'short retirement' to deliver its verdict. It is also clear from the report, that Lodge complied with all requirements of the police and courts after his arrest, despite the poor treatment he and his family and guests had received during the ham-fisted raid of 23–24 February 1865.

If the case was so easily dismissed and Lodge acquitted, why do the modern writers persist in believing as fact what both judge and jury doubted? The assumption of guilt first seems to emerge in a badly drafted article in the *Illustrated Sydney News*. Of course, this monthly was not known for its journalistic merit.[51] Its account of the raid on the Breadalbane Hotel used a number of earlier newspaper reports

48. For Faucett, later, a puisne judge of the Supreme Court, see WB Perrignon in *ADB*, volume 4, 157–8.
49. For leading Sydney counsel, Isaacs, see JR Forbes in *ADB*, volume 4, 464. For Dalley, a high-profile barrister and friend of Archbishop Polding, see B. Nairn and M Rutledge in *ADB*, volume 4, 6–9.
50. For Cheeke, see H T E Holt in *ADB*, volume 3, 384–5.
51. For Example *SMH* (October 1853): 2.

to construct an erroneous retrospective summary. The writer did not seem to understand the earlier press reports, nor took any trouble to check the information. A number of key facts were botched.[52] In particular, it is riddled with errors in relation to the raid on Byrne's farm. Yet most pundits since have taken either the repudiated testimony of Jones or this sloppy piece of journalism in the *Illustrated Sydney News* as fact. Many of them have even gone on to exaggerate the errors even further and assumed all manner of sinister motives for Lodge.[53]

Further Punitive Action

One of the immediate financial impacts of the trial was loss of income as the local postmaster. The role was stripped from Lodge due to his alleged association with Hall, which is not surprising. But the manner in which this was undertaken confirms the prejudices of the Goulburn judiciary.

A box of post-office archives for Breadalbane (known as Mutt Billy) now housed in the National Archives shows how Zouch, McLerie, Huthwaite and Chisholm all became involved.[54] At first, an opportunist, Algernon Jones, (who does not seem to be a relative of Jones, the informant in Lodge's trial) wrote to the Postmaster General. Just thirteen days after the police raid he seeks his own appointment as Breadalbane Postmaster. This is five months before Lodge's trial. The Postmaster General seeks urgent advice from McLerie and Zouch. The latter says that Lodge is 'unfit' for the office, but also does not support Jones. He says that rumour has it that Jones too is in league

52. The errors include: the location of Lodge's inn (the wrong part of the Breadalbane district is cited); the claim that Lodge was not present (he had been in Goulburn, but was back in Breadalbane on bail when the inn was raided by police); the reported number of alleged 'bush telegraphs' ('several', when only Sullivan and Walsh were briefly detained); the claim that information was extracted at Lodge's that led them to Byrne's (on information from Daniel Supple the intention was always to raid Byrne's farm from the moment they left Goulburn); Byrne's name (misspelt as 'Burns'); and the claim that the horses were left at Lodge's with two constables (it was the reverse, with the horses stabled at Hilton's Red House).
53. For example, Weatherstone (*Parkesbourne*, 36) quotes the *ISN* passage word for word (without identifying his source) and accepts what was said as fact without any reference to contrary newspaper reports or other evidence.
54. NAA, SP 32/1 (item 433412), Breadalbane (Mutt Billy) Post Office file (box 99).

with the bushrangers (letter dated 15 April 1865). Instead, Zouch recommends that the position be given to John O'Keeffe within 'half a mile'. In fact, O'Keeffe is almost four miles away. It also happens that one of the sureties offered for O'Keeffe's bond is by none other than Augustus Huthwaite (application dated 9 May 1865) and Huthwaite mentions him as one of his informants in the raid on Lodge's (page 2 of the statement appended to the letter of complaint).

Lodge accepts his fate and politely writes to the Postmaster General stating that he will comply with the provisions of his removal, but states that O'Keeffe is not a local and that, as he is leasing his hotel to John Hannan, the role of Postmaster should remain at Breadalbane (letter dated 7 May 1865). The suggestion is ignored and O'Keeffe is installed. This stirs up immediate discontent in Breadalbane with a number of letters (with sixty one memorialists supporting Jones and eighty two supporting Hannan) sent to the Postmaster General arguing about the location of the post office. The punitive nature of Zouch's misleading advice is clear. Huthwaite and Chisholm are eventually consulted. Not surprisingly, Huthwaite favours his man (O'Keeffe) and Chisholm recommends setting up a post office at Hilton's; that is, his tenant at the Red House on his own land (letter dated 8 August 1865). Self-interest abounds, if not, vindictiveness.

Post Office archive boxes are usually mundane bundles, but the flurry of heated correspondence triggered by McLerie and Zouch's attempt to punish the village is an exception. The action is consistent with his prejudice against the Breadalbane Catholics and Lodge. The police chose to ignore Lodge's letter of complaint about the raid in February. They chose not to interview the twenty plus witnesses at the hotel and now we learn that months before the trial had even commenced, they tried to punish the Breadalbane community by removing its post office.

Rebuilding in Marulan, Jacqua and Mandurama

The year 1865 was not just a bad one for Lodge in terms of the damage to his reputation and the loss of the fruits of twelve-years hard work, but he also had to face the tragic loss of a child. Thomas junior died in September.

The hotel struggled on, but Lodge had two mortgages at high interest and it was only a matter of time before foreclosure.[55] Lodge did, however, have a road contract with the government to construct a section of the Yass Road.[56] But, for whatever reason, the Commissioner of Roads delayed remittance of £305 for work that had already been undertaken. This may have been a matter of bureaucratic incompetence, but given the authorities' other actions against him, the matter begs suspicion. On balance, the delay seems deliberate. At this time, Lodge's father, Henry, filed a claim in Goulburn to recoup a sum of £174 from his son.[57] Henry himself had been declared insolvent and may have been forced by his creditors to seek the money owed him by Thomas. This, of course, had the effect of bankrupting Thomas, who lost the hotel and land. Thomas was declared insolvent within twelve months.[58]

The next we hear of the Lodge family is in late 1867 at Marulan (then, Mooroowoolen), where they purchased a block of land. They appear to have been among those hoping to take advantage of the building of the railway.[59] But after Marulan's short-lived boom, the Lodges moved to Jacqua. Mary applied for the position of Postmistress and was even supported in her application by the emancipated Irish rebel, John Hurley, who had become MP for Narellan and whom she had probably known from her Campbelltown days.[60] But Mary's appointment was delayed until Thomas's character could be ascertained, as Lodge had been 'considered a great rascal'.[61] Eventually, Mary commenced postal duties in November 1869. At Jacqua, Lodge had a quarter-share of a contract for sinking a 140-foot shaft in the 'Sir Hercules Robinson' claim at Spring Creek for the Kiama Company. Within four years 'bad air' forced the closure of the mine and Lodge turned his attention to the alluvial diggings.[62] At this time, he and two other men came into conflict with a miner named Que Sing over sluice boxes and water

55. Small Debts Registers (1863–1970) of the Goulburn Court of Petty Sessions, item NRS-3038.
56. Supreme Court: Bankruptcy Administration File, item 8046.
57. *GHC* (16 September 1865): 4.
58. *SMH* (6 December 1866): 6.
59. See Booth, 'Lodge Family News', 47–8.
60. For Hurley, see M Rutledge in *ADB*, volume 4, 450.
61. NAA, SP 32/1 (item 10787686), Jacqua Post Office file (box 339).
62. *GHC*, (19 October 1872): 4; *cf* Booth, *'Lodge Family News'*, 48–9.

rights, a common conflict at the diggings. Lodge was found guilty of a violent assault with a shovel and was sentenced to fourteen days imprisonment in Goulburn Gaol.[63] At this time, the Jacqua goldfield was in severe decline.

By January 1876 the Lodges moved to Mandurama.[64] Mary was appointed to run an unofficial post office from their home for which they were paid £20 rent and a salary of £78 per annum.[65] She became admired by the townsfolk, who commemorated twenty years' service as Postmistress by presenting her with an illuminated address and a purse of sovereigns.[66] Thomas established a carrier business and took up mail contracts as well as a short-lived butcher's shop at nearby Carcoar.[67] To his credit, Lodge gave up drinking again and went on to lead a productive and peaceful life in the new community. Their daughter, Alice, became the teacher at Thommond, where Lodge himself built the slab schoolhouse at a cost of £45.[68] But the Lodge family is most fondly remembered in these years for its compassion in stepping in when Thomas' sister and brother-in-law, Ann and Henry Curran, suddenly died in Sydney in 1880 and 1882, respectively, leaving five children orphaned. The Lodges adopted two of the girls, despite their limited means. In this way, the family became a loved part of the local community, just as it had been at Breadalbane. In 1899 Mary died of pneumonia. Her husband followed seven years later.

---

63. *GHC* (6 June 1874): 4; *Goulburn Gaol Entrance Books*, 1874, 101 (entry 1,476); *Goulburn Gaol Discharge Books*, 1874, 75 (discharge number 1,476).
64. NAA, SP 32/1 (item 10787686), Jacqua Post Office file (box 339).
65. NAA, SP 32/1 (item 435884), Mandurama Post Office file (box 404).
66. *The Blayney Advocate and Carcoar Herald*, (24 January 1899, 2), *Cf* Booth, '*Lodge Family News*', 52
67. For the butchery, see *The Carcoar Chronicle*, 24 September 1881, 2. For the carrier contracts see *NSW Government Gazettes*: January–March 1889, 802; January-February 1890, 1,408; November-December 1890, 8,720; January-February 1891, 1,318; November-December 1891, 8,856; January–February 1892, 1,550. These entries cover a range of services over the years, including mail deliveries for Mandurama, Eganton, Walli, Canowindra, Belmore, Galley Swamp, and even Bourke. Mary Lodge, as we have seen, was Mandurama postmistress for many years. See Mary Lodge's death notices in *SMH* (17 January 1899): 5; *Carcoar Chronicle* (20 January 1899): 2. The postmistress position is also noted in her obituary in *The Catholic Press* (9 July 1936): 26.
68. Thommond School Files, State Archives and Records NSW (box 5/17830.3).

Reactions to Thomas Lodge will vary from those who see him as an informant of violent criminals to those who might suggest that he was a class hero who stood alongside benevolent larrikins in an ill-fated struggle against the law. Neither view rings true. As we have seen, there is no worthwhile evidence to suggest that Lodge abetted the bushrangers, but there does seem to be a valid argument to suggest that he, like most other local people, were never going to be perceived as compliant citizens by a hostile Protestant constabulary based in Goulburn. His great mistake – or strength – was to complain about his treatment and to resist intimidation. Lodge certainly had his demons, but the actions of his later life support the view that he was an honourable man. He continued his battle with alcoholism and forged a solid new life in Mandurama. The evidence against him in 1865 shows that only one spurious and minor charge was ever laid. The allegation of buying a stolen saddle at full price defies logic and the charge rested uneasily on the uncorroborated testimony of a compromised youth. The case was dismissed by judge and jury at the time. In the absence of anything to the contrary, so should we.

Journal of the Australian Catholic Historical Society, Volume 41/2020

Edward Gell—The Catholic Architect How a little-known immigrant from Yorkshire influenced the emergent Catholic Church in Bathurst and regional New South Wales

*Graham Lupp**

On 27 February 1858, a 649 ton merchant ship, *The Centurion*, left London for New South Wales. After a journey of just over three months the ship sailed into Sydney Harbour on 7 June 1858.[1] Keeping each other company on the voyage were five passengers; Revd. J. Kinross, Mr and Mrs Pinnock, Mr. Hammond, and Mr Gell. We don't know why four of the passengers made the journey, but the fifth, the forty-year-old Edward Gell (1818–99) was taking up a special invitation that would shape the rest of his life.

Edward Gell (1818–1899). From Gell's photo album, with his own inscription. Collingridge Family Collection

As a newly-certified architect, Gell had been invited to the colony by the

* Graham Lupp is a Bathurst architectural historian and painter, author of Building Bathurst (2018). His website is www.grahamlupp.art

1. NSW Australia Unassisted Passenger Listing 82015439, and *SMH* (7 June 1858): 4.

Archbishop of Sydney, John Bede Polding (1794–1877), to supervise construction of a new church in Bathurst, then a remote town 125 miles west of Sydney. To understand why Polding would import an unknown and relatively inexperienced architect like Gell, we first need to briefly consider some aspects of the early development of the Catholic Church in Australia.

Ordained a bishop in London in 1834, Polding then became Vicar Apostolic of New Holland, Van Diemen's Land and adjoining islands. He arrived first in Hobart on 6 August 1835, but soon sailed for Sydney, arriving on 13 September. Polding's mission was to establish the Catholic faith throughout the huge region of NSW, which then comprised most of the eastern seaboard.

In this task Polding found invaluable assistance in another Benedictine monk, William Bernard Ullathorne (1806–89). Polding and Ullathorne had met in 1824 while the latter was training as a priest at the Benedictine monastery at Downside Priory, near Bath in England. Polding had been at the priory since 1814 and in his role as Prefect, and Novice-Master from 1823, he mentored the young monks such as Ullathorne.[2] With long careers that frequently overlapped, Ullathorne and Polding were among the founders of Catholic Australia.

When Polding arrived in Australia he was faced with an urgent need for ecclesiastical buildings of all kinds—churches, schools, presbyteries and convents. While the colony had a surprising number of well-qualified tradesmen, both convicts and free-settlers, there were few architects, so Polding began using plans sourced from England. Among his other duties at Downside, Polding had been responsible for raising loans and supervising the construction of new buildings.[3] In 1823, when new monastic buildings and a chapel were built, Polding became acquainted with the appointed architect, Henry Edmund Goodridge (c1800–63) of Bath.

Architectural historian Brian Andrews examines the nineteenth-century use of English architects in Australia in great detail in his account, *Polding's English Architects.*[4] Over a period of thirteen years from 1834, Polding purchased plans from three English architects:

2. Frances O'Donoghue, *The Bishop of Botany Bay: The Life of John Bede Polding* (Sydney: Angus & Robertson, 1982), 3.
3. O'Donoghue, *The Bishop of Botany Bay*, 6–7
4. Brian Andrews, 'Polding's English Architects', *Tjurunga*, 47 (1994): 21–44.

first Goodridge, the Downside architect, then the celebrated Augustus Welby Northmore Pugin (1812–52) and, finally, a Coventry-based architect, Charles Francis Hansom (1817–88).[5]

When Polding returned to England in 1841 on his first trip home from Australia, he was drawn to the growing reputation of Pugin and, abandoning Goodridge, he purchased a number of Pugin's designs. As the recognised father of the Gothic revival in England Pugin advocated a return to a pure form of Gothic architecture, while Goodridge's work suffered from the influence of an eighteenth-century amateurish and short-lived style called Gothick which, in the hands of untrained designers, affected the trappings of medieval architecture without the understanding of the style that Pugin so famously revived. In Australia, at least eight Pugin's buildings can now be identified,[6] although, like Goodridge and Hansom, Pugin never visited the colony.

Inspired by Polding's talk of Australia, Ullathorne was only twenty-seven when he arrived on *The Thomas Munro* as the Vicar General of NSW on 18 February 1833.[7] To help address a chronic shortage of priests in NSW, Ullathorne later undertook recruiting trips to England, although he had more success in Ireland. Recruiting in Ireland may have been Polding's suggestion because, although a native of Lancashire and a staunch believer in an English Benedictine future for Australia, Polding empathised with the numerous Irish pupils at Downside.

Irish immigration largely determined the development of Catholicism in Australia. Despite English Benedictine intentions, the future was decided by waves of Irish immigrants, first as convicts after the ill-fated Irish rebellion of 1798 and, later, as thousands escaped the Irish Potato Famine of 1845–49. This can be seen in the history of the Church in Bathurst, where the earliest Catholic services were given in November 1830 by a devoted Irishman, Fr John Joseph

---

5. Charles Hansom trained under his architect brother, Joseph Aloysius Hansom (1803–82), known for publishing the influential architectural journal, *The Builder*, in 1842, and as the inventor of the Hansom cab.
6. Brian Andrews, *Australian Gothic* (Melbourne: Melbourne University Press, 2001), 151–153.
7. Cuthbert Butler, *The Life and Times of Bishop Ullathorne, 1806–89* (London: Burns, Oates and Co, 1942), 29–30.

Therry (1790–1864), who had arrived as the first official Catholic priest in the colony in 1820.[8]

Polding, Ullathorne and Charles Hansom

Regarding his choice of architects, Polding turned to Charles Hansom because Pugin's increasing fame meant his services had become too expensive.[9] As a skilled practitioner of Pugin's pure Gothic style, throughout his career Hansom designed numerous churches in the West Country of England, most notable among them St John's in Bath, built 1861–63. To quote Brian Andrews, 'It would be fair to say that the majority of Charles Hansom's English churches are scholarly, competent and at times above ordinary examples of the early Gothic Revival genre.'[10] As a far less expensive, but highly-considered architect, Hansom would have been a natural alternative for Polding. However, Hansom's involvement was not accidental.

Born in York in 1817, Hansom was the Town Surveyor in Coventry in 1843 when William Ullathorne, who had just returned from his eight-year mission in Australia, commissioned him to design a new parish church in Coventry, to be called St Osburg's. This was Hansom's first major church design.

Ullathorne was born in Pocklington about thirteen miles from York. Working together on St Osburg's, the two Yorkshiremen soon discovered a mutual passion for Gothic architecture. This led to a lifelong friendship which saw them travel together through Europe studying medieval church design. Their travels included Bruges, Ghent, St Troud, Leau, Louvain, Aix-la-Chapelle, Liege and Cologne.[11] The depth of their friendship can be measured by the fact that Ullathorne became godfather to Hansom's son, Edward,[12] who later joined his father's architectural firm.

When Polding visited England between February 1846 and March 1848 seeking church designs, he replaced Pugin with Hansom. No doubt this was at the urging of Ullathorne, because Pugin himself

8. Graham Lupp, *Building Bathurst* (Bathurst: Bathurst Regional Council, 2018), Volume I, 132–136.
9. Andrews, *Polding's English Architects,* 36–37.
10. Andrews, *Polding's English Architects,* 36.
11. Judith Champ, *William Bernard Ullathorne* (Leominster: Gracewing, 2006), 116.
12. Champ, *William Bernard Ullathorne,* 403.

recommended Hansom to Ullathorne when he was looking for an architect for St Osburg's.[13] When Polding asked for plans for clerestoreyed churches, Hansom duly provided two sets of drawings, one for a small church Polding intended for Mudgee, eighty miles north of Bathurst. The second design was for a large church in Bathurst, which later became the Cathedral of St Michael and St John.[14] The Bathurst church was a rework of the design of St Osburg's. To accommodate antipodean orientation, Hansom simply mirror-reversed his plans so the side entry moved to what became the sunny northern elevation.[15]

Very Revd Dr John Grant (1816–64), Dean of Bathurst. Gell's photo album. Collingridge Family Collection

Rev Dean John Grant

Although Polding returned to Australia in 1848, it was not until 13 September 1853 that he finally brought Hansom's plans to Bathurst.[16] Earlier that year an Irish priest, John Grant (1816–64), was appointed to Bathurst. Grant had been studying at St Kieran's College, Kilkenny, when Ullathorne recruited him as a volunteer for NSW. The twenty-year-old Grant

13. Champ, *William Bernard Ullathorne*, 115–116.
14. Monsignor Leo Grant, *Salt of the Earth*, undated, 250.
15. Hansom's Australian buildings include the cathedrals of St Patrick's, Ballarat, 1852 and St Francis Xavier, Adelaide, designed in 1854–58. Smaller parish churches, mostly in Victoria, include St Peter's, Daylesford; St Augustine's, Creswick; St Patrick's, Kilmore; and St Mary of the Holy Rosary, Kyneton. Two further examples in Victoria worth visiting are St Patrick's, Port Fairy and All Saints' Church, Portland. Andrews, *Australian Gothic*, 146–148.
16. Grant, *Salt of The Earth*, 250.

arrived in Sydney on 21 September 1836. He entered St Mary's Seminary and was ordained Priest on 20 August 1843. After serving as Chaplain at Darlinghurst Gaol, he was sent to Appin, Picton and Berrima. However, while serving at Windsor in 1851 his health began to fail. While on leave in Europe, he received his Doctor of Divinity from Pope Pius IX.

Returning to Australia he was posted to Bathurst and put in charge of building the new church of St Michael to replace an early and, by then, dangerously decrepit church of the same name, built 1839–1843. By the time Polding visited Bathurst to lay the foundation stone for the new church in November 1857,[17] John Grant had quietly added the name St John, thus creating the church of St Michael and St John. The church became the cathedral after Matthew Quinn was consecrated first Bishop of Bathurst in Dublin Cathedral on 14 November 1865.

In addition to his ill-health, Grant's struggle with the onerous task of building this large church was made worse by other matters. Although Bathurst was well supplied with capable builders,[18] one major problem was the lack of a suitably qualified professional to ensure proper supervision of the project, which involved solving problems such as building on Bathurst's notoriously bad reactive clay. This problem was solved almost by chance when a surveyor and engineer, Peter Edwin Henderson (1813–1904), came to Bathurst in early in 1858 to survey the last leg of the intended railway line over the Blue Mountains, commissioned by Governor Denison.[19]

Henderson solved the problem of reactive clay by his use of mass concrete for the footings. Over five feet deep and totalling 460 cubic yards, the concrete footings provided a massive foundation which is still in excellent condition 150 years later.[20] *The Bathurst Free Press,*

17. On the same journey Polding laid foundations stones for churches in the NSW towns of Orange, Carcoar and King's Plains (Blayney). *Bathurst Free Press* (28 November 1857).
18. Lupp, *Building Bathurst,* Volume I, 91–121.
19. Lupp, *Building Bathurst,* Volume I, 309–310.
20. In February 2013 the Roman Catholic Diocese started a major restoration of the Cathedral. The heritage architect, Christo Aitken, confirmed that the structural integrity of the building, including the tower on which it is hoped to erect the spire shown on the original drawing, but not built, is very much intact with little evidence of movement or cracking.

20 January 1858, stated that this was the first time concrete had been used this way in the colony. With this major section of the work completed little more is heard of Henderson after he departed Bathurst to resume his railway survey, this time in the Hunter Valley.

Edward Gell[21]

Dean Grant must have been relieved when later in the year architect Edward Gell arrived in Bathurst to take over the construction. Having arrived in Sydney in June, Gell stayed only long enough to make contact with Archbishop Polding, and familiarise himself with life in the colony. He made time to complete several sketches of the original St Mary's Cathedral (destroyed by fire in 1865), which was undergoing an extensive remodelling to a design by Welby Pugin. Only six weeks later, on 21 July 1858, *The Bathurst Free Press* carried a tender notice calling for tenders for the Catholic Presbytery in Orange, '. . . application to Mr. GELL, Architect, Bathurst.'

A number of sources give explanations of why Gell came to Australia. Revd John Hall, in his *History of St Stanislaus' College, Bathurst,* 1944, claims that Archbishop Polding invited Gell. Adrian Mitchell and Joan Kerr both state that Gell, under the patronage of Ullathorne, then Bishop of Birmingham, was formally invited by Polding to work on Hansom's Bathurst church.[22]

Edward Gell was born in 1818 in Hedon, a small village east of Hull in East Riding, Yorkshire. When Gell's father, Edward senior (1790–1819), a shipwright, drowned when Gell was only a few months old, Gell's mother, Elizabeth Pickering (1788–1875), was left to bring up the family.

Among his siblings Gell had an older brother, John (1812–94), a carpenter, who emigrated with his family to New Zealand in 1842 where he became a successful builder. Gell also had two sisters, Mary (1810–70) and Frances (Fanny) (1815–91). By 1841 Gell, now twenty-two, was living with sisters Fanny and Mary in St Nicholas Cliff, Scarborough, on the North Yorkshire coast.

---

21. Gell is pronounced with a soft 'G', as in 'to gel'.
22. Adrian Mitchell, *Plein Airs* and *Graces, the Life and Times of George Collingridge* (Kent Town SA: Wakefield Press, 2012), 68. Joan Kerr, 1977 PhD thesis, Designing a Colonial Church, York University, 343.

As noted above, William Ullathorne was born at Pocklington, about 30 miles from Hedon where Gell was born. In 1817, when Ullathorne was only ten, his entire family moved to Scarborough. In June 1841, having just returned from Australia, he was living briefly with his family in Scarborough at the same time that Gell was there with his sisters Mary and Fanny.[23] It was then that Gell and Ullathorne would have met, because Ullathorne's brother James (1810–65) was courting Fanny. The couple were married in 1842. Contact between the families must have been constant, as they lived within an eight-minute walk.

It is assumed, therefore, that Ullathorne, who had recruited Grant from Ireland and would have known of his difficulties in Bathurst, must have discussed with Polding that Gell would be in a position to emigrate to NSW to complete the church. As for his qualifications, research has to date failed to establish how Gell became an architect. The 1851 census shows he was living in Morpeth, Northumberland working on the artistic decorations for a new Catholic church, St Robert's. In the census Gell gave his profession as 'artist'.[24]

In a letter to the editor of the *Morpeth Herald* on 27 July 1867, a contributor signed 'RC', who was an acquaintance of Gell's, names him as the artist who, in 1851, completed the '. . . scriptural and ornamental painting in St Robert's Roman Catholic Church . . .' Gell was also described as 'possessing considerable abilities as a portrait, historical and ornamental painter', and, regarding his whereabouts, 'Previous to going out to New South Wales he resided for some time in Morpeth.'

Throughout his later life he comes across as a consummate professional, forthright and assertive in all he did, so we can assume that if Gell had been a qualified architect, he would have said so in the 1851 census. When Gell arrived in Sydney on 6 June 1858 he presented himself as an architect and took up immediate work for the Catholic Church.

---

23. 1841 UK Census, 6 June.
24. Gell also gave that he was married. No record of this marriage can be found. Gell described himself as a bachelor, not a widower, when he married, Elizabeth Haselden in Bathurst in 1861. He also decided to give his age as thirty-seven, when he was actually forty-three. If Gell had been widowed, it may help explain, why he accepted a new start in NSW.

William Munro, Archdiocesan Architect

It has been suggested that Gell was invited to Sydney to supervise Pugin's remodelling of St Mary's Cathedral in Sydney, but this seems unlikely. By the time Gell arrived, Polding had, two years earlier, given the project to a Scottish Presbyterian builder William Munro (1812–81). Acting initially as the clerk of works on St Mary's, Munro, a good builder, had turned architect around 1856 when he secured the position of Archdiocesan Architect under Polding.

Two years before Gell arrived in Bathurst, on 25 October 1856 *The Empire* reported that Dean Grant had received plans and specifications for a new church in Bathurst, and that work would start 'as soon as the necessary arrangements can be completed.' On 15 August 1857, an interesting tender notice appeared in *The Sydney Morning Herald*. Lodged by Munro, it said 'In consequence of certain alterations and reductions, fresh Tenders are desired for the Roman Catholic Church at Bathurst. Plans and specifications to be seen at St Mary's . . .'

The 'certain alterations and reductions' of Munro's notice refer to the need to convert Hansom's original St Osburg's design from a stone to a brick structure, because of the lack of good building stone anywhere near Bathurst. In reworking the design, in Free Gothic Revival style, Munro lost or altered a great deal of Hansom's refined architectural purity. For example, Munro's octagonal spire, set within a pinnacled, crenellated parapet, is an easier, less elegant solution, and compares poorly with Hansom's traditional broach spire of St Osburg's. Neither the spire nor the pinnacles were built.

In 2006 in the Bathurst Catholic Diocesan Archives, the author uncovered one of Munro's 1857 working drawings for the Cathedral. The drawing is one of two sheets and shows a transverse section, the west elevation facing William Street, and part of a longitudinal section. A second drawing which would have shown the floor plan has been lost. However, Hansom expert, Brian Andrews, has examined the different styles of drafting by Hansom and Munro, and argues that the building we see in Bathurst, despite overall similarities to St Osburg's, owes much more to Munro than to Hansom; and that the one surviving drawing was not by Hansom, but is in Munro's hand.[25]

---

25. Brian Andrews, Who Designed St Michael's Church, Bathurst? Unpublished. Andrews carefully examines the differences in architectural treatment of the two very different men, and their architectural drafting. Original drawings by Hansom are held by Woods Bagot, Architects, Adelaide.

Elevation and sections, St Michael and St John's Cathedral, Bathurst. c 1856. by William Munro, Archdiocesan Architect, redrawn from original plans by Charles Hansom. Catholic Diocesan Archives, Bathurst

The final confirmation of Munro's involvement with St Michael's comes just after Gell arrived in Bathurst to take full control from the ailing and exhausted Dean Grant. On 29 September 1858 a tender notice appeared in *The Sydney Morning Herald* for stone and brickwork for the Catholic church at Bathurst in the joint names of the Architect (Munro) at St Mary's Cathedral, Sydney and Edward Gell, Bathurst. Only a week later, on 6 October 1858, Gell placed the first tender notice for the cathedral in his own name in *The Bathurst Free Press.*

It must have been a great relief to Grant when his beloved church was finally opened on 11 April 1861. Not inappropriately, he took control of proceedings when Archbishop Polding could not complete the journey from Sydney because of bad weather. As expected, there was 'a large assemblage' of about 1,200 people, with the procession starting at eleven o'clock at the old original church of St Michael and making its way down Keppel Street to the new church at the other end of the block.

Despite the magnitude of the occasion for Dean Grant, he had earlier that morning already performed another special duty in the new St Michael and St John's. When Edward Gell married Elizabeth Haselden (1826–1907),[26] it was Dean Grant who officiated in what was the first marriage celebrated in the new church, only hours before it was officially opened.[27] This marks what must have become a special friendship between the two men as they worked together to complete the church.

Unfortunately, the struggle cost John Grant the last of his health. He died of diphtheria in early 1864 aged only forty-eight. It is most appropriate that he is buried in the Cathedral, alongside another tireless worker for the Catholic Church in Bathurst, the first bishop, Matthew Quinn—a man he would no doubt have admired, but was two years short of knowing. As John Grant came from Kilkenny, it is fitting that his memorial stone, made by Hardman Brothers of Birmingham, is in black Kilkenny marble and was designed by his friend, Edward Gell.

26. Elizabeth was one of six teachers at the Catholic Denominational School in Keppel Street. She taught grammar, geography, arithmetic, reading, reading, writing and spelling to an enrolment of seventy-eight girls. Eventually in January 1860, Elizabeth established her own finishing school for girls within the Catholic system.
27. Gell's marriage certificate 11 April 1861, Catholic Chancery, Bathurst.

Bshop Matthew Quinn

After eight years in Bathurst, Edward Gell, the Yorkshireman who became a fervent convert to Catholicism in 1835, and with personal connections to the most powerful Benedictines, Ullathorne and Polding, was well positioned to develop a solid working relationship with the Irish Catholics when Matthew Quinn (1821–85) was installed as first Catholic bishop of Bathurst on 1 November 1866. The arrival of Bishop Quinn marked the beginning of an era in which the Catholic Church in rural NSW developed at an unprecedented rate.

The new Catholic Diocese of Bathurst was created and the church became the Cathedral of St Michael and St John. The Catholic population of the new diocese at that time was about 13,000, so an urgent need for churches, convents, schools and presbyteries triggered an extraordinary building programme that extended over the huge diocese which covered much of central NSW.

With his wife Elizabeth fully engaged teaching Catholic children, and an abundance of architectural commissions for Gell—a church and mill in Cowra, a hospital in Carcoar, a presbytery in Orange, and in Bathurst, numerous shops and dwellings, a Presbyterian school and a new bank, he was the natural choice for a much needed diocesan architect.

When Quinn arrived he brought with him an entourage that ensured he would not be alone in the task ahead. He and his cousin, James Murray (1828–1909), had been consecrated together on 14 November 1865 in Dublin Pro-Cathedral—Quinn as bishop of Bathurst, and Murray as bishop of Maitland. The pair arrived in Sydney on *The Empress* on 21 October 1866. The event was reported in a detailed article in *The Empire*, noting that both bishops were greeted by Archbishop Polding, numerous dignitaries of the Catholic church, and a crowd of between 2000 and 3000. Accompanying the bishops were nine priests, eighteen nuns, and six postulants.[28]

Despite the distance between their respective dioceses, Quinn and Murray worked closely together over the years. On numerous occasions they attended important ceremonies, such as the opening of new buildings, where one often officiated as a guest in the other's diocese. For example, Murray laid the foundation stones of St Mary's Convent, Bathurst (1868), St Joseph's Church, Orange (1869), Catholic school, Wellington (1875) and St Ignatius, Bourke (1876).

28. *Empire* (23 October 1866): 8.

Right Revd Dr Matthew Quinn, Bishop of Bathurst, Gell's photo album. Collingridge Family Collection

He also opened St Brigid's, Moorilda (1875) and St Mary's, Mudgee (1876), and assisted with the opening of the Carcoar presbytery (1878).

Apart from James Murray in Maitland, Bishop Quinn was further supported by his older brother, James Quinn (1819–1881), who had been appointed bishop of Brisbane on 14 April 1859, arriving in March 1861. In 1873 James Quinn and James Murray were among the eight bishops who attended the opening of Matthew Quinn's finest achievement, St Stanislaus' College in Bathurst. James Quinn also assisted at the opening of the St Francis of Assisi church at O'Connell in 1869 and in 1876 laid the foundation stone of St Charles de Borromeo Seminary, now part of St Stanislaus' College.

It is important to note that Gell designed all the buildings mentioned above, including an extension to St Bede's Church, Morpeth, at which Bishop Quinn officiated for Murray in 1870. Despite a number of architects in the Maitland region, most notable among them being John W. Pender,[29] Murray, no doubt because of his working relationship with Quinn, used the services of the Bathurst based Edward Gell.

In one of Gell's notebooks, kept between 1872–79, we find his notes and designs relating to the Maitland diocese as well as the Bathurst region.[30] For example, in 1874 Gell noted 'for Dr. Murray'

29. Les Reedman, *Early Architects of the Hunter Region* (Sydney: Boraga Academic, 2010), 60–69.

30. The book belongs to Gell's great-great-granddaughter, Mrs Susan Gore of Cornwall. The author is grateful to have had this invaluable primary source in his possession for a number of years, during which time it was thoroughly scanned and studied.

against his sketch design of an (unsuccessful) entry in a competition for St Nicholas' Church in Tamworth. Also for the Maitland diocese, Gell designed a new school and significant additions to the convent in Newcastle for the Dominican order in 1876.

Further north, in the Armidale diocese of Bishop O'Mahony, in 1874 Gell designed All Saints' Catholic Church at Kempsey, and a convent in Armidale 1874 which was either demolished or never built.

Because of the difficulty of travel and the distances involved, it is most unlikely Gell travelled to any of the above buildings. Once plans were delivered either by courier or a travelling priest, supervision was left to a local clerk of works or the integrity of the builder. We know that in 1871 Gell's plans for a church at distant Wentworth where the Murray and Darling rivers join, were delivered by Bishop Quinn as part of a three month round trip via Bourke.[31]

In 2006 the author discovered a collection of Gell's original drawings in the Catholic Diocesan Archives, Bathurst. These included a number of linen tracings Gell did as a record of his original watercolour drawings. Among them was a tracing of the Wentworth church, dated 6 October 1871, and with a note by Gell of his estimated cost for the church of £450. Once sent off, few original drawings survived the rigours of a construction site, so tracings were made as a record.

We do know, however, that Gell personally supervised buildings closer to Bathurst. For example *The Freeman's Journal* of 27 August 1859 recorded that while returning the thirty-three miles from Carcoar, where Gell had been inspecting construction of his hospital, just past Kings Plains (Blayney) his horse fell into a deep shaft located just off the road. Gell was thrown clear, but the horse, ten feet down and with a broken leg, could not be rescued even with the help of 'eight or nine miners' from nearby Whittaker's Inn. For the sake of the suffering animal Gell acted quickly and 'discharged the contents of a brace of pistols into its body'.

In the context of Gell's significance, it may be asked what is it about this country architect that warrants attention? Settling in Bathurst in 1858, Gell accepted the limitations of a country practice and never benefitted from the opportunities of his better known Sydney-based

31. *Bathurst Times* (17 May 1871).

peers, such as Edmund Blacket, Benjamin Backhouse, George Allan Mansfield or Thomas Rowe—although all designed buildings for Bathurst and the district.[32] Gell did, however, bring from Yorkshire a quirkish style, which is at times clumsy and quaint but nevertheless distinctive.

One example is his use of unique brickwork patterns known as diaper work. Originating from medieval Hanseatic Germany, diaper patterns in architecture derive from the patterns women embroidered into babies' diapers utilising the warp and weft of the linen. The not dissimilar checkered coursing of brickwork lends itself to similar patterning using different coloured bricks. The influence spread to Britain, and in part focused in Yorkshire where Hull was a major trading port with northern Europe. Most of Gell's ecclesiastical buildings between 1858 to about 1876 feature diapers, with darker bricks being created by simply dipping a heated brick into hot tar—the resulting uptake of tar produced a contrasting black brick which was also more waterproof. Although others, such as Benjamin Backhouse, used diaper patterning, Gell's use made his work distinctive in the remote Bathurst region.

In her 1977 doctoral thesis, Designing a Colonial Church, the late Joan Kerr describes Gell as '. . . the most interesting of the Catholic architects working in NSW in the 1870s, and it is a pity that the Bathurst diocese only offered limited opportunities for experiment. He was at least fortunate in his main patron, Bishop Quinn of Bathurst.'[33]

As for the 'limited opportunities', in his relatively brief twenty-two years in Bathurst, Gell managed to complete some 162 confirmed buildings, including alterations and additions and those few buildings which can only be attributed.[34] Of this total number, fifty-seven known buildings were designed for the Catholic Church. These

32. Lupp, *Building Bathurst*. The contribution these figures made to rural NSW is well documented in Chapters 4 and 7.

33. Joan Kerr, Designing a Colonial Church: Church Building in New South Wales 1788–1888, PhD thesis, University of York, 1977, 352.

34. It is very likely there are other buildings which may never be identified. Tender notices were the most reliable method of identifying an architect's buildings, however, this method is not infallible. In some cases the client may have known a builder and the work proceeded privately without the need to call tenders. For a catalogue raisonné of Gell's work see Lupp, *Building Bathurst*, Volume I, 321–382.

include minor projects such as a number of sepulchral monuments, and planning the layout of the Catholic Section of Bathurst Cemetery in 1862. In addition, like most architects and builders of the day, Gell worked for other denominations, both the Anglicans and the Presbyterians, on at least fourteen occasions.

Obviously, most of Gell's important buildings were built in Bathurst. While many private commissions, such as the impressive row of shops, *Britannia House,* at 55–61 William Street, built for Thomas Kite in 1871, are outside the scope of this article, our focus here is on a selection of significant buildings done for the Catholic Church during Gell's time in the city.

St Mary's Convent

Upon their arrival the Sisters of Mercy were accommodated in *The Deanery*, John Grant's old cottage in Keppel Street, but when a further seven sisters arrived in mid 1868 it became obvious a convent was needed. Designed by Gell in mid 1868, St Mary's Convent is illustrated here showing how it was linked to the Cathedral by the nun's chancel, later the Blessed Sacrament Chapel, but which is now incorporated into the nave as a public transept. What is unique about this image is that both the convent and cathedral are shown exactly as Gell finished them before later alterations. The crucifixion scene halfway up the tower was carved by Gell.

Gell's St Mary's Convent with adjoining chapel to the Cathedral of St Michael and St John. Both buildings shown as Gell completed them before later alterations. Photo c1869, RC Archives, Bathurst

The Freeman's Journal, 22 August 1868, described the convent as being Venetian Gothic because of its numerous windows and doors, the decorative blind arcading at the eaves, and the diaper patterns in the brickwork. The arcading is more Romanesque revival, with similar detailing found on other Gell buildings around Bathurst—St Thomas' at O'Connell; St Joseph's Orange and the towers of St Stanislaus' College.

In 1887 a third storey was added to the convent, under a distinctive Mansard roof that matched Gell's wing facing William Street. St Mary's Convent, which opened in July 1869, was demolished in 1983[35] and remains a great loss to the architectural heritage of Bathurst.

St Stanislaus' College

Rising above the city like a great Gothic cathedral, this huge building was Bishop Quinn's greatest contribution and Gell's most important building. As a fervent advocate of denominational education, Quinn first established the college as a boys' school in another Gell building, the 1864 Denominational School for boys, girls and infants at the corner of Keppel and George Streets. This was on the site of the old St Michael's Church, which had housed a school since 1842. It was decided to build the present St Stanislaus' College when the 1864 building was handed over to the nuns to become the Girls' and Infants' School.

Stage One of St Stanislaus' College, or 'Stannies' as it is fondly known, was built in 1871–73 at a cost of £4,000. The builder was James Douglas. Quinn furthered his dream of Catholic education when in 1876 he started on Stage Two, St Charles de Borromeo Seminary, built by John Willett. St Charles', which has started in cramped conditions in *Redruth Villa* (also designed by Gell) at 172–174 George Street, was the second stage in Quinn's vision to establish a Catholic educational facility based on the university college and seminary in Harcourt Street, Dublin, where he had been vice-president, and where his brother James had been president, before both were sent to Australia.

---

35. In 1983 the author was commissioned by the Mitchell Library to carry out a measured drawing of the convent with photographic documentation both before and during demolition.

St Stanislaus' College, Bathurst. Stage Three, on right, completed by architect John Copeman in 1907 to Edward Gell's original design. Photo c1915, Catholic Diocesan Archives, Bathurst.

Quinn didn't live to see the fate of his seminary. With the opening of St Patrick's Seminary in Manly in 1888, and the centralising of seminarial training by Cardinal Moran, St Charles' became redundant. It closed at the end of 1891, but was soon absorbed into St Stanislaus'. This central section of the complex, which now houses the Marble Hall designed by James Hine in 1892, is distinguished by the Decorated stained glass window of 1915 on the eastern end of the first-floor chapel.

Gell's masterplan was completed in 1905–07 by Bathurst architect John Copeman and builder William McLean. Copeman faithfully extended Gell's overall design, including the diaper patterns. Although the college has continued to expand, Gell's original design still remains the heart of the complex.

Regional Churches and Convents

Perhaps the next most important contribution by Gell is to be found in the network of regional churches, convents and schools he designed for Quinn and the Sisters of Mercy. Although scattered throughout the district, if visited systematically, these complexes present a pleasing harmony of style and use of materials. Although often much altered, extended or part-demolished, good examples can be found at Cowra 1859 (and second church 1877), O'Connell 1864, Carcoar

1867–70, Orange 1869, Dubbo 1869–74, Bourke 1871–76, Mudgee 1873, Wellington 1875 (demolished c 1890), Blayney 1877, and Forbes 1878. Stand-alone Catholic churches by Gell are at Peel 1859, Kirkconnell 1863, Rockley 1869, Rydal 1869, Rylstone 1873, Molong 1874 and Lithgow 1879 (demolished).

St Mary's RC Church, Mudgee, 1873–76, built over an original church of 1857, reusing the stonework but retaining the old sanctuary and sacristy. The stonework was done by John Burns, monumental mason of Bathurst. Steeple added by Dubbo architect J.P. Watson 1911. Photo, G. Lupp 2011

The small church of The Immaculate Conception at Carcoar is perhaps the most interesting. Perched precariously on a steep site, it is of local basalt in varying shades of ochre with windows and doors framed in pink sandstone. The most splendid of Gell's churches must be St Mary's Mudgee, 1873–76. The sumptuous interior has stencilling by Lyon, Cottier & Co, stained glass windows by Hardman Brothers, and a superb marble altar designed by Bathurst architect William Dryden in 1922. With Dubbo and Cowra, St Mary's is only one of three large stone churches by Gell.

In most cases the convents and schools were built after the churches, and usually in local brick, which invariably featured Gell's Romanesque blind arcading and trademark diaper patterns. At Mudgee, St Matthew's Convent 1878 is in warm-coloured local brick with an interesting corbelled variation on diaper work. In Maitland, Gell's Dominican Convent and Chapel of St Mary and St Laurence O'Toole 1870–72 are also good examples.

At Moorilda, past Newbridge, Gell's three churches, St Andrew's Anglican 1870, St Brigid's Catholic 1871–75 and St David's Presbyterian 1874, are within sight of each other. Gell's other Anglican churches are O'Connell 1865 (attributed), Georges Plains 1867, Rockley 1867, East Guyong 1870, Blayney 1870 and Hill End 1872 (now a ruin). In 1872 Gell designed a vestry, porch, and bell-tower with spire for the 1861 Presbyterian church in Carcoar. As was sometimes his tendency, Gell's tower was overly grand for the modest brick chapel. Of course, it was also richly decorated with diaper patterns.[36] Unfortunately, the design was not built and his drawings are now in The Ferguson Memorial Library Archives, Surry Hills.

Miscellaneous Church Buildings

Some of Gell's most interesting designs fall slightly outside the categories listed above. In 1859 his now-demolished Presbyterian school on the corner of George and Church Streets, Bathurst, is the only known case where he collaborated with another architect—the talented Henry Sadlier (1836–72). This little school and teacher's residence was unusual for its Dutch gables and clustered chimneys.[37] It was replaced by a petrol station in 1929.

Two other schools, St Michael's Denominational School 1864 (demolished 1909) and All Saints' Denominational School 1867, show Gell's use of the picturesque Victorian Rustic Gothic style popular between 1840 and 1890. With its domestic-scaled asymmetrical massing, steeply pitched roofs, and obligatory bell tower, the style was preferred for denominational schools probably because of its religious connotation.[38] Until about 1890 the style was also adopted for public schools, particularly in the work of George Allan Mansfield, architect for the Council of Education 1867 to 1879.[39]

Only a few months after the Sisters of Mercy arrived, in May 1867 two orphaned girls were found deserted by their mother in an untenanted house. They were brought to Bishop Quinn who handed them over to Mother Ignatius Croke, saying, 'Here, Mother,

36. Lupp, *Building Bathurst,* Volume I, 357.
37. Lupp, *Building Bathurst,* Volume I, 324.
38. Lupp, *Building Bathurst,* Volume I, 331–333.
39. Rural examples of Mansfield's schools are Bathurst and Mudgee 1876, and Orange 1879.

is the beginning of your Orphanage.' The first orphanage in Bathurst, housing fifteen orphans, was a weatherboard shed and converted stable. In October 1871 Gell called tenders for a two-storey brick orphanage, which became known as *The Academy*. It was located to the west of the convent approximately where the new school hall stands today and can be seen in several of the 1873 Holtermann photos taken from the tower of the cathedral. Despite Gell's additions in 1876, the building eventually became too small. It was closed in 1909, but reopened in 1915 in *Holmhurst*, a large home at 306 William Street. This spacious residence, designed by John Copeman for James Holmes in 1904, was bought by the Church when Holmes died in 1914.

Conclusion

During his years in Bathurst, Gell's architectural output may have been far greater had it not been for a consuming interest in mining. As early as 1861 Gell was the manager of the Creek Junction Quartz Crushing Company at Mitchell's Creek, Kirkconnell. A few years later he was a director of the Amy Gold Mining Company, also at Kirkconnell, and the Bathurst Gold Mining Company at Trunkey Creek. By 1871 Gell was one of four partners in the Lithgow Valley Colliery Company (LVCC), a demanding enterprise which eventually saw him abandon architecture and leave Bathurst, when he became the Company manager on 30 March 1880.

It is not surprising Gell had an affinity with mining. North-eastern England is one of the oldest coal mining regions in Britain, and Gell, who had travelled throughout the neighbouring counties and lived for some time in Morpeth just north of Newcastle, would have been totally familiar with the mining industry. Arriving in Bathurst between the first and second gold rushes, at a time when rich deposits of copper, silver, lead, zinc and tin were also being discovered in the region, particularly at Mitchell's Creek (Sunny Corner), Gell would have immediately felt at home.

Once he relocated to Lithgow in 1879 to manage the LVCC, his architectural output is difficult to trace. As an architect, Gell would obviously have been involved in building the company's colliery and its successful pottery works, both workers' housing and Company buildings. Some of these are known but it is almost certain that other

Convent of the Good Samaritan, Queanbeyan, 1879-81. This commission given to Gell, on the recommendation of Fr Patrick Birch, with whom Gell had worked on St Patrick's Church in Lithgow. Photo, G. Lupp 2013

buildings by Gell remain to be identified.[40] Among his last known buildings was St Patrick's Catholic Church in Lithgow 1879–80, (demolished in the 1970s), at 68 Left Street. Despite the ready availability of fine sandstone in the district, this relatively small church (56 x 24 feet) was built in brick, no doubt provided by the Company's brickworks to help reduce costs.

Also in 1879, Gell designed the Good Samaritan Convent of St Benedict for the Sisters of St Benedict at 39 Isabella Street in Queanbeyan. The commission came through Revd Fr Patrick Birch who had been the priest at Lithgow before taking charge of the Queanbeyan parish. This handsome building still exists. The windows are of particular interest. A simple flat arch, supporting what is probably rendered brick presently painted cream, supports an unpainted corbelled triangular arch of single bricks which gives a decorative rhythm across the facade that repeatedly catches the eye. Bathurst's most famous son, Ben Chifley, Prime Minister of Australia 1945–49, owed his name to a suggestion made by the Mother Superior to Chifley's mother, Mary Anne, who had served as a domestic servant in the convent.

40. Lupp, *Building Bathurst,* Volume I, 365–366. See also Ian Evans, *The Lithgow Pottery* (Sydney: Flannel Flower Press, 1982).

Much more on the life and work of Edward Gell is covered in Chapter 6, *Edward Gell, The Catholic Architect,* of the author's book *Building Bathurst.* Although there exists a number of sketchbooks, scrapbooks and photo albums, these relate mostly to his work. Nothing to date has been discovered by way of letters, diaries or journals to reveal something of his personality. In the few newspaper reports relating to his activities he comes across as straightforward and decisive.

During the years spent in Bathurst, Gell was the town's first City Surveyor in charge of sanitation and improving the town's appalling roads and footpaths. He was an active alderman for nine years, eventually becoming Bathurst's sixth Mayor in 1867. In the same year, on 3 April, *The Government Gazette* announced that he had been appointed a magistrate of the colony. Gell was also a trustee on the board of the Bathurst Hospital and the Bank of NSW, and a life member of the School of Arts.

The captions in his photo albums reveal a typical Victorian reserve. For example, on a charming photograph of his late mother, Elizabeth Gell (Pickering), taken in Scarborough towards the end of her life, Gell has simply written 'Late Mrs. Gell. Scarboro.' The two portrait photos we have of the man himself are slightly conflicting. The earlier one portrays a certain self-importance, tempered by a hint of self-consciousness, perhaps not unexpected in a formal Victorian photograph. Gell put this in his album with the caption, 'Mr E. Gell.' In the later portrait, labelled simply 'E. Gell, Esq.', he appears to have mellowed.

Edward and Elizabeth had seven children. Of the four who survived childhood, Frances Mary (1862–1937) never married, Mary Josephine (1862–1942) married Louis Francis Heydon and Angela (1866–1948) married Charles Graham Hepburn.

The only surviving son, Edward Augustine (1867–1951), became a highly respected priest. Educated at St Stanislaus' College, Edward Jnr then studied for three years at Oscott Benedictine College in England. After returning to Australia he studied engineering for several years before finally settling on the priesthood. After briefly attending St Charles' Seminary at his old school in Bathurst, in 1888 he transferred to Propaganda College, Rome and was ordained in 1894. Returning to Australia, he served in the parishes of Orange, Wellington and Dubbo, and finally at Ryde in 1906, where he succeeded Samuel

Sheehy (1827–1910) who had been Polding's Vicar-General. During his illustrious career, Fr Gell oversaw the construction of churches at Epping, Meadowbank and Gladesville. He also made additions to the Catholic school at Ryde, and erected the first Catholic school in Gladesville.[41]

Edward Gell Snr continued as manager of the Lithgow Valley Colliery Company until the late 1890s when ill health forced him to move to Potts Point in Sydney, where he had the prominent architect John Kirkpatrick design a house, *Ebor* (now demolished).[42] Gell died at *Ebor* on 31 October 1899 and is buried in Waverley Cemetery. The last rites and the service at the grave were given by Fr O'Gorman of St Canice's Church, Bayswater, assisted by Gell's son, Edward. When St Charles' at Ryde was rebuilt in 1934, Fr Gell donated a window, *The Assumption of Mary into Heaven*, in memory of his parents.

Gell left an estate of £16,674[43] which passed to their children after Elizabeth's death in 1907. In 1913 this inheritance allowed Fr Gell and his sister, Frances Mary, to become the principal benefactors of Eileen O'Connor when they generously purchased a house in Dudley Street, Coogee, which became the home of Our Lady's Nurses for the Poor.[44]

41. *The Catholic Press* (14 May 1931): 18–19.
42. *The Freeman's Journal* (11 November 1899).
43. Gell's Will, State Archives and Records, NSW.
44. www.ourladysnurses.org.au/history

Journal of the Australian Catholic Historical Society, Volume 41/2020

The First Vatican Council (1869–1870)

*Paul Collins**

The notion of the First Vatican Council would have been unimaginable in 1799. The monarchy had been swept away by the French Revolution and revolutionary ideas were spread across Europe by war and conquest. It certainly seemed to contemporary revolutionaries and progressive intellectuals that the papacy, the oldest monarchy in Europe, would disappear with the rest of the detritus of the *ancien regime*. The Papal States had been abolished and Pope Pius VI died as a prisoner of the French in Valence in late-August 1799. However, a conclave managed to gather in Venice under Austrian protection in late-December 1799, and on 14 March 1800 Pius VII was elected. The papacy emerged from the Napoleonic period strengthened by the resistance of the pope against Napoleon and the diplomacy of his Secretary of State, Cardinal Ercole Consalvi.

After the defeat of Napoleon, the victorious powers at the Congress of Vienna in 1815 tried to stabilize Europe by partially restoring the *status quo* before 1789. Despite the opposition of Austria and France, the Papal States were re-established with support from British Foreign Secretary, Viscount Castlereagh. But what seemed a victory at Vienna, in the long term became a noose around the papal neck, with the Papal States often described as the 'sick man of Europe.' With the exception of the period of Pius VII, Leo XII and Gregory XVI restored the old-style clerical government which excluded the laity, and corruption, maladministration and inefficiency reigned supreme. The reactionary Gregory XVI, much given to condemnations of modernity, saw even

* Paul Collins is a writer, historian and broadcaster. His recent book *Absolute Power* is a history of the papacy from the French Revolution to Pope Francis.

steam trains as *chemins d'enfer*. Clerical maladministration led to resistance and revolt manifested particularly in anti-clerical secret societies like the *Carbonari*.

More broadly across Europe the ideas of liberty, equality, democracy, freedom of religion and the separation of church and state continued to spread. As the nineteenth century progressed these ideas gained traction and gradually came to be summed-up in two words, 'progress' and 'liberalism'. Also, a profound shift was occurring as Europe's population increased rapidly (it doubled from 180 million in 1800 to 390 million in 1900), with the focus shifting from a predominately rural-based society to an urban, industrialized one, with mechanization demanding an around-the-clock workforce. Industrialisation soon led to exploitation, with men, women and children working in horrendous conditions, leading to acute social problems and ultimately to a series of revolutions in 1848.

Intimately linked to the ideas of progress and liberalism was the emergence of romanticism, succinctly defined by Kenneth Clark in his TV series *Civilization* as 'I feel therefore I am.' This dynamic movement emphasized nature and feeling; it reacted against the intellectualism of the Enlightenment and the symmetry of classicism. With an emphasis on the beauty of the natural world, it reacted against industrialisation, vividly symbolized by William Blake's 'dark satanic mills.' Beethoven's Third Symphony in E flat major, *Eroica*, composed in 1803–1804, gave expression to the restless energy and struggle that underpinned romanticism and his opera *Fidelio* to the desire for liberty from political repression.

In the Catholic world romanticism found expression in a feeling-centred, more tactile religiosity focused on a merciful, loving, human image of Jesus and on the powerful intercession of Our Lady in contrast to the abstract spirituality and absentee landlord vision of a remote God in the Enlightenment. This new religiosity found expression through devotion to the Sacred Heart, the Passion of the suffering Christ, the Blessed Sacrament and Marian apparitions and pilgrimages to shrines like La Salette and Lourdes. Newly founded, active religious orders of sisters, priests and brothers, embraced these devotions and promoted this more feeling-based spirituality. It led to a century-long emphasis on devotion to the Blessed Virgin. Historian, Roger Aubert, comments that this spirituality 'had a weak theological foundation,' but that it was seen as 'the best means to protest against the rationalistic and pleasure-seeking trends of the time.'[1] As the nineteenth century progressed this kind of religiosity appealed to many, particularly the *bourgeoisie*, who from the 1830s onwards became increasingly conservative and returned to Catholicism and the social stability it offered.

However, there is a remote but more profound theological background to Vatican I, ultimately reaching back to the fifteenth century, to the Council of Constance (1414–1418). Constance was called to resolve the Great Western Schism when there were three claimants to the papacy. On 30 March 1415 the Council issued the decree *Haec sancta synodus* which declared that a general council representing the universal church, held its authority immediately from Christ; it could not be dissolved or prorogued without its consent; everyone, even the pope, was bound to obey it in matters of faith, resolving the schism and the reform of the church; that the council had authority over the pope, just as over other christians, and that when it was in session it was the supreme authority in the church. There has, of course, been much debate surrounding the actual ecumenicity of the council when *Haec sancta* was passed, but nowadays most historians accept that Constance was 'ecumenical from the start.'[2] There is a sense in which *Haec sancta* expresses a constitutional understanding of the Church, whereas Vatican I articulates a monarchical one.

Conciliarism, in turn, gave ecclesiological shape to the kind of Gallicanism expressed in the 'Four Articles' of 1682, the second of which asserts the validity of *Haec sancta* on the authority of general councils over the pope. The fourth article claims that 'In questions of faith the pope has the chief part . . . yet his judgment is not irreformable unless the consent of the church be given to it.' The Four Articles also limited papal power in France with the church there regulated 'by the laws and customs of the Gallican church,' essentially handing over control to the monarch. In 1690 Pope Alexander VIII condemned the Four Articles. Two eighteenth century movements reflected the Gallican position in the Holy Roman Empire. The more ecclesiologically developed of these was Febronianism which

1. Roger Aubert quoted in *History of the Church,* edited by Herbert Jedin and John J Dolan (London: Burns & Oates, 1981), volume 8, 222–223.
2. August Franzen, 'The Council of Constance: Present State of the Problem', *Concilium*, 7 (1965): 29–68.

advocated keeping as much power as possible at the local level in the hands of the bishops and the civil authorities. Josephism, after the Hapsburg Emperor Joseph II (1765–1790), was really just a form of Austrian political Gallicanism. Gallicanism was swept away by the French Revolution, although elements of it survived at the Sorbonne influencing a few bishops at Vatican I.

If Constance represented ecclesial constitutionalism, Ultramontanism (from *ultra montes*, beyond the Alps, that is, all truth and authority is to be found in Rome) represented a monarchical papacy. This was developed in its classical form by Saint Robert Bellarmine in his *Controversies against the Heretics of the Times* (1586). He held that the basic implications of the Petrine texts were that Christ intended that the church be a monarchy and that Christ made Saint Peter monarchical ruler of the church. The Bishop of Rome succeeds to the primacy and prerogatives of Peter *iure divino*, by divine right. Christ is the supreme head of the church, the pope his ministerial head on earth. The pope rules the church with absolute power making promulgations that are binding in conscience. Popes alone can convoke general councils; the pope is above a general council and popes cannot be judged, punished or deposed by a council, or by any human authority and the decrees of councils need his authorisation for validity. The pope is supreme judge of faith and morals and when he teaches the church formally on faith and morals, he cannot err.

But in the nineteenth century a more extreme form of Ultramontanism emerged. It was rooted in traditionalism, a kind of anti-revolutionary ideology that maintained that it was only through adherence to an imagined 'perennial tradition' that truth, peace and stability could be maintained. Revolutions were wrong because they interfered with this process. Family and state were both God-given and there was an indissoluble union between the (Catholic) church and monarchy.

In the ecclesiastical sphere traditionalism found expression in so-called 'Neo-Ultramontanism'. The sources of this were the laymen Louis de Bonald, Joseph de Maistre and the Vicomte François-René de Chateaubriand, he of steak and sauce fame. In his book *Du pape*, De Maistre saw an infallible papacy as a symbol of spiritual authority, truth and stability. Essentially, Neo-Ultramontanism is the conflation of papalism and traditionalism, the ecclesial and the socio-political. Traditionalism was a kind of culture war against liberalism, progress, democracy, equality, the separation of church and state, rationalism and the forces of change. The emerging nineteenth century *bourgeoisie* increasingly longed for a society characterised by a kind of social and economic stability that traditionalism promised. Many of them found this in Neo-Ultramontane Catholicism. Nevertheless, the same *bourgeoisie* were happy to embrace all of the advantages that nineteenth century modernity brought them, particularly freedom of expression.

A key Neo-Ultramontanist was the French journalist Louis-François Veuillot, editor of *L'Univers*. After a wayward youth as a non-believer, Veuillot returned to a Catholicism characterised by a kind of papal idolatry. Typical of Veuillot are statements like 'When the Pope thinks, it is God who is thinking in him' and 'We must affirm squarely the authority and omnipotence of the pope, as the source of all authority, spiritual and temporal' or 'No man knows anything except the Man with whom God is forever, the man who carried the thought of God.'[3] Despite strong criticism from bishops like Archbishop Georges Darboy of Paris, *L'Univers* was widely read by the French clergy.

In the English-speaking world Neo-Ultramontanism was espoused by converts like the pugnacious William George Ward, the grandfather of Maisie Ward who married Sydney-born Frank Sheed, founders of the publishing house Sheed and Ward. WG Ward actually invented the term 'Neo-Ultramontanism'. Ward had a saving sense of humour; it was he who said he wanted 'a new Papal Bull every morning with the *Times* at breakfast.' He was editor of the *Dublin Review*. He was also the theological advisor to another convert, Henry Edward Manning, archbishop of Westminster, who became the 'chief Whip' of the extreme pro-infallibilists at the Council. It was above all Veuillot and to a lesser extent Ward who kept Neo-Ultramontanism on the boil in the press before the Council.

Meanwhile in Rome Giovanni Maria Mastai-Ferretti was elected pope in 1846 as Pius IX. After a brief flirtation with liberalism, he found himself facing a revolution in Rome in late-1848 led by Italian nationalist Giuseppe Mazzini who established a short-lived Roman Republic (1849), forcing him to flee to Gaeta in Neapolitan territory.

---

3. Quoted in Cuthbert Butler, *The Vatican Council, 1869–1870* (London: Collins and Harvill, 1962), 49, 59–60.

The pope returned to Rome in April 1850 after the recapture of the city by French forces sent by then President Louis Napoleon, later Emperor Napoleon III. Profoundly shaken by the seizure of Rome, Pius IX retreated to a kind of integralist Neo-Ultramontanism. From the early-1860s he became myopically focused on his view of himself as pope becoming increasingly narcissistic as he progressively lost the Papal States to the forces of the Italian *Risorgimento*. His mood swings increased and he often castigated people, becoming something of a bully. This is partly what John Henry Newman meant when he said that the Pius' papacy became 'a climax of tyranny.' Pius also became a kind of papal 'personality', appealing to the enormous influx of pilgrims who were able to come to Rome because of the development of public transport, particularly railways and shipping. He was witty and charming and in tune with the romantic spirituality of the time.

The years after 1860 saw the almost complete seizure of the Papal States by a resurgent Italy led by the kingdom of Piedmont under King Victor Emmanuel II and Prime Minister, Count Camillo di Cavour. By 1865 all that was left to the pope was the Patrimonium Petri, the region immediately around Rome. Increasingly the Pope played the role of a martyr and living saint who was being deprived of his kingdom by a resurgent Italy. Pius IX turned increasingly inward, rejecting modernity almost entirely. In the ecclesiastical sphere the best example of this is the Syllabus of Errors (1864), a grab bag of condemned propositions from papal encyclicals and allocutions including rationalism, pantheism, indifferentism, socialism, bible societies, secret societies and attacks on the rights of the church and the pope's civil power. The Syllabus is summed-up when it condemns the proposition that 'The Roman pontiff can and ought to reconcile himself with liberalism and modern civilization'.

As long as the French garrison remained the *Patrimonium Petri* was safe, but the Franco-Prussian War (1870) sounded the death-knell. The French withdrew their troops, and all that was left was an international troop of papal Zouaves and the Swiss Guards who put up a token resistance leading to the final occupation of Rome on 20 September 1870. Pius IX now cast himself in the role of the prisoner in the Vatican and he refused to negotiate with the Italian government.

The irony is that as he lost his civil power, Pius IX increased his ecclesiastical power as the Neo-Ultramontanist revolution shifted the ecclesial focus from the local church to the Roman church as the micro manager of the universal church. There are several elements in this process. The most important was Rome's increasing control of the appointment of bishops. The Congregation of Propaganda Fide had been appointing bishops in missionary territories for two centuries and this became even more highly centralised in the nineteenth century, particularly under the long-serving Propaganda Prefect, Cardinal Alessandro Barnabò. Mission countries included not only the new churches in Asia, Africa and the Pacific, but also included the United States, Canada, the United Kingdom and Australia. Bishops in all mission countries required quinquennial or decennial faculties from Propaganda to fulfill the most basic functions in their dioceses or vicariates. But beyond that Rome gradually gained control of all episcopal appointments as secular governments lost interest in church matters. The influence of papal nuncios increased and cathedral chapters, which had previously had a major say in the appointment of bishops, decreased in influence. Bishops were now expected to come to Rome every five years on *ad limina* visits to report on their dioceses to the pope and the Holy See. Increasingly, they stated to resemble branch managers.

At the same time national colleges for training priests were established in Rome where students were expected to imbibe *Romanità* ('Romanness'), the Roman, clerical-hierarchical way of doing things in the church. This is what John N. Molony is referring to in his book on the 'Roman mould' of the Australian church, although not all of Australian bishops were by any means besotted by *Romanità*.[4] Archbishop Daniel Mannix of Melbourne was distinctly ambivalent towards papal representatives like Apostolic Delegates. As Patrick O'Farrell points out: 'the fact was that to most Australian Catholics, the papacy, its politics and pronouncements seemed remote and irrelevant,' but this doesn't mean that they didn't see the papacy as pivotal in the church.[5]

Since most see papal infallibility as the central issue at Vatican I, I will turn now to the origins of this doctrine. Several recent historians have examined this issue. The distinguished medievalist,

4. John Molony, *The Roman Mould of the Australian Catholic Church* (Melbourne: Melbourne University Press), 1969.
5. Patrick O'Farrell, *The Catholic Church and Community: An Australian History*, 3rd edition (Sydney: New South Wales University Press, 1992), 407.

Brian Tierney, argued the doctrine entered the tradition with Petrus Johannes Olivi and the Franciscan Spirituals in early-thirteenth century. They wanted the pope to declare infallibly that Franciscan poverty is of the essence of Christian faith.[6] But Tierney's view has been questioned by Klaus Schatz who asserts that notions of infallibility gradually entered the tradition as late as the fifteenth century, but that respect had always been shown to the Roman see as the touchstone of orthodoxy. 'The Roman church,' said Pope Hormisdas (514–523), 'has never erred (and will never err),' but this is not the kind of personal infallibility that Vatican I claimed; rather it refers to the Roman tradition of orthodoxy.[7] In a study of the Dominican theological tradition on the papacy, Ulrich Horst shows that, beginning with Aquinas, Dominican ecclesiology held that it was the Roman church that was infallible and that the pope was bound to consult the church before acting infallibly. This was certainly the view expressed by the Dominican Cardinal and theologian Filippo Maria Guidi at Vatican I.[8]

Nevertheless, Pius IX was determined to declare papal infallibility in an extreme Neo-Ultramontane form. For him this seemed to act as a kind of unconscious compensation for the loss of the Papal States and he tried to bully the bishops into accepting that. Vatican Council I began on 8 December 1869. The average attendance at the council, which was held in the apse of Saint Peter's basilica behind the high altar, was between 600 and 700 bishops.

However, Italy and Spain were over-represented. There were 293 Italian bishops for some thirty million Catholics, whereas Germany and Austria-Hungary had a Catholic population of seventy million, but were represented by only seventy seven bishops. There were almost 200 bishops from outside Europe, including ten from Australia. The over-representation of Latin countries has led to some questioning the ecumenicity of the Council, which was called into doubt at the time by the historian Johann Ignaz von Döllinger and subsequently

6. Brian Tierney, *Origins of Papal Infallibility, 1150–1350* (Leiden: Brill, 1988).
7. Klaus Schatz, *Papal Primacy: From Its Origins to the Present* (Collegeville: Liturgical Press, 1996), 118ff.
8. Ulrich Horst, *The Dominicans and the Pope* (Notre Dame: University of Notre Dame Press, 2006).

by contemporary theologians such as Luis Bermejo.[9] On the question of infallibility there were three constellations of bishops at Vatican I. There were the Neo-Ultramontane, extreme pro-infallibilists; the Bellarmine Ultramontanes, moderate pro-infallibilists; and the inopportunists, including those who actually opposed the notion of papal infallibility. All up, there were about 140 bishops in this final group.

First the Neo-Ultramontane pro-infallibilists. One of the leaders of this group was Westminster archbishop (later cardinal), Henry Edward Manning. He was 'an unattractive, ambitious man who was utterly convinced that he was right, and the overwhelming absolutism of his views made dialogue with him almost impossible.'[10] Manning's advisor WG Ward, believed that 'all direct doctrinal instruction of all encyclicals, all letters to individual bishops and allocutions published by the pope, are *ex cathedra* pronouncements and *ipso facto* infallible.'[11] Similar views were expressed by Oxford Movement convert and hymn writer, Frederick William Faber. He is typical of the silly extremes to which Neo-Ultramontanists went: 'What is done to the Pope, for him or against him, is done to Jesus Himself. All that is kingly, all that is priestly, in our dearest Lord is gathered up in the person of His Vicar, to receive our homage and our veneration . . . Both His Mother and His Vicar are parts of our Lord's Gospel.'[12] Another leader of the Neo-Ultramontanists was Paul Cullen, Archbishop of Dublin, who had considerable influence on diaspora Irish bishops, including the Australian bishops. The Jesuit order generally was Neo-Ultramontanist, especially the prominent Jesuit theologians Joseph Kleutgen and Clemens Schrader. Kleutgen's scandalous association with the Roman convent of Sant'Ambrogio has only been recently revealed.[13] The French bishops were divided into pro-definition and anti-definition groups. There were about thirty-five pro-infallibilists,

9. Luis Bermejo, *Infallibility on Trial: Church, Conciliarity and Communion* (Westminster Md: Christian Classics, 1992).
10. Paul Collins, *Absolute Power: How the Pope Became the Most Influential Man in the World* (New York: PublicAffairs, 2018), 43.
11. Cuthbert Butler, *The Life and Times of Bishop Ullathorne, 1806–1889* (London: Burns Oates and Washbourne, 1926), volume 2, 41.
12. FW Faber, *Devotion to the Pope* (London: T Richardson, 1860), pamphlet.
13. Hubert Wolf, *The Nuns of Sant'Ambrogio. The True Story of a Convent in Scandal* (New York: Vintage, 2015).

including several extremists like Gaspard Mermillod, bishop of Geneva and the Redemptorist Victor Dechamps, Archbishop of Mechelen.[14]

The majority of bishops were moderately pro-infallibilist, possibly because many of them had not given the matter much thought. Most of the missionary bishops fitted in here, including the ten Australian bishops who attended, as well as most of the English bishops.[15]

The final constellation of about 140 bishops who opposed the definition were themselves divided into two groups: first, the inopportunists who believed that it wasn't the right time to define infallibility. Most of the bishops who held this view lived in non-Catholic countries and didn't want further alienation between church and culture, including most of the United States' bishops led by Archbishop Patrick Kenrick of St Louis. Among them was Bishop Edward Fitzgerald of Little Rock, Arkansas, who remained behind to be one of the two bishops who voted *non placet* to *Pastor aeternus*, the 'Dogmatic Constitution on the Church of Christ', defining the infallibility and primacy of the pope. The Irish bishops John MacHale of Tuam and David Moriarty of Kerry and the outspoken Serbo-Croatian bishop, Josip Štrossmayer of Djakovo, in present-day Croatia, were also inopportunists. Interestingly, several prelates from Catholic countries were part of this group: Bishop Félix Dupanloup of Orléans and Cardinals Friedrich von Schwarzenberg of Prague, Joseph Othmar Rauscher of Vienna and Filippo Maria Guidi of Bologna. Also, among those concerned about the reaction of civil governments were some members of the Roman Curia, including Cardinal Giacomo Antonelli, the Secretary of State. A number of bishops, like William Bernard Ullathorne of Birmingham and Cardinal Rauscher, were concerned about the effect of the Vatican I definitions on the episcopal and pastoral authority of bishops.

There were also those who opposed the definition on historical or theological grounds. The most important of these was Bishop Karl Josef von Hefele of Rottenburg, the distinguished historian of the ecumenical councils. Inspired by his theological mentor, Johan Adam Möhler, Hefele viewed the church as an organic rather than a

14. Butler, *Council*, 140.
15. Peter Price, *Australian Catholic Bishops and the First Vatican Council* (Northcote, Vic: Morning Star, 2017).

hierarchical structure that primarily expressed itself through synods. In this, Pope Francis has much in common with Hefele, who spent twenty-five years compiling a history of ecumenical councils which remains a standard work. He was appointed an advisor on the rules governing the council in 1868, and in 1869 he was appointed bishop of Rottenburg. He opposed infallibility on historical grounds and left before the vote. A deeply pastoral bishop utterly opposed to schism, he struggled long and hard before publishing the Vatican decrees in his diocese. Another German opponent of infallibility was the priest-historian, Johann Ignaz von Döllinger, writing as Janus, in the book *The Pope and the Council.*[16] Its 425 pages in the English edition constituted a massive assault on the papacy from the medieval period onwards, according to Butler 'probably the most damaging ever compiled'.[17] It caused a sensation in Germany and in the English-speaking world.

Another small group of bishops who theologically opposed infallibility were the Gallicans, specifically Bishop Henri Maret, dean in the theology faculty at the Sorbonne in Paris and the very pastoral Bishop Jean Auguste Vérot, whose ministry in the southern states of the United State of America included being Vicar Apostolic of Florida, Bishop of Savannah, Georgia and then Bishop of St. Augustine, Florida.

While subsequent theological attention has been largely focused on infallibility, in the long-term papal primacy has become the most intractable problem that Catholicism has inherited from Vatican I. It was defined 'almost by default and apathy'.[18] The problem is the wording of the definition; it claims all-embracing and unlimited power for the pope. It is best summarised in the anathema at the end of *Pastor aeternus*:

> If anyone says that the Roman pontiff has merely an office of supervision or guidance, and not the full and supreme power of jurisdiction over the whole church, and this not only in matters of faith and morals, but also in those which concern the discipline and government of the church dispersed throughout the whole world; or that he has only the principal

16. English translation published by Rivington, London, 1869.
17. Butler, *Council*, 89.
18. Price, *Australian Bishops*, 97.

> part, but not the absolute fullness of this supreme power; or that this power of his is not ordinary and immediate both over-all and each of the churches and over-all and each of the pastors and faithful: let [them] be anathema.

This is a breath-taking statement. There is something almost demented about the repetition of the term 'supreme power' and the phrase 'the absolute fullness of this supreme power'. These claims are especially over-stated in light of the humility of the crucified Christ who had washed his disciples' feet. The ironic thing is that this claim was made on the very eve of the final annihilation of the Papal State, so popes had nowhere to exercise this absolute power except within the life of Catholic community.

Certainly, the primacy of the Bishop of Rome has been recognized from early Christianity, but it was always contextualised by an ecclesiology of communion in which Rome was seen as the heart of the church and court of appeal in disciplinary and doctrinal matters. In the debate at Vatican I the bishops focused on what the terms 'ordinary' and 'immediate' meant in practice. But these are not theological, but legal words. 'Ordinary' here is used in the canonical sense meaning 'not delegated', that is the power of office comes with the bestowal of the office. The word 'immediate' means that the pope can act directly in any part of the church without going through another person or structure. Where does this leave the bishops? Are they simply branch managers? Can the pope go over their heads and interfere in their dioceses? As successors of the apostles they also have ordinary jurisdiction, but this definition says that the pope can and has overruled, ignored or dismissed them without any process. An example is Benedict XVI's treatment of Bishop Bill Morris of Toowoomba.

Many bishops saw clearly that the vision of the church underpinning *Pastor Aeternus* was defective, inadequate and incomplete. 'Here . . . is a summary of Catholic doctrine on the church,' says Butler, 'in which there is no account taken of the hierarchy, episcopate, ministry, ecumenical councils" and, he might have added, laity. 'Simply church and pope.' *Stupefacti sumus* said one bishop.[19] Actually, the anathema quoted above originally didn't contain the phrase 'or that he has only the principal part, but not the absolute fullness of this supreme power.'

19. Butler, *Council*, 332.

In what Butler calls 'a grave error of judgement,' this was added at the last minute in a way that 'was clearly irregular.' After protests the theological deputation was ready to withdraw the clause, but then the chairman, Cardinal Luigi Bilio, was told that the pope wanted the clause inserted.[20] It was another example of the restriction of the freedom of the bishops who accepted this *fait accompli.*

The core problem with this definition is that scriptural and ecclesiological language was replaced with canonical, legal rhetoric which gives the impression that the pope owns the church, lock, stock and barrel The reason why the bishops didn't focus on primacy was that many wanted to get on to the infallibility debate and simply let it slip past.

Pastor aeternus was passed in the midst of a summer storm by the concluding session of the council on 18 July 1870. Almost all of the minority bishops had already left Rome, so the result of the voting was *placet* 533, *non placet* two. Besides Fitzgerald of Little Rock, the other *non placet* was Bishop Luigi Riccio of Caiazzo in the Kingdom of Naples. Both immediately accepted the Constitution after papal approbation.

To conclude, a final word on the role that Birmingham bishop William Bernard Ullathorne, the organizational founder of the Australian church in the 1830s, played at Vatican I. Butler positions Ullathorne in the majority of moderate pro-infallibilists as 'a sober ultramontane of the . . . Bellarmine type.'[21] However, Ullathorne's biographer, Judith Champ, shows that Ullathorne's views were far more complex and drew on his vast ministerial experience of the church in both England and Australia. Originally formed at Downside Monastery in a moderate Gallican ecclesiology by his mentor and friend, Thomas Joseph Brown, OSB, later bishop of Newport and Menevia, Ullathorne came to detest any form of extremism, especially Manning and Ward's Neo-Ultramontanism. Ullathorne was profoundly conscious of the way in which Catholicism was viewed in non-Catholic countries, especially in countries like England and Australia, where anti-Catholicism is still a default position. He believed in good order in the church. As Champ says Ullathorne 'had not struggled to bring order and good ecclesiastical government to

20. Butler, *Council*, 345–346.
21. Butler, *Council*, 119.

the church in Australia and England, only to have that order disrupted and unbalanced . . . His attitude to the matter of papal infallibility had more to do with ensuring order and . . . unity in the church than with his personal loyalty to the papacy.'[22] Ullathorne's position was that papal infallibility only existed because of the infallibility of the church and that an over-emphasis on the papacy created the danger of neglecting the proper role of bishops as successors of the apostles. In this he was absolutely right. Between Vatican I and Vatican II ecclesiology was very out of joint with undue importance being given to the papacy and Vatican centralization. This issue was recognized and righted at Vatican Council II.

The council was adjourned *sine die* on 20 September 1870 after Italian troops had occupied Rome and Pius IX retired to the Vatican as a 'prisoner'. Small groups from Germany, Austria and Switzerland, including Döllinger, rejected *Pastor aeternus* and formed their own church which received episcopal succession from the Old Catholic Church of Utrecht in the Netherlands. Pius IX lived on for eight years to become the longest serving pope in history—a papacy of thirty two years.

22. Judith Champ, *William Bernard Ullathorne. A Different Kind of Monk* (Leominster: Gracewing, 2006), 359.

Journal of the Australian Catholic Historical Society, Volume 41/2020

On the 150th Anniversary of the First Vatican Council and the document *Pastor Aeternus*

*Robert Gascoigne**

The First Vatican Council was an attempt to respond to the beginnings of the democratic era and to the Enlightenment. It had only limited success in doing so, and most of the work in achieving this response was left to Vatican II, nearly a century later. For Catholics, it is encouraging to think that, despite its severe limitations, Vatican I did teach theological truth, even though some of the truths it did teach—especially Papal infallibility—were not a necessary or even opportune response to the demands of the time.

It is very important to bear in mind that Vatican I was convened in the midst of two of the greatest changes in human history: in the first place, the monumental change in political order from a monarchical to some form of nascent democratic order; in the second place, the challenge to Christian faith from a range of philosophical and scientific developments, accompanied by an industrial revolution, that purported to erect a secular civilization in the place of Christendom. Since the time of Constantine, the Catholic Church had lived in close conjunction with monarchical order, with varying degrees of harmony and success. This monarchical order had been radically threatened by the French Revolution and the Napoleonic wars, and these revolutionary upheavals—in conjunction with some of the more radical secularizing and anti clerical trends—had led to the widespread confiscation, theft and destruction of church and monastic property and the murder of priests and religious. In its wake,

* Robert Gascoigne, DPhil, Dtheol, is an emeritus professor of the School of Theology, Australian Catholic University. This paper was given at a meeting of the Australian Catholic Historical Society, 19 July 2020.

the Papacy allied with the anti-Napoleonic forces at the Congress of Vienna in 1815 and assumed a radically reactionary stance in the political order.

During the 1830s, Félicité de Lamennais and his followers offered the Catholic Church the possibility of another response to the democratic and liberal movements. The 'pilgrims of liberty' proposed to Gregory XVI that the Papacy could ally itself with democratic movements and national aspirations. Lamennais' advocacy was rejected, and in 1832 the Pope condemned the Catholic Polish noblemen who were attempting to liberate their country from Tsarist rule.[1] His hopes for an alliance between the papacy and movements of liberation dashed, Lamennais left the church and wrote his impassioned *Paroles d'un croyant, Words of a Believer* (1834), in sorrow at the crushing of the Polish uprising.

The papacy had thrown in its lot with monarchical restoration, and the trauma of revolutionary and Napoleonic destruction was a key reason. Yet the Catholic Church had suffered greatly from the old order as well—the suppression of the Society of Jesus, engineered by monarchical forces, the confiscation of German Church and monastic land and property in the last years of the Holy Roman Empire,[2] and

1. Gregory rejected any rapprochement between the Church and democratic movements in his encyclicals Mirari Vos: *On Liberalism and Religious Indifferentism* (1832) and *Singulari Nos*: *On the Errors of Lamennais* (1834). In his 'Metternich, Pope Gregory XVI and Revolutionary Poland, 1831–42', in *The Catholic Historical Review*, 86/4 (Oct 2000): 603–619, Alan J. Reinerman discusses the context of Gregory's letter to the Polish bishops, emphasizing Metternich's influence on the Pope: 'On June 9, 1832, Gregory addressed Cum primum to the Polish bishops . . . It denounced the "artificers of trickery and deceit who . . . under the cover of religion" turned the people against the "legitimate power of princes."'(609) Reinerman also notes that, ten years later, disillusioned by the Tsar's persistently repressive policies, and no longer persuaded by Metternich's arguments that he should avoid any public criticism of the Tsar, Pope Gregory published the allocution *Haerentem diu*, forcefully describing 'the persecution of the Church, the Pope's unsuccessful efforts to halt it by appeals to the Tsar, and the resulting complaints that he had abandoned the Catholics in the [Russian] Empire, which now had made this public protest necessary' (618).
2. In 1803 the 'Reichsdeputationshauptschluss' ('Imperial Recess'), the last major law of the Holy Roman Empire before its dissolution in 1806, secularized numerous religious estates and abbeys, giving their land to secular rulers who had lost lands on the west bank of the Rhine during the French Revolutionary wars.

the secularisations of Emperor Joseph II of Austria are just some of the most radical examples of despoliation of the Church under the pre-revolutionary order.

The 'alliance of throne and altar' established in 1815 was challenged by a number of revolutionary episodes in subsequent decades, culminating in the European-wide wave of revolutions in 1848, the 'springtime of the peoples' as it was called in Germany. The 1848 revolutions, which included national, democratic and proletarian elements to different degrees in different countries, and occurred against the background of radical impoverishment and hunger in the 1840s, were generally unsuccessful in their key goals, although they did lead to some amelioration of the lot of the poor in some contexts.[3] Once again, the papacy condemned these movements, and Pius IX's forced exile from revolutionary Rome to Gaeta (a town in the Kingdom of the Two Sicilies) had much to do with that. Other Church leaders also fell victim to revolutionary movements, such as Archbishop Affre of Paris, who, in response to the pleas of Frédéric Ozanam, sought to conciliate during the 'June days' of the revolution and was hit by a stray bullet in the melée.[4]

Despite such tragic events, the democratic revolutionary movements of the first half of the nineteenth century did embody aspirations that contemporary Australians can readily identify with. The Eureka Stockade and the development of representative government in the Australian colonies were influenced by these events; the Chartist movement in Britain, although rejected by Parliament, did inspire and energise men like Henry Parkes to continue the development of democratic institutions. These movements, although deeply flawed and sometimes destructive, were the harbingers of the democratic societies we value so much today. Yet, because they challenged the monarchical, authoritarian order that the Catholic Church still identified with, they were rejected and seen as the forces of darkness. In this, they were grouped together with other, less democratic forces, such as the nascent Kingdom of Italy, which was gradually absorbing the Papal States, a development culminating in the storming of the Vatican's Porta Pia in 1870.

---

3. For example, the final abolition of serfdom in the Austrian empire.
4. See the detailed account in Thomas Bokenkotter, *Church and Revolution: Catholics in the Struggle for Democracy and Social Justice* (New York: Image, Doubleday, 1998), Chapter Four, 'Frederick Ozanam (1813–1853): A "Yes" to the Revolution', in particular 126.

These developments brought an apocalyptic tone to Church documents and piety. The English Benedictine Archbishop of Sydney, Roger Bede Vaughan, wrote a pastoral letter entitled 'Pius IX and the Revolution' in 1877, warning his flock against the dangers of contemporary movements, materialism in particular.[5] In his hymn 'O Purest of Creatures', written about 1850, Frederick Faber combined Marian piety with an apocalyptic note:

> Deep night hath come down on this rough-spoken world,
> And the banners of darkness are boldly unfurled;
> And the tempest-tossed Church—all her eyes are on thee;
> They look to thy shining, sweet Star of the Sea!

The documents of Vatican I themselves provide a number of examples, such as these words in the preamble to *Pastor Aeternus*: 'since the gates of hell trying, if they can, to overthrow the Church, make their assault with a hatred that increases day by day against its divinely laid foundation.'[6] Yet the upheavals of the nineteenth-century could be seen with different eyes. Charles Dickens and George Eliot, for example, in their very different ways, portrayed the lives and struggles of ordinary people in an industrializing Britain, illuminating their aspirations for a better life. In her great poem *The New Colossus*, written in 1883, the American Jewish poet Emma Lazarus also used the phrase 'tempest-tost', but about the poor and oppressed of Europe, who saw their hopes illuminated by the Lady of Liberty as they approached New York harbour:

> 'Keep, ancient lands, your storied pomp!' cries she
> With silent lips. 'Give me your tired, your poor,
> Your huddled masses yearning to breathe free,
> The wretched refuse of your teeming shore.
> Send these, the homeless, tempest-tost to me,
> I lift my lamp beside the golden door!'[7]

---

5. See the discussion in Peter Cunich, 'Archbishop Vaughan and the Empires of Religion in Colonial New South Wales,' in Hilary Carey, ed., *Empires of Religion* edited by (London: Palgrave Macmillan, 2008), Chapter 7, 147–9.
6. English translation of Pastor aeternus, provided by John O'Malley as an appendix to his Vatican I: *The Council and the Making of the Ultramontane Church* (Cambridge, Mass: Belknap Press Harvard University Press, 2018), 252.
7. Given on the website of the Statue of Liberty National Monument, https://www.nps.gov/stli/learn/historyculture/colossus.htm>.

I note this contrast in an attempt to illustrate the limitations of the papacy's vision of its contemporary world leading up to Vatican I. It was only in Vatican II, perhaps because the experience of twentieth-century totalitarianism had assisted the Church to value democracy and religious freedom, that a profound re-assessment of the relationship between the Church and democratic movements took place. The great document *Gaudium et spes, On the Church in the modern world*, was the most important fruit of this re-assessment. Thanks to Leo XIII, and all his predecessors in the field, notably Wilhelm von Ketteler, Bishop of Mainz, author of *Die Arbeiterfrage und das Christentum* ('The Labour Question and Christianity') in 1864, the needs and aspirations of the working classes began to be addressed by the Papacy from the 1890s, after Vatican I. In our time, Mary as Star of the Sea, prayed to by those suffering persecution for their faith, is also Mary of the Magnificat, who rejoices as 'He hath filled the hungry with good things: and the rich he hath sent empty away' (Lk 1:53).

Notoriously, Pius IX's *Syllabus of Errors* condemned religious freedom as 'indifferentism'[8] and it was Vatican II's *Declaration on Religious Freedom, Dignitatis humanae* (1965), drawing on the thought of John Courtney Murray, that gave its blessing to religious freedom, within appropriate constraints in terms of the common good, out of respect for the dignity of conscience. Here also, the nineteenth-century Catholic church was not able to resolve the foundational questions stemming from the end of the Constantinian era. Vatican I's declaration of Papal primacy rightly ended the pretensions of secular rulers in relation to Church governance and the appointment of bishops, but at the same time the Papacy sought to maintain the Church-state nexus by insisting that states give special privileges to the Catholic Church and avoid 'indifferentism'. Vatican I did not attempt to resolve this issue, and, until the 1960s, it remained official church doctrine that non-Catholics should, in effect, suffer disabilities in states governed or ruled by Catholics. The Church in fact owes a great debt of gratitude to Félix Dupanloup, Bishop of Orleans and a key figure

8. Among many other notions, the Syllabus condemned the propositions 'that every man is free to embrace and profess the religion he shall believe true, guided by the light of reason . . . That the eternal salvation may (at least) be hoped for, of all those who are not at all in the true Church of Christ.' H Bettenson and C Maunder, edited by *Documents of the Christian Church*, 4th edition (Oxford: Oxford University Press, 2011), 275.

at Vatican I, who made a brave attempt to resolve this contradiction through his distinction between the 'thesis' and the 'hypothesis', which was not rejected by Pius IX.[9] Australian Catholics in particular benefited from this. Having received permission to worship according to Catholic rites from the time of Governor Lachlan Macquarie onwards, Australian Catholics welcomed and benefited from a liberal and pluralist society in religious terms, pursuing political integration, especially through the Australian Labor Party, and religio-cultural segregation, especially through canonical marriage legislation and the Catholic school system. In the world church, during and after Vatican II, and in particular during the papacies of John XXIII, Paul VI and John Paul II, the Catholic Church affirmed its identity as a servant Church, ready to uphold and assist the cause of human rights on a global scale and renouncing worldly power.

I have attempted to sketch this historical background in order to illustrate the severe limitations of the official Church's perspective at the time of Vatican I, as well as the intensely conflictual atmosphere in which it was held. This was exacerbated by the personality of Pius IX, the aftermath of his trauma of exile to Gaeta, and his own view of his Papal role, shockingly exemplified by his response to Cardinal Guidi: '*La tradizione sono io*!', 'I am tradition!'[10] By the time of Vatican I, the liberal ultramontanism of Lamennais and his followers had given way to conservative ultramontanism, often with an apocalyptic note.

9. In Dupanloup's skilful and eirenic rendering, the 'thesis' was that the Catholic faith must have privileged support as the true religion, and the 'hypothesis' was that religious pluralism could be accepted under current circumstances. He 'pleaded for the necessity to distinguish "the absolute and the relative, for what might be admissable in certain conditions (hypothèse) would often be false if advanced as an absolute (thèse)."' Marvin R O'Connell, 'Ultramontanism and Dupanloup: The Compromise of 1865', in *Church History*, 53/2 (June 1984): 200–217, here at 215.
10. As John O'Malley writes in his *Vatican I*, 'In reaction to Guidi's insistence that before issuing a definition the pope had to investigate the tradition of the church, Pius broke out with the famous words, "I, I am tradition! I, I am the church" (*Io, io sono la tradizione! Io, io sono la chiesa*!). To defend himself Guidi could say only that he had spoken according to his conscience and according to the teaching of Saint Thomas and Cardinal Bellarmino. This incident is so shocking that it hardly seems credible. Did it actually happen, and did it happen as it has consistently been described? Historians and theologians have time and again sifted the evidence. Their conclusion is unambiguous: there is no reason to doubt the incident occurred and occurred as it has commonly been told' (212–213).

Let us then consider the key documents and definitions of Vatican I, bearing this background in mind; in the first place, the document *Dei Filius, On the Catholic Faith*, promulgated early in the Council's proceedings. This document, prepared in draft by a number of Roman theologians, including the outstanding neo-scholastic thinker, Jesuit Johann Baptist Franzelin, was essentially a response to the secular strands of the Enlightenment, affirming the roles of reason and faith in a complementary relationship. I noted at the beginning of this essay the two great challenges to the Church in the nineteenth century, the first political, the second intellectual. *Dei Filius* was a response to the intellectual challenge, emphasising that God could be known by reason without the benefit of Biblical revelation, that divine revelation imparted higher truths that could not be known by reason as well as confirming the truths known by reason, and that the propositional truths of revelation are received by faith. As such, within significant limitations, it was a timely and important document, which responded directly and confidently to fundamental challenges to a Catholic intellectual and believing vision. Its fundamental limitation was its ahistorical character. Biblical 'higher criticism' had been under way in earnest since the early nineteenth century, but was not reflected in this document since it was an essentially Protestant, especially German Protestant, endeavour. Indeed, this 'higher criticism' was resisted by the Catholic magisterium essentially until Pius XII's *Divino Afflante Spiritu* of 1943, and only came fully into its own after Vatican II. Vatican II's *Dei verbum*, the *Dogmatic Constitution on Divine Revelation*, while drawing on and affirming *Dei Filius*, sets revelation in a biblical and interpersonal context in terms of the divine, trinitarian self-communication.

Our principal focus in this commemoration is Vatican I's second key document *Pastor Aeternus*, essentially concerned with papal primacy and papal infallibility. In some ways, a contemporary Catholic can view the definition of papal primacy as a positive and necessary development of Catholic teaching. In the first place, as already noted, it rightly ended any pretensions of secular powers to control the Church or vet the appointment of bishops and similar privileges. In this sense, it would prove a helpful response to the end of the Constantinian era, since the new era would throw up a medley of rulers, ranging from the benignly democratic to the most savagely totalitarian, none of whom had any right to claim powers over church structures and appointments. Papal primacy meant that local bishops were responsible to the pope, rather than to governments and rulers, and that the pope had the right to intervene in any church around the world, against and in defiance of the pretensions of local rulers. Among many possible examples, one thinks of Pope Pius XI's ordering of the Viennese Cardinal Innitzer to Rome, to reprimand him for his enthusiastic support of Hitler at the time of the Anschluss of Austria into the Nazi Reich.[11] Papal primacy would also give renewed impetus to the Church's global missionary efforts, and all the ways in which this is important for Australian Catholic history.

At the same time, the definition of papal primacy had limitations bound up with the context of Vatican I. The despoliation of the Church in the late eighteenth and early nineteenth centuries, by both monarchical and revolutionary forces, had led to an intense focus on the papacy as the source of the Church's life, confidence and faith. This ultramontanism included profound personal respect, for example, for Pius VII, who was captured by Napoleon and imprisoned in France for several years, and later for Pius IX himself. This atmosphere, together with the desire to free the church of any bonds to local rulers and conditions, summed up by the word 'Gallicanism' or its equivalents in Germany and Austria, meant that the majority at Vatican I were focussed on Papal prerogatives. It was—once again—only at Vatican II that papal primacy was put in the context of the college of bishops informed by a theology of communion. Further, it has only been Pope Francis' recent initiatives that have taken the theology of communion

11. At the time of the Anschluss, in March 1938, 'the Austrian bishops under Cardinal Innitzer issued a proclamation celebrating the "extraordinary accomplishments of National Socialism in the sphere of völkisch and economic reconstruction as well as social policy."' Karl Dietrich Bracher, *The German Dictatorship: The Origins, Structure and Consequences of National Socialism* (Harmondsworth: Peregrine Books, 1978), 386. Soon after, Innitzer was summoned to Rome by Pius XI and Cardinal Pacelli, the Vatican Secretary of State (and future Pius XII). The Austrian episcopate's position 'was completely at odds with the position of the Holy See in its struggle with National Socialism. On April 5 Cardinal Innitzer arrived in Rome to undergo difficult and exhausting conferences with Pius XI and Cardinal Pacelli. The following day the Osservatore Romano printed a revised declaration regarding the Anschluss which was signed by Cardinal Innitzer on behalf of the entire Austrian episcopate.' William M. Harrigan, 'Pius XI and Nazi Germany, 1937–1939', in *The Catholic Historical Review*, 51/4 (January 1966): 457–486, here at 476.

further to a theology of synodality, which he attempted to put into practice in the two synods on the family in 2014 and 2015, bearing fruit in the Apostolic Exhortation *Amoris Laetitia, The Joy of Love,* in 2016. Papal primacy is the affirmation of a Catholic truth, but a truth which was without its proper context when it was promulgated.

Let us conclude with some reflections on the definition of papal infallibility. Here I am drawing in particular on two theological sources. In the first place, the book *Sign and Promise: A Theology of the Church for a Changing World* (1988), by our dear departed John Thornhill SM, who died on 29th July 2019. John's life and work is itself a distinguished episode in Australian Catholic history. Second, I will cite two recent articles in the German Jesuit periodical *Stimmen der Zeit*, by the eminent Church historian Klaus Schatz, articles published to mark this anniversary: 'Papal Infallibility: Its Slow Genesis' and 'Papal Infallibility Today: between Immobility and Irrelevance?'[12]

In Chapter Four of *Sign and Promise,* entitled 'Sharing in a Call to Serve', Thornhill considers the document *Pastor Aeternus.* He notes that what was intended by the definition of Papal infallibility can only be properly understood in the light of the exposition by Vinzenz Gasser, Prince Bishop of Brixen in South Tirol, now the city of Bressanone in Italy. Gasser, spokesman for the doctrinal commission of the Council, made an important speech to the Council shortly before the vote on the definition. He attempted to address some of the concerns of the minority by emphasizing that the exercise of papal infallibility cannot be anything but an expression of the Church's tradition. The definition does not imply 'that we separate the pontiff from the remarkably regulated union he has with the Church . . . Exercising the office of teacher of all, therefore, he makes his judgement as representing the universal Church.'[13] In this light, although *Pastor Aeternus* affirms that papal teachings about

12. Klaus Schatz SJ, 'Päpstliche Unfehlbarkeit: Ihr langsames Entstehen' (*Stimmen der Zeit*, June 2020, 451–464) and 'Päpstliche Unfehlbarkeit heute: Zwischen Immobilisierung und Irrelevanz?' (*Stimmen der Zeit*, [July 2020], 493–505). Schatz is also the author of a number of other writings on *Vatican I*, including the magnum opus *Vaticanum I*, 3 volumes. (Paderborn: Ferdinand Schöningh, 1992–1994.)

13. Quoted from Gasser's speech, translated from the documents of Vatican I, in John Thornhill, *Sign and Promise: A Theology of Church for a Changing World* (London: Collins, 1988), 137.

the content of divine revelation are irreformable in themselves and not from the consent of the Church, they cannot be informed and articulated except as an expression of the faith of the Church. In this way, Gasser's statement did link the papal teaching office to the witness of the bishops, as successors of the apostles, but the Vatican I definition lacked a context of collegiality and communion.

Thornhill emphasizes the role of the petrine ministry in making possible this collegiality and communion. The truth in papal primacy is how it can serve universal communion: the key point is to ensure that the task of the episcopal college is discharged in all circumstances, so it therefore must have leadership commensurate with the college as a whole, otherwise there could be an appeal beyond the Papacy to the college, leading to the confusion displayed at the late medieval 'Conciliarist' councils of Constance and Basel. This papal primacy can also be expressed as infallibility, especially if the college is so divided that only a Papal statement can preserve the Church from doctrinal anarchy. If this is sound 'it follows that the exercise of papal infallibility should only occur in a situation of extraordinary crisis in the Church's life. An ultimate expression of the Petrine leadership, providing for that terrible possibility of a moment in which even the apostolic group may be wavering (*cf* Lk 22:32), it should not be used for other purposes.' For Thornhill, the exercise of papal authority to define Marian dogmas, 'in effect no more than the expression of the Church's devotion', was a luxury we could scarcely afford.[14]

Intriguingly, Klaus Schatz notes that Papal infallibility was first seen as a limitation on Papal power, since it meant a definition was irrevocable for all time. The Franciscan Petrus Olivi taught around 1280 that a papal definition in favour of the stricter school of thought in the dispute about Franciscan poverty could not be changed by subsequent popes. In 1323 Pope John XXII declared the notion of the complete poverty of Christ heretical and rejected the idea of papal infallibility.[15] However, since the fifteenth century, and the failure of conciliarism, a doctrine of papal infallibility has been a strong theological opinion and was developed by Robert Bellarmine into what became essentially the teaching of Vatican I.[16] Like Thornhill,

14. Thornhill, *Sign and Promise*, 171.
15. Schatz, 'Päpstliche Unfehlbarkeit: Ihr langsames Entstehen', 451–3.
16. Schatz, 'Päpstliche Unfehlbarkeit: Ihr langsames Entstehen', 459.

and with Gasser's statement as background, Schatz emphasises that the dogma's statement 'irreformable in themselves, and not from the consent of the Church' means that papal statements meeting the relevant conditions do not need further confirmation by the Church—it is not a statement restricting how much the pope should consult beforehand in order to authentically express the faith of the Church.[17]

While endorsing the definition's theological truth and consistency, like Thornhill, Schatz emphasizes its lack of context. He emphasises the 'long shadow' thrown by the definition (what has sometimes been called 'creeping infallibility') and at the same time the fact that it has only once been invoked in the strict sense since it was defined, in Pius' XII definition of the Assumption of Mary in 1950. In a striking simile, he compares papal infallibility to the possession of nuclear weapons, which once possessed can never be used. In his judgement, the expectations of the proponents of the definition have not been fulfilled, because they were expectations marked by the conflicts and polarisations I have briefly described.[18] It has become clear that we must live with internal church controversies—they cannot simply be solved by the pope. Like Thornhill, Schatz questions the invocation of Papal infallibility to define the Marian dogmas, since these were the expressions of Church devotion, rather than solving a crisis or conflict. He also notes that, despite considerable efforts by proponents of other Marian themes during the pontificate of Pius XII and at Vatican II, they have not become dogma.[19] For Schatz, expressions of papal infallibility in the sense of Vatican I's dogma are legitimate and possible, but should be seen as a deficient mode of exercising the highest magisterium, which is best exercised by the Pope together with an ecumenical council.

On this 150th anniversary of Vatican I, there is much to learn and ponder from the events leading up to the Council and its deliberations. We have seen how much perspective can change with the passage of time—that a definition of papal infallibility that appeared so intensely important and urgent to many in 1870 has not played a

17. Schatz, 'Päpstliche Unfehlbarkeit: Ihr langsames Entstehen', 463.
18. Schatz, 'Päpstliche Unfehlbarkeit heute: Zwischen Immobilisierung und Irrelevanz?', 493.
19. For example, the requests to define as dogma that Mary is the 'Mediatrix of All Graces' and 'Co-Redemptrix'.

crucial role since that time. In the turmoil of the revolutionary age, papal primacy was invoked as a way of giving the rock of Peter its due role, yet it was left without a complementary context until Vatican II. *Dei filius* re-asserted fundamental Catholic teaching concerning the relationship of faith and reason, yet it also need enrichment from a new engagement with Scripture which only came later. Reflecting on Vatican I, we need to be conscious of the fundamental and bewildering revolutions in political and intellectual life that it attempted to respond to. The magnitude of these revolutions was reflected in the sometimes partial and one-sided responses it made. Yet the truths it did affirm have been received into Catholic tradition, in particular by Vatican II. In many ways, it is helpful to consider Vatican I and Vatican II as two great episodes in a process, as the Catholic Church responds to the modern world. Today, Pope Francis has opened up a new path of synodality, so that the gifts of more and more members of the Church may contribute to the Church's self-awareness and response to the Spirit's presence through 'the signs of the times'.

Journal of the Australian Catholic Historical Society, Volume 41/2020

Father George Tuckwell: Missionary Priest in the Australasian Colonies

*Tim O'Sullivan**

The seemingly little-known Catholic priest George Tuckwell was a convert who spent a significant part of his priestly ministry in Auckland and Sydney. His story is an interesting example of a parish priest's life in the 1880s when church building and the growing Irish population came to dominate Catholic life in the Australasian colonies.

George Tuckwell was born in Edinburgh in 1843 to parents Samuel and Charlotte Tuckwell. Little is known about George's parents except that Tuckwell family lore relates that Samuel Tuckwell was a member of the Royal Household Band. The name of one Samuel Tuckwell does appear as a member of the King's (and Queen's) household in the years 1825–1854.[1] The family professed membership of a staunch variety of Presbyterianism. No trace of this family appears in the Census records of England or Scotland.

Father Tuckwell's first sister, Charlotte married a Catholic, Henri Marin de Kioux in the Anglican Cathedral in Mauritius in 1858.[2] Charlotte was received into the Church by Bishop Collier of Mauritius

---

* Tim O'Sullivan, of Christchurch, is the author of *Early History of the Society of St Vincent de Paul in New Zealand, 1867–1925* (2017).

1. See for example, The Royal kalendar, and court and city register for England, Scotland, Ireland, and the colonies year.1825, https://hdl.handle.net/2027/uc1.a0004033155 and The Royal kalendar, and court and city register for England, Scotland, Ireland, and the colonies. London, 1854. https://hdl.handle.net/2027/uiug.30112073208172
2. http://www.cgmrgenealogie.org/actes/acte_mari.php?xid=233977&xct=5920

prior to 1863.[3] Apart from sister Charlotte, George Tuckwell had another known sibling, Blanch Mary. Blanch married New Zealander Alexander Gerrard Allan on 21 April 1887 at the Archbishop's Chapel in Manly. Father Tuckwell officiated at the marriage.[4] Both sisters became Catholics though the influence of their brother and both died in Australia. There was another unknown brother who also converted through the influence of George.

Father Tuckwell himself often referred to his conversion from the Presbyterianism of his parents to the Catholic Faith as arising from the love of the Blessed Virgin Mary 'at an early age,' and after becoming aware of the scriptural teaching supporting Catholic doctrine, felt that he was 'bound to defend her honour against all assailants'.[5] At the age of six the young George came across the Hail Mary and after discussion with his mother, he was forbidden to repeat it on the grounds that it was idle superstition. His mother's words were 'Go away you naughty boy! Don't ever repeat that again!' Young George's reading of the New Testament confirmed to him that the archangel's salutation in Saint Luke's gospel was anything but "superstitious" and he somehow managed to teach himself the rosary. At the age of thirteen his reading of the scriptures led him to the Magnificat and he tried to discuss protestant theological inconsistency on Our Lady in his parent's polite company, for which he received a 'sound

3. 'Family Notices', in *The Sydney Morning Herald* (7 September 1893): 1: http://nla.gov.au/nla.news-article13917765 and 'Obituary,' *Freeman's Journal (Sydney),* (2 September 1893), 15: http://nla.gov.au/nla.news-article115574472 Family information: 'Mrs Kioux, Obituary', in *Freeman's Journal,* (2 September 1893): 15: http://nla.gov.au/nla.news-article115574472, death notice: 'Family Notices' *The Sydney Morning Herald,* 25 August 1893, 1: http://nla.gov.au/nla.news-article13927956 and 'Obituary,' *Freeman's Journal* (2 September 1893): 15: http://nla.gov.au/nla.news-article115574472 and 'Requiem at Redfern,' *Freeman's Journal,* (30 September 1893): 15, from: http://nla.gov.au/nla.news-article115579162 and 'Family Notices,' *Freeman's Journal* (2 September 1893): 11: http://nla.gov.au/nla.news-article115574436.
4. 'Family Notices' *The Sydney Morning Herald,* 6 May 1887, 1: http://nla.gov.au/nla.news-article13655850 'Marriages,' Observer, Volume 8, Issue 439, 21 May 1887, 10: https://paperspast.natlib.govt.nz/newspapers/TO18870521.2.25. The Allan family had two children, George (born 1888) and Vivian Rose (born 1890).
5. 'At St Benedict's Roman Catholic Chapel . . .' Auckland Star, 12 October 1885, 2, https://paperspast.natlib.govt.nz/newspapers/AS18851012.2.13.

reprimand' in front of the guests.[6] His mother apparently saying 'Oh dear, That child will surely become a Papist one day.'[7]

The workings of grace were to result in George's conversion to the one true Faith as an adult, an event which can only have disconcerted his parents. The depth of anti-Catholic feeling in his family is indicated by the story of one of George's sisters, who would have apparently wished her children dead rather than become papists.[8] As Grace would have it, the two children became ill with croup and were in danger of death. The now catholic George suggested to his sister that they should pray the Hail Mary asking for the cure of the children. The mother's distraught prayer was heard in heaven, the children were cured, and their mother converted. Father Tuckwell would recount how both he and his sister were converted by the Hail Mary.[9]

In 1862, George Tuckwell received a commission in the Army as Captain, and for some years held high official positions in the Mauritius Civil Service. The *Mauritius Almanac and Colonial Register* for 1878 records George Tuckwell's career in Mauritius from 1st May 1855 in the Customs Department on a salary of 2,700 rupees.[10]

An outcome of George's conversion in Mauritius was that he joined the Society of St Vincent de Paul and became the president of the Conference. He was instrumental in encouraging visitations of the poor in their own homes and encouraging the practice of the Faith.[11] One of those who encouraged him in his vocation was well known French priest and spiritual writer Révérend Père Justin Etcheverry SJ of Port Louis, Mauritius.[12]

---

6. 'Converted by the Hail Mary', *New Zealand Tablet*, 11 May 1899, P 10, https://paperspast.natlib.govt.nz/periodicals/NZT18990511.2.22.
7. 'Death of a Convert Priest'. *The Catholic Press (Sydney)*, (31 October 1918): 31. http://nla.gov.au/nla.news-article105968336.
8. This is repeated more than once, see also No title, *Le Mémorial des Pyrénées: politique, judiciaire, industriel et d'annonces*, (Pau) 18 July 1882 p 2. https://www.pireneas.fr/ark:/12148/bpt6k52395959/f3.item.
9. "Converted by the Hail Mary", *New Zealand Tablet*, 11 May 1899, P 10, https://paperspast.natlib.govt.nz/periodicals/NZT18990511.2.22.
10. John B Kyshe, *The Mauritius Almanac and Colonial Register for 1878*, 252.
11. No title, *Le Mémorial des Pyrénées: politique, judiciaire, industriel et d'annonces*, (Pau) 18 July 1882 2: https://www.pireneas.fr/ark:/12148/bpt6k52395959/f3.item
12. No title, *Le Mémorial des Pyrénées: politique, judiciaire, industriel et d'annonces*, (Pau) 18 July 1882 2: https://www.pireneas.fr/ark:/12148/bpt6k52395959/f3.item

George moved on from Mauritius and arrived in Hobart with his sister Charlotte (Mrs Marin de Kioux) on July 19 1874 after a six week voyage.[13] He also spent time prior to the realisation of his vocation working for the Crown Lands Office of Victoria.[14]

After resignation from the Crown Lands Office, George sailed for France where he began studying for the priesthood at the Major Seminary of Aire in 1879. Father Tuckwell was ordained by the Bishop of Tarbes on Sunday 16 July 16th, 1882 in the Cathedral of Aire.[15] Such a short seminary career of three years indicates that his superiors in religion considered him an excellent prospect and in this their expectations were fulfilled.

After ordination there are two possible explanations as to why Father Tuckwell accepted an offer to become a missionary in New Zealand. It is possible that Father Tuckwell and the new Bishop of Auckland John Edward Luck OSB. met sometime between August and November 1882. Father John Edward Luck O.S.B. was at the Benedictine Priory at Ramsgate when he was appointed Bishop of Auckland. Cardinal Manning consecrated him there on 3rd August 1882, and the new Bishop Luck arrived in Auckland on 14 November 1882.[16] A more likely possible first meeting date for Bishop Luck and Father Tuckwell is in mid-1884 when Bishop Luck was on a trip to Europe to recruit priests and religious for service in the Auckland Diocese.[17] Bishop Luck brought out to New Zealand three Benedictine priests (Fathers Osmund Egan, Gabrielle Areguy and Raphael Wissell[18]) with another to follow. Bishop Luck had also recruited

13. 'Shipping Intelligence,' *The Tasmanian Tribune (Hobart)*, 20 July 1874, 2: http://nla.gov.au/nla.news-article201169585
14. *The Argus*, (29 January 1885): 5: http://nla.gov.au/nla.news-article6066037
15. *Donohoe's Magazine*, volume 8, October 1882, 379 and 'Nouvelles Diverses,' *L'Univers* (Paris), 1882-07-22, 4: https://gallica.bnf.fr/ark:/12148/bpt6k704174r/f1
16. Hugh Laracy. 'Luck, John Edmund', Dictionary of New Zealand Biography, first published in 1993. Te Ara - the Encyclopedia of New Zealand, https://teara.govt.nz/en/biographies/2l19/luck-john-edmund.
17. 'News of the Week,' *New Zealand Tablet*, 7 November 1884, 11: https://paperspast.natlib.govt.nz/periodicals/NZT18841107.2.15 Bishop Luck left Auckland on 6th May 1884. Mentioned in *L'Univers* (Paris), 15 November 1884, 2: https://gallica.bnf.fr/ark:/12148/bpt6k705017s/f2
18. 'Arrival of His Lordship the Bishop of Auckland,' *New Zealand Tablet*, Volume XII/42, (6 February 1885): 20: https://paperspast.natlib.govt.nz/periodicals/NZT18850206.2.30 and 'Shipping Telegrams,' *Evening Star*, Issue 6799 (14 January

two members of the secular clergy, Father Tuckwell and E Morgan.[19] (It appears Father Morgan did not arrive).

By October 1884, prior to his arrival in Auckland, Father Tuckwell was in Paris preparing for his trip to New Zealand. Bishop Luck had asked him to solicit funds for the diocese of Auckland before leaving and provided him with this letter:

> We, Jean-Edmond Luck, O.S.B., by the grace of God and the Apostolic Holy See, Bishop of Auckland (New Zealand), instruct R. P. [Révérend Père] Tuckwell to call upon the charity of the faithful of France to help us, through their alms, in our apostolic work in our poor mission of New Zealand. The zeal and piety of French Catholics give us the assurance that it is not in vain that we have asked them to cooperate in the work of salvation of so many thousands of infidels in those lands. Donated under our seal. Monastery of St. Augustine, in Ramsgate (England). October 16, 1884.
> John Edmund Luck, O. S. B., Bishop of Auckland.[20]

Father Tuckwell's journey to New Zealand began on 17 December 1884 when he boarded the steamship *Caledonien* in Marseilles for the six-week voyage to Sydney via Suez, Aden, Mauritius, Adelaide, and Melbourne. On board with him were five Marist priests: Fathers Ferrier, Forestier, Courceti, Lepetit, and Lepretre. There were also two priests, two brothers and five nuns of the order of Our Lady of the Sacred Heart on board heading to New Guinea and two Sisters of Mercy.[21] The *Caledonien* arrived in Sydney on 31 January 1885 and the Marists headed on to New Caledonia.[22] Father Tuckwell departed

---

1885): 3: https://paperspast.natlib.govt.nz/newspapers/ESD18850114.2.19 and no title, *Auckland Star* (14 January 1885): 2: https://paperspast.natlib.govt.nz/newspapers/AS18850114.2.12

19. 'Return of Bishop Luck,' *Auckland Star*, 14 January 1885, 2: https://paperspast.natlib.govt.nz/newspapers/AS18850114.2.27
20. 'Le R.P. Tuckwell . . .', *L'Univers* (Paris), 27 October 1884, 3: https://gallica.bnf.fr/ark:/12148/bpt6k704999t/f3
21. *The Argus* (29 January 1885): 5: http://nla.gov.au/nla.news-article6066037 and "Chronique Religieuse," *L'Univers*, 13 January 1885, 4: https://www.retronews.fr/journal/l-univers/13-janvier-1885/132/966425/4
22. 'Shipping', *The Sydney Morning Herald* (2 February 1885): 6: http://nla.gov.au/nla.news-article28365150

Sydney on 6th February on the steamship Waihora and arrived in Auckland on 11th February 1885.[23]

Father Tuckwell was soon at work as assistant priest at St Patrick's Cathedral in Auckland and on Sunday 15th February he celebrated a High Mass with Father Walter McDonald as deacon and Father Egan as sub-deacon. Father Tuckwell preached on the necessity of good works without which Faith is dead, a subject upon which a convert from Protestantism would be knowledgeable. At the Mass, a pastoral letter was read in which the Bishop pleaded with his catholic flock to support the Church. Bishop Luck's strategy to strengthen the Faith in his struggling Diocese was to bring in religious orders. New orders which arrived in the Diocese included the Marist Brothers, the Fathers of St Joseph's Society known as the Mill Hill Fathers (for the Maori mission), the Sisters of the Good Shepherd (for the Magdalen asylum) and the Little Sisters of the Poor.[24] One of the 'new missionary priests' was Father Tuckwell who was eminently qualified due to his apostolic zeal and language skills in German, Hindustani, English and several dialects of French.[25]

Father Tuckwell had not been in Auckland very long before the *Tablet* reported that, 'The zeal of this good Father is making him endeared not only to Catholics but to the Protestants of the district his zeal and charity know no bounds'.[26] Father Tuckwell was instrumental in the foundation of the foundation of the first Conference of the Society of St Vincent de Paul (July 1885), the "League of the Cross" for the encouragement of total abstinence (January 1886) and the encouragement of the Rosary.[27] The Hibernians were also quick to recruit Father Tuckwell as chaplain, a role he fulfilled with zeal for the members.[28]

---

23. 'The Wairarapa,' *Auckland Star* (12 February 1885): 2: https://paperspast.natlib.govt.nz/newspapers/AS18850212.2.3.6
24. 'Ecclesiastical', *New Zealand Herald* (16 February 1885): 5: https://paperspast.natlib.govt.nz/newspapers/NZH18850216.2.22
25. Friday February 20, 1885, *New Zealand Herald* (20 February 1885): 4: https://paperspast.natlib.govt.nz/newspapers/NZH18850220.2.15
26. 'Auckland', *New Zealand Tablet*, (5 March 1886): 9: https://paperspast.natlib.govt.nz/periodicals/NZT18860305.2.11
27. 'Presentation to the Rev Father Tuckwell', *New Zealand Herald*, (4 May 1886): 5: https://paperspast.natlib.govt.nz/newspapers/NZH18860504.2.34
28. 'Auckland,' *New Zealand Tablet* (29 January 1886): 21: https://paperspast.natlib.govt.nz/periodicals/NZT18860129.2.34

The arrival of Cardinal Moran in Auckland on Monday 1st March 1885 was an event of significance for the Catholic community of Auckland who turned out by the thousands to welcome him. At the reception held at St Patrick's Cathedral Cardinal Moran acknowledged the flourishing of the Hibernians, the League of the Cross and the Society of St Vincent de Paul in Auckland.[29] Moran's subsequent conversations obviously led him to discover the name of the energetic priest who was involved with all three organisations, Father Tuckwell.

Cardinal Moran was concerned for his own pastoral responsibilities in Sydney and was obviously not above poaching talent if the opportunity availed. So, Father Tuckwell accepted the Cardinal's invitation to take a parish in Sydney,[30] much to the disappointment of St Patrick's Cathedral parishioners in Auckland.

On Father Tuckwell's departure from Auckland the *Tablet* reported that:

> During the short time Father Tuckwell has been here, he has made himself endeared to all classes, by his zeal, charity, and gentlemanly demeanour. Connected with illustrious French and Irish families, and an ex-officer of Her Majesty's Civil Service, be had the entree to the best society here, but he preferred to spend his time among the poor, the sick, and the afflicted, who never appealed to him in vain for help, in their spiritual and temporal distress. He founded the St. Vincent, the Rosary, and the League of the Cross Societies. Everything he took in hand prospered and was blessed. The League of the Cross, which was commenced with 40 members three months ago, now numbers nearly 300. There is nearly the same number in the living Rosary, and the St. Vincent de Paul's is in ample funds for its requirements. It is scarcely necessary to say that such a priest is not to be allowed to leave the scene of his successful labours without a suitable recognition, and that a movement is on foot for that purpose, in which all the Catholics of Auckland will take part. His well-known Irish sympathies will soon be recognised, and duly reciprocated by the patriotic Irishmen of Sydney.[31]

29. 'Arrival of Cardinal Moran in Auckland', *New Zealand Tablet* (12 March 1886): 15: https://paperspast.natlib.govt.nz/periodicals/NZT18860312.2.21
30. 'Auckland', *New Zealand Tablet*, XIII/52 (23 April 1886): 7: http://paperspast.natlib.govt.nz/periodicals/NZT18860423.2.6
31. 'Auckland', *New Zealand Tablet*, Volume XIII, Issue 52, 23 April 1886, 7: http://paperspast.natlib.govt.nz/periodicals/NZT18860423.2.6

Prior to his departure from Auckland there was a round of farewells and the organisations he had been involved with presented him with purses of sovereigns. The Society of St Vincent de Paul Conference presented him with a 'magnificently bound album of New Zealand scenery.' The disappointment felt by many of the parishioners must have been keenly felt as Bishop Luck felt it necessary to warn the members of the League of the Cross not to be too attached to their chaplain (or any other material things) so as to lose sight of the workings of Divine Providence.[32] On the day of departure, a procession led by Fathers Thomas Kehoe[33] and Patrick Costello and the League of the Cross, accompanied by 'thousands' of parishioners, saw Father Tuckwell off at the wharf.[34] Father Tuckwell sailed from Auckland on May 10 on the Mararoa[35] and arrived in Sydney on May 14 1886.[36]

Father Tuckwell's first appointment in Sydney was to Manly Parish of Mary Immaculate, where he succeeded the outgoing parish priest Dean Hanley.[37] In the next year Father Tuckwell embarked on a fundraising program to build a new church at Manly to replace the church described as an 'antiquated weatherboard structure.'[38] He solicited funds throughout Sydney as the working class suburb of Manly was used as a summer retreat by the well off from town who he expected to be able to donate.[39] Parish life developed under Father Tuckwell's leadership and the 1887 Easter celebrations were

---

32. Presentation to Bishop Luck, *New Zealand Herald* (3 May 1886): 6: https://paperspast.natlib.govt.nz/newspapers/NZH18860503.2.47
33. Father Kehoe took over leadership of the League of the Cross: The League of the Cross Concert and Dance, *New Zealand Herald*, 27 April 1886, 5: https://paperspast.natlib.govt.nz/newspapers/NZH18860427.2.27
34. Auckland, *New Zealand Tablet* (28 May 1886): 13: https://paperspast.natlib.govt.nz/periodicals/NZT18860528.2.13
35. 'Shipping Summary: Departures,' *New Zealand Herald*, Volume XXIII, Issue 7645, (24 May 1886): 4: https://paperspast.natlib.govt.nz/newspapers/NZH18860524.2.65
36. 'Shipping.' *Australian Town and Country Journal* (22 May 1886): 43: http://nla.gov.au/nla.news-article71077436
37. 'Dean Hanly.' *Freeman's Journal* (29 May 1886): 14: http://nla.gov.au/nla.news-article119444511
38. 'New Catholic Church at Manly,' *The Sydney Morning Herald* (13 June 1887): 4: http://nla.gov.au/nla.news-article13654388
39. 'Simple Obsequies,' *Freeman's Journal* (15 January 1887): 16: http://nla.gov.au/nla.news-article115449839

spectacular with a full Church on Maundy Thursday evening and an 'imposing' procession to the Altar of Repose. Adoration all night followed. The Good Friday memorial of the Passion was in keeping with Baldeschi's Roman Ceremonial and was followed by Stations of the Cross in the evening. Easter Sunday's Mass of the Resurrection was the first High Mass in Manly with music by Novello (Kyrie and Sanctus) and Bateman (Gloria and Credo). Father Tuckwell preached on the Resurrection. Vespers later that evening was crowded.[40] He was clearly a popular and devoted priest.

Soon after Pentecost 1887, the foundation stone of the new Church of Mary Immaculate at Manly was laid. Although a heavy squall of rain and hail pushed the formal celebrations inside the old church, the rain ceased, and Cardinal Moran was able to lay the stone.[41] This was an era of Catholic construction and competition for funds was strong. Not only was the Manly Church being built but also Cardinal Moran's new seminary at Manly was under construction. Fundraising was also still going on for the St Mary's Cathedral building fund in Sydney to which Father Tuckwell contributed two guineas.[42]

It was not only the Catholics who respected the parish priest of Manly. After Father Tuckwell wrote to the council about a "fever breeding nuisance" at Manly (whatever that was) he attracted the usual comments about the clergy. The *Manly Signal* defended Father Tuckwell:

> 'Father Tuckwell is a very estimable citizen, and is respected by all creeds and classes in Manly, as he has ever been elsewhere throughout his almost world-wide travels; and it goes against our grain as advocates for, and guardians of, the liberty of conscience, to see a gentleman of his standing snubbed up by a fossilized alderman who apparently gauges the claims of the ratepayers by the church they belong to.'[43]

---

40. 'Manly Beach,' *Freeman's Journal* (16 April 1887): 16: http://nla.gov.au/nla.news-article115449789
41. 'New Catholic Church at Manly,' *The Sydney Morning Herald* (13 June 1887): 4: http://nla.gov.au/nla.news-article13654388
42. 'St Mary's Cathedral Building Fund,' *Freeman's Journal*, (8 February 1890): 19: http://nla.gov.au/nla.news-article111123297
43. 'Bigotry at Manly,' *Freeman's Journal* (21 May 1887): 9: http://nla.gov.au/nla.news-article115446867

Father Tuckwell was obviously not too worried about the odd Manly bigot as he was part of the Council's organising committee for the borough's wild flower festival.[44] Half the proceeds of the flower show were to be donated to the Catholic Church building fund.[45] The flower show was a great success especially as it was patronised by New South Wales State governor Lord Carrington, Lady Carrington and Cardinal Moran.[46] Fundraising for the Manly church continued with all sorts of community activities and Father Tuckwell was usually heavily involved. One such was the 'Moonlight serenade and Promenade Concert' held at a crowded Manly Aquarium and a steamer was hired to bring the dignitaries and the band of the Second Regiment over from Sydney.[47]

Father Tuckwell also kept up the high standard of liturgy and the spiritual lives of the parishioners were much enriched. At Easter 1889 over ninety parishioners received Holy Communion.[48]

Sometime around 1890 Father Tuckwell was moved from Manly to the parish of Saint Vincent de Paul in Redfern and, conscious of the destitution in the neighbourhood, sought to establish a Conference of the Society of St Vincent de Paul in the Parish. Once the appropriate parishioners were identified, the Conference was established in January 1891 with the help of Charles Gordon O'Neill, president of the Sydney Council of the Society.[49] Further news reports show that Father Tuckwell supported the Redfern Conference of the Society and regularly attended meetings.[50]

---

44. 'News of the Day,' *The Sydney Morning Herald* (9 August 1887): 7: http://nla.gov.au/nla.news-article13649843 accessed on
45. 'The Manly Flower Show,' *Freeman's Journal* (13 August 1887): 20: http://nla.gov.au/nla.news-article115447696
46. 'Wild flower shows,' *The Sydney Morning Herald* (29 September 1887): 11: http://nla.gov.au/nla.news-article28349889
47. 'Moonlight serenade and Promenade Concert,' *The Sydney Morning Herald* (19 January 1889): 12: http://nla.gov.au/nla.news-article13710919
48. 'New Church at Pittwater,' *Freeman's Journal* (4 May 1889): 16: http://nla.gov.au/nla.news-article115378440
49. 'Society of St Vincent de Paul', *Freeman's Journal*, (24 January 1891): 15: http://nla.gov.au/nla.news-article115565495 This article mentions that Father Tuckwell had been a president of a Conference and vice-president of a Council. Presumably in the period when he was in Mauritius and before he was ordained.
50. 'General News,' *The Daily Telegraph* (23 February 1891): 4: http://nla.gov.au/nla.news-article235887395 and "Charity in more than name," *Freeman's Journal*, (28 February 1891): 15: http://nla.gov.au/nla.news-article115569543

Regular parish work included fundraising and Father Tuckwell was in full support of his parish reducing the debt on their buildings. Fetes involved large numbers of parishioners and the support of the parish priest was crucial to their success.[51]

A bout of ill health affected Father Tuckwell while he was living at Redfern. What it was is not known but by November 1891 he had recovered sufficiently to resume his parish duties thanks to Doctor McDonagh's care.[52]

Redfern was a diverse area in the 1890's and when Syrian (Melkite) priest Father Sylvannus Mansur arrived in Sydney, Cardinal Moran posted him to Father Tuckwell's hospitality at St Vincent's Church. Holy Mass in Greek was celebrated regularly in Redfern after morning Holy Mass in the Roman rite.[53] Father Tuckwell lent his support to the establishment of a church for the Syrian clergy at Waterloo, Sydney. In due course the new Syrian (Melkite) Church of Saint Michael in Elizabeth Street was constructed and the first wedding there in December 1892 saw Father Tuckwell take the "concession" of the couple before the Syrian Priest, Father Mansur, performed the rest of the marriage ceremony.[54]

In September 1894, Father Tuckwell was moved from Redfern parish to Holy Trinity Parish Granville and it was noted with gratitude that many of the decorations of the Redfern St Vincent de Paul Church were provided at Father Tuckwell's own expense.[55] Father Tuckwell's removal was an unpopular move as far as the parishioners of Redfern were concerned, and a meeting was called to discuss whether a deputation should visit Cardinal Moran or Bishop Higgins to see if the decision could be reversed. It was also noted that Father Tuckwell's charitable benevolence was well known in Redfern,

---

51. 'St. Vincent De Paul, Redfern,' *The Sydney Morning Herald* (3 October 1892): 5: http://nla.gov.au/nla.news-article13881085
52. 'Catholic Notes.' *Freeman's Journal* (7 November 1891): 18: http://nla.gov.au/nla.news-article115565351
53. 'A Novel Religious Service,' *Illustrated Sydney News* (15 October 1892): 4: http://nla.gov.au/nla.news-article64031509
54. 'A Syrian Wedding.' *Evening News* (20 December 1892): 5: http://nla.gov.au/nla.news-article113320347
55. 'Father Tuckwell's Removal,' *Freeman's Journal* (18 August 1894): 15: http://nla.gov.au/nla.news-article115546352 and 'Clerical Changes,' *Freeman's Journal* (8 September 1894): 15: http://nla.gov.au/nla.news-article115547718

even among non-Catholics.[56] Nothing eventuated with the protest and Father Tuckwell moved to Granville at the end of October 1894 where he was heartily welcomed by the parishioners and Mayor with a banquet and dance. In his response to the Granville welcome Father Tuckwell remarked that he hoped to remain for many years.[57]

It seems that Father Tuckwell's health was not the best at the time of his move to Granville and this may explain him taking a job as a private chaplain for a "French gentlemen's family" on the north side of the Pyrenees in France despite his initial hope to remain many years. He planned to leave in April 1895.[58] In the meantime there were still parish matters to attend to and Father Tuckwell was present at a Concert at the Paramatta Town Hall to raise funds to fix the Holy Trinity Church, damaged in a recent wind storm.[59] The funds were raised by Easter and Father Tuckwell remarked that this was 'thanks to the spirit of faith displayed by his people'.[60] His Granville parishioners were not at all happy to see him go.[61] Part of Father Tuckwell's appeal to the people of the parishes he pastored was in the habit of wearing his clerical cassock when out around the town.[62]

Father Tuckwell departed Sydney for Marseilles on the Steamship *Australien* on Saturday 27 April 1895.[63] The ship voyage may have done Father Tuckwell a world of good as on arrival his health had vastly improved. On arrival in France Father Tuckwell went to the family in the Pyrenees, but early in 1896 he was appointed by

56. 'The Rev. Father Tuckwell,' *The Cumberland Mercury* (1 September 1894): 6: http://nla.gov.au/nla.news-article252759453
57. 'Welcoming a pastor,' *Evening News* (30 October 1894): 6: http://nla.gov.au/nla.news-article108880864 A fuller report of the event is here: 'The Rev. Father Tuckwell.' *The Cumberland Mercury* (3 November 1894): 6: http://nla.gov.au/nla.news-article252760440
58. 'Personal,' *Table Talk* (15 March 1895): 2: http://nla.gov.au/nla.news-article145920319
59. 'Organ Recital,' *The Daily Telegraph* (23 March 1895): 6: http://nla.gov.au/nla.news-article235994750
60. 'Holy Trinity Church, Granville,' *The Cumberland Mercury* (20 April 1895): 4: http://nla.gov.au/nla.news-article252767392
61. 'The Rev. Father Tuckwell.' *The Cumberland Mercury* (27 April 1895): 4: http://nla.gov.au/nla.news-article252767516
62. 'News of the Day,' *The Age* (20 February 1896): 4: http://nla.gov.au/nla.news-article193983377
63. 'English and French Mails,' *The Australian Star* (27 April 1895): 11: http://nla.gov.au/nla.news-article227111971

Cardinal Rickards to the parish of *Notre Dame des Victoires* (Our Lady of Victories) in Paris.[64] Whatever health problem Father Tuckwell had previously must have cleared up sufficiently for him to take this new appointment in Paris. At *Notre Dame des Victoires* he was to be chaplain to the English-speaking community which at that time included a sizable number of Irish.[65] His good health did not last, and he was struck by an attack of pleurisy just after Christmas 1897.[66] Pleurisy may be the health explanation for Father Tuckwell's short stay in Granville and return to France.[67]

Nevertheless, Father Tuckwell remained in Paris for six years where he was known as a confessor, hearing confessions in English, German, French and Italian. In Paris he was known as *Abbe Restiaux de Tuckwell.*[68] He supported his expat Irish parishioners through the Saint Patrick's Society in Paris.[69] In both 1896[70] and 1897,[71] the Irish ex-pat community in Paris celebrated St Patrick's day with a function held in Paris attended by Father Tuckwell. Both events included Irish revolutionary Maude Gonne and although this indicates father Tuckwell's well connected social circle it leaves hidden his actual thoughts on the topics of Irish politics, not to mention the rather 'progressive' opinions of Maude Gonne. The *Association Artistique et Literaire de Sainte Patrice* to which Father Tuckwell loaned his support was not just political but also hosted concerts and historical lectures. The May 1897 meeting was to be a lecture on the Irish at the

64. 'Local and District Items,' *The Cumberland Argus and Fruit Growers Advocate,* (11 January 1896): 2: http://nla.gov.au/nla.news-article85762167 and "Catholic News," *The Catholic Press* (15 February 1896): 17: http://nla.gov.au/nla.news-article104411666 and 'Rev. Father Tuckwell,' *Evening News* (20 February 1896): 6, http://nla.gov.au/nla.news-article109913069
65. "A Distinguished Priest," *The Daily Telegraph,* (20 February 1896): 5: http://nla.gov.au/nla.news-article238693292
66. "Personal," *The Catholic Press* (20 February 1897): 8: http://nla.gov.au/nla.news-article104405450 and 'Personal.' *The Catholic Press* (20 February 1897): 8: http://nla.gov.au/nla.news-article104405450 which cites the French magazine *Verite.*
67. "L'Angleterre Catholique," *La Croix* (27 September 1898): 3: https://gallica.bnf.fr/ark:/12148/bpt6k218079n/f3
68. The origin of the *de Restiaux* part of his surname is not known.
69. 'Paris notes,' *Freeman's Journal,* (5 October 1898): 6, Gale Primary Sources database.
70. 'La Sainte Patrice,' *Le Gaulois: littéraire et politique* (19 March 1896): 2: https://gallica.bnf.fr/ark:/12148/bpt6k5294388/f2
71. 'Chronique Parisienne,' *L'Univers* (20 March 1897): 3: https://gallica.bnf.fr/ark:/12148/bpt6k7094352/f3

battle of Fontenoy at which 'Irish soldiers fought so effectively for the success of France'.[72] Irish politics was obviously not far below the surface and again it is hard to know Father Tuckwell's thoughts as an Englishman although earlier reports suggest that he was sympathetic to the Irish situation.

In France, Father Tuckwell was not averse to verbal pugilism and standing up for the Faith. One example from 1897; the clearly anti-clerical newspaper *La Lanterne* took issue with a stand Father Tuckwell took in another newspaper *La Verite* where he lamented the defection of Abbe Charbonnel from the Church. Ex priest Charbonnel had become a proponent of free thought and secularism. La Lanterne derided Father Tuckwell as a 'broker in colonial papism' ridiculing him for illogicality in condemning the Abbe Charbonnel for trading religions when he himself was a convert from the protestant religion. Clearly the editors of *La Lanterne* subscribed to the illogical creed that all religions are equal.[73]

By 1898, Father Tuckwell decided that the Paris climate was not conducive to his good health and he decided to move the more clement environment of Pau in the Diocese of Tarbes.[74] In Pau, Father Tuckwell was well known socially among the expat English speaking community and the socially well connected. One reported musical reception at the *Hotel de la poste* in Pau hosted by *Madame de Coigny* at which Father Tuckwell was present included people with twenty-four recognisably English surnames.[75] Father Tuckwell's spiritual care for his flock of English-speaking exiles in Pau was a happy one.

Father Tuckwell's death was preceded by an attack of sunstroke contracted during a procession of the Blessed Sacrament through the

72. 'Paris Notes,' *Freeman's Journal* (27 April 1897): 5, Gale primary Resources.
73. 'Illogisme,' *La Lanterne: Journal Politique Quotidien*, (19 October 1897): 1: https://gallica.bnf.fr/ark:/12148/bpt6k7513731s/f1. I have not been able to trace the *Verite* article.
74. M. L'Abbe Tuckwell, *Église d'Albi: la semaine religieuse de l'Archidiocèse d'Albi*, (8 October 1898): 652, https://gallica.bnf.fr/ark:/12148/bpt6k6395010b/f12 and "Echoes,"*Gazette Nationale ou leMoniteur Universel* (29 September 1898): 3: https://www.retronews.fr/journal/gazette-nationale-ou-le-moniteur-universel/29-septembre-1898/149/2624137/3 and 'Nouvelles Religieuses,' *Le Gaulois: littéraire et politique* (28 September 1898): 3: https://gallica.bnf.fr/ark:/12148/bpt6k5304080/f3
75. 'Social Jottings,' *New York Herald (European Edition)* (16 December 1904): 2, Gale Primary Sources.

streets of Pau on the Octave Day of Corpus Christi 1918. He died on June 17 that year aged 75 years.[76] The *Catholic Press* in Sydney reported his death saying:

> 'He loved Our Blessed Mother—how she must have loved him, who as a child had defended her honour! Peace be to his noble soul!'

Acknowledgement: Thanks to Keith Smiley, of Melbourne (great nephew of Father Tuckwell) for family information.

76. 'Death of a Convert Priest.' *The Catholic Press (Sydney, NSW: 1895—1942)* (31 October 1918): 31: http://nla.gov.au/nla.news-article105968336 and Extrait, *L'Indépendant des Basses-Pyrénées*, (18 June 1918): 2: https://www.pireneas.fr/ark:/12148/bpt6k5275647f/f2 Also noted in 'In the French Provinces,' *New York Herald (European Edition)* (21 June 1918): 2.

Journal of the Australian Catholic Historical Society, Volume 41/2020

Fanaticism, Frisson, and *fin de siècle* France: Catholics, Conspiracy Theory, and Léo Taxil's 'Mystification'—Part 1

*Bernard Doherty**

On November 21, 1907, the Sydney-based *Catholic Press*—a forerunner to the modern *Catholic Weekly*—published an anonymous (and probably syndicated) article entitled 'The World's Worst Liar', subtitled 'Gabriel Jogand and His Hoax'.[1] This somewhat distasteful piece of post-mortem polemic gave a brief and highly selective account of the late nineteenth century 'mystification' of the erstwhile French anticlerical, expelled and disgraced Freemason, and later feigned convert to the Roman Church, Gabriel Jogand-Pagès (1854–1907). A figure better known to posterity by his *nom de plume*: Léo Taxil. The article, with some morbid satisfaction, held that Taxil had 'died despised by those who had known him and by the great world he had cheated'. Among other pieces of invective, the *Catholic Press* article referred to Taxil as a 'horrible buffoon', whose 'thrilling fairy tale under the guise of fact took the Catholic world by storm'. More accurately perhaps, however, it called him 'the most successful fraud of the nineteenth century'—an appellation Taxil would have savoured.

To most Australian Catholics, both then and now, Taxil's name was likely unfamiliar, but only a decade earlier he had made international headlines when he brought a dramatic conclusion to a twelve-year-

* Dr Bernard Doherty is a lecturer at St Mark's National Theological Centre, Canberra, and a research fellow in the Centre for Public and Contextual Theology (PaCT) at Charles Sturt University. Part of this paper was delivered as the St Mark's National Theological Centre Commencement Lecture on 31 March 2020.

1. 'The World's Worst Liar, Gabriel Jogand and his Hoax', *Catholic Press*, (21 November 1907): 8.

long and highly lucrative literary masquerade which some American commentators called 'the biggest hoax of modern times'.[2]

Playing on wider societal fears, Taxil almost single-handedly created a frisson in the French *fin de siècle* by convincing influential figures in the French (and wider European) Roman Catholic hierarchy and press of the existence of a vast and thoroughly fantastical conspiracy involving what he alleged were Satanic machinations taking place among the upper echelons of Freemasonry (what Taxil called 'High-Masonry')—in particular those of a fictional group he dubbed the Palladists.[3]

This article is the first instalment of a two-part historical examination of the 'Taxil Hoax', its historical background, and its reception. In this first instalment I will introduce the salient features of the hoax, highlight some important features of the French Third Republic (1870–1940) which made it conducive to conspiracist thinking, and give a very brief overview of recent historiography on the hoax. In the second instalment I will examine the very distinct initial reception within the Anglosphere—particularly amongst non-Catholic writers in Europe and America.

2. For Taxil's full confession see 'The Confession of Léo Taxil', Translated by Alain Bernheim, A. William Samii and Eric Serejski, in Arturo de Hoyos and Morris S. Brent, *Is it True What they Say About Freemasonry? 195–228* (New York: M. Evans, 2010).
3. The bibliography, particularly recently, on the Taxil Hoax is extensive. For the most detailed recent accounts see John Dickie, *The Craft: How the Freemason Made the Modern World* (New York: Public Affairs, 2020), 222–245; David Allen Harvey, 'Lucifer in the City of Light: The Palladium Hoax and "Diabolical Causality"', in Fin de Siècle France', *Magic, Ritual, and Witchcraft*, 1/2 (Winter 2006): 177–206; Massimo Introvigne, *Satanism: A Social History* (Leiden: Brill, 2016), 158–226; WR Jones, 'Palladism and the Papacy: An Episode of French Anticlericalism in the Nineteenth Century', in *Journal of Church and State* 12/3 (1970): 453–473; Ruben van Luijk, *Children of Lucifer: The Origins of Modern Religious Satanism* (Oxford: Oxford University Press, 2016), 205–280; Christopher McIntosh, *Eliphas Lévi and the French Occult Revival* (London: Rider, 1972), 206–218; Gordon Wright, *Notable or Notorious? A Gallery of Parisians* (Harvard: Harvard University Press, 1989), 87–95; Robert Ziegler, *Satanism, Magic and Mysticism in Fin-de-siècle France* (Basingstroke: Palgrave Macmillan, 2012), 50–73. For an account which includes many of the important primary sources see Eugen Weber's *Satan franc-maçon: La mystification de Léo Taxil* (Paris: Julliard, 1964).

Taxil's 'Mystification'

In 1885 Léo Taxil renounced his earlier position as a notorious anticlerical journalist and publicist.[4] Hitherto, Taxil had been responsible for a series of scurrilous and scandalous works aimed squarely at the clergy, with such memorable titles as *Les Soutanes Grotesques* (1879); *Les Fils du Jesuite* (1879–featuring an introduction by Giuseppe Garibaldi (1807–1882); *Les debauches d'un confesseur* (1884–with Karl Milo); *Les Pornographes sacrés: la confession et les confesseurs* (1882); and *Les Maîtresses du Pape* (1884).[5]

At this time, Taxil feigned conversion to Catholicism, an event which achieved international media attention, and over a twelve-year period, beginning with an anti-Masonic work entitled *Les frères trois-points* (1885), began to cumulatively construct what would today be called a wild conspiracy theory about a fictional higher echelon group of Masons known as the Palladists.

Cashing in (quite literally[6]) on the anti-Masonic enthusiasm occasioned by Pope Leo XIII's 1884 encyclical *Humanum Genus*,[7] Taxil's earliest post-conversion writings plagiarised numerous pre-existing texts and fabricated others, taking well-worn anti-Masonic tropes regarding alleged sexual deviancy and political intrigue and weaving these into an increasingly fantastical narrative in writings with titles like: *Les Sœurs maçonnes* (1886); *Les Mystères de la franc-maçonnerie* (1886); and *La France maçonnique, liste alphabétique des francs-maçons, 16 000 noms dévoilés* (1888)—the latter of which is, quite literally, an alphabetical list of members of the Grand Orient. These works, like Taxil's earlier anticlerical writings, were one-part anti-Masonic propaganda, one-part plagiarism, and one-part scandal mongering. It was not until late 1891, however, in the wake

4. This account draws *inter alia* on the works cited in N.
5. Most of Taxil's anticlerical and anti-Masonic writings are now available online through http://archive.org/ accessed on
6. The entire hoax was particularly lucrative, a point made before its exposure by F Legge, 'Devil Worship and Freemasonry', *Contemporary Review*, 70 (July-December 1896): 481f.
7. On Pope Leo XIII and the Freemasons see especially Giovanni Miccoli, 'Leone XIII e la massoneria', *Studi Storici*, 47/1 (January–March 2006): 5–64, especially 38–56. See also Geoffrey Cubitt, 'Catholics versus Freemasons in Late Nineteenth-Century France', in edited by, F Tallett and N Atkin *Religion, Society and Politics in France Since 1789* (London: Hambledon Press, 1991), 121–136.

of the success and controversy occasioned by Joris-Karl Huysman's infamous Satanic novel *Là-Bas* earlier that year, that Taxil began to elaborate on his most diabolical creation: the Palladists.[8]

In *Y a-t-il des femmes dans la franc-maçonnerie?* (1891), an expanded version of his earlier *Les Sœurs maçonnes*, Taxil elaborated on the Palladists, who he had vaguely alluded to in the earlier text. Now referred to as the 'New and Reformed Palladium,' which (according to Taxil) had been formed in America in 1870, Taxil waxed lyrical about the Palladists' alleged worship of Lucifer and their blasphemous rites.

These so-called Palladists, Taxil later claimed, controlled a worldwide Satanic cult from their headquarters in Charleston, South Carolina, initially under the leadership of Albert Pike (1809–1891)—a former Confederate General and high-level Scottish Rite Mason who had publicly denounced Pope Leo XIII's anti-Masonic encyclical *Humanum Genus* in 1884,[9] in a pamphlet.

In order to create a veneer of authenticity—certainly enough to convince many credulous clerics—Taxil also included numerous other well-known figures as *dramatis personae*. Among these were well-known anticlerical Freemasons like the Italian banker Adriano Lemmi (1822–1906) and figures connected with the fringes of masonry and the occult revival like John Yarker (1833–1913) and Dr William Wynn Westcott (1848–1925)—the latter two of whom were less than impressed when informed about their alleged involvement with the Palladists.[10] In addition to this, Taxil created a series of characters out of whole cloth, notably the dreaded sapphic Templar mistress Sophie Walder, who Taxil described as 'an incarnate she-devil, wallowing in sacrilege, a true Satanist, such as one meets in Huysmans' books.'[11]

8. Taxil's indebtedness to Huysmans was a point not lost on writers at the time, see for example Legge, 'Devil Worship and Freemasonry', 468 and Arthur Edward Waite, *Devil-Worship in France, or The Question of Lucifer* (London: George Redway, 1896), 11.
9. See Albert Pike, *A Reply for the Ancient and Accepted Scottish Rite of Free-Masonry to the Letter 'Humanum Genus' of Pope Leo XIII* (Charleston: Grand Orient of Charleston, 1884). For a discussion of Pike's reply and Taxil's reasons for choosing Pike as a figurehead see Harvey, 'Lucifer and the City of Light', 191–194.
10. See for example Waite, *Devil-Worship in Modern France*, 214–21, 280–282.
11. 'The Confession of Léo Taxil', 210.

Over the next four years much more would be written about these alleged Palladists and particularly the (possibly fictitious) professed apostate from the Luciferic cult, Dianna Vaughan, who became the *belle de jour* of anti-Masonic writers. As time passed, however, the claims made about the Palladists became increasingly unbelievable.

With the assistance of his co-conspirator, a merchant surgeon named Dr Karl Hacks (alias Dr Bataille), the unwitting Italian dupe Domenico Margiotta, and the mysterious alleged Franco-American type-writer saleswoman Dianna Vaughan, between 1892 and 1895 Taxil produced, among other works, a monumental near 2000-page serialised work entitled *Le diable au XIXème siècle*. This adventure story, compared by some to the writings of Jules Verne,[12] convinced all manner of credulous Roman Catholic anti-Masons not only of the existence of the Palladists, but also that since the final loss of the Papal States in 1870 this group had been working piecemeal to destroy the Church and ferment revolutions across Europe. Unsurprisingly, and importantly, Taxil found ready allies here, not least amongst reactionary anti-Masonic and antisemitic clerics like Monsignor Leo Meurin SJ (1825–1895), then Archbishop of Port Louis (Mauritius) and author of *La franc-maçonnerie, synagogue de Satan* (1893) and Monsignor Armand-Joseph Fava (1826–1899), then Bishop of Grenoble and editor of the anti-Masonic periodical *La Franc-Maçonnerie démasquée* published from 1884.[13]

It was at this point, according to Taxil's confession, that things moved from relatively standard anti-Masonic tropes into the more absurd and clearly both Taxil and his collaborators were testing how far they could push the envelope. *Le diable au XIXème siècle* included, among its more sensational elements, Dr Bataille's alleged visit to Sri Lanka in which he encountered Satanists who had a monkey that spoke Tamil and a spiritualist séance in which the pagan god Moloch was invoked and appeared in the form of a crocodile who proceeded to play a piano and drink the house dry! While some more sensible Roman Catholics cottoned onto the dubious nature of these claims, Taxil and particularly the mysterious Dianna Vaughan, continued

---

12. See for example Arthur Edward Waite, *A New Encyclopedia of Freemasonry* (New York: Wings Books, 1970 [1921]), 257.

13. On these two figures see especially Norman Cohn, *Warrant for Genocide: The Myth of the Jewish World Conspiracy and the Protocols of the Elders of Zion* (London: Serif, 2005 [1967]), 46–65 and also Introvigne, *Satanism*, 178–9, 190.

to elicit great support amongst European clerics and religious who perceived in their writings proof positive of both the Masonic threat suggested in a series of papal encyclicals going back to Clement XII's *In Eminenti* (1738), and moreover, of the fundamentally 'Satanic' nature of Masonic rites.[14] As Taxil's confession noted, he received 'the most encouraging episcopal congratulations' adding 'not counting those of the grave theologians who didn't bat an eyelid when our crocodile played piano'.[15] While many of Taxil's clerical supporters, one of whom sent him a gift of particularly expensive gruyere cheese from Switzerland, were clearly unsophisticated and pious dupes, others were far more culpable in swallowing the charade, including, according to Taxil, 'illustrious theologians, eloquent preachers, eminent prelates' all of whom 'congratulated him, each louder than the other'.[16]

The hierarchy of the Church and more sceptical journalists soon began to privately doubt Taxil's claims, but in an astounding act of at best face-saving expediency, at worst duplicity, failed to publicly acknowledge their reasons—likely out of a fear that Pope Leo XIII's tacit support of Taxil (whom he had given an audience in June 1887) and other anti-Masonic writers would bring the Church into disrepute and threaten the Pope's (ultimately doomed) policy of *ralliement*.[17] Amid doubts expressed at a major anti-Masonic congress held at Trent in Italy in late September and early October 1896, coupled with Hacks' public admission that it had been a hoax, Taxil saw the writing

14. On the anti-Masonic Papal documents and the wider background to anti-Masonic writing among Roman Catholics see José A Ferrer Benimeli, 'The Catholic Church and Freemasonry: An Historical Perspective', in *Ars Quatuor Coronatorum* 119 (2006): 234–255 and 'Freemasonry and the Catholic Church', in Henrik Bogdan & Jan AM Snoek, *Handbook of Freemasonry*, 139–154; Cubitt, 'Catholics versus Freemasons in Late Nineteenth—Century France', 121–136; Alec Mellor, Our Separated Brethren: The Freemasons, translated by BR Feinson (London: George G Harrap & Co, 1964), 149–279 and 'The Roman Catholic Church and the Craft', *Ars Quatuor Coronatorum*, 89 (1976): 60–69
15. 'The Confession of Léo Taxil', 213.
16. 'The Confession of Léo Taxil', 198. Taxil's confession includes several letters from clergy and bishops. For two excellent surveys of various Catholic responses see *inter alia* Introvigne, *Satanism*, 158–226 and van Luijk, *Children of Lucifer*, 207–241.
17. On this policy and its eventual failure see especially Henry Chadwick, *A History of the Popes 1830–1914* (Oxford: Oxford University Press, 1998), 290–301 and Eamon Duffy, *Saints and Sinners: A History of the Popes*, 3rd edition (New Have: Yale Nota Bene, 2006), 305–318.

was on the wall for what he called his 'mystification'. He eventually appeared before an audience at the Geographical Society in Paris on April 19, 1897—Easter Monday—to give a speech later published in the Paris weekly *Le Frondeur* as 'Twelve Years Under the Banner of the Church'.[18] In this speech Taxil confessed all, providing extensive detail about the entire farce before declaring that 'Palladism is now dead for good. Its father just murdered it'.[19] Taxil then exited the hall under police guard. The gathered audience of Masons and anti-Masons subsequently engaged (according to at least one account) in an all-in brawl—mercifully, weapons had been confiscated upon entry, so no one was seriously hurt![20]

An irrepressible prankster, Taxil considered this whole affair a source of 'inexpressible joy' to be savoured and which he hoped would lead to 'a worldwide outburst of laughter'.[21] To this end, Taxil prefaced his extensive disclosure with an account of his earlier mischievous escapades involving the good citizens of his native Marseille, who he persuaded through a series of forged letters, were being beset by a plague of shark attacks; and other Europeans he had convinced of the existence of a subaquatic city which could be viewed from Lake Geneva in Switzerland.

However, as will be discussed below, there was a more serious side to this mystification and even Taxil referred to it as 'this funny as well as instructive hoax'.[22] Once we move beyond its more ridiculous elements we arrive at a more sobering conclusion—many people, especially Catholics, clearly took Taxil and his co-conspirators at their word and spread these ludicrous ideas. Even today, as a cursory internet search will reveal, in some reactionary Roman Catholic circles and amongst fundamentalist Protestants, aspects of Taxil's hoax are still taken *aux sérieux* and have provided the historical roots

18. 'Douze ans sous la Bannière de l'Eglise', *Le Frondeur* (April 25, 1897): 1.
19. *Confessions*
20. See the account of Henry C Lea, 'An Anti-Masonic Mystification', in *Lippincott's Magazine* 66 (1900): 948–960. This work was later translated as a pamphlet into French by Salomon Reinach as *Léo Taxil, Diana Vaughan et l'Eglise romaine, histoire d'une mystification* (Paris: Sociéte nouvelle de librairie et d'edition, 1901).
21. 'The Confession of Léo Taxil', 205.
22. 'The Confession of Léo Taxil', 203.

for later conspiracy theories.[23] To begin to make sense of this, it is necessary to look briefly at the context in which the hoax occurred and its relationship with the wider conspiracist milieu of the Third Republic.

The Conspiracist Context

The Taxil Hoax was, in the words of the British historian JM Roberts (1928–2003), an example of conspiracist 'ideas now generally thought to be nonsense'. However, in a period where once again the often-powerful lure and seductive explanatory simplicity offered by conspiracy theories has wielded influence among sectors of wider society in several countries, it is worth also recalling along with Roberts that, at least historically, these ideas 'were often elaborately articulated'. Historical conspiracy theories like the Taxil Hoax were, in a word, 'an area of highly organized nonsense', replete with their own alternative experts, periodicals, and reading publics, which spanned much of Europe and beyond.[24] Moreover, these ideas were both effective and influential in their political impact, especially among the significant number of Roman Catholics in the Third Republic who had—not always unreasonably—been caught up in what one historian fairly described as the 'persecution mania' that swept what another called the 'Catholic underworld' of post-Revolutionary France and which found their greatest articulation in the closing decades of the nineteenth century and the reactionary Catholic search for real and imagined enemies.[25]

The Third Republic was a period of frequent political defeat for conservative French Catholics.[26] Monarchists saw any serious hope of a Legitimist restoration of the monarchy die with the last

23. For a list of examples see de Hoyos and Brent, *Is it True What they Say About Freemasonry?*, 39–41.
24. JM Roberts, *The Mythology of Secret Societies* (London: Watkins, 2008 [1974]), 15.
25. John McManners, *Church and State in France 1870–1914* (London: SPCK, 1972), 123; C.S. Phillips, *The Church in France 1848–1907* (London: SPCK, 1936), 323.
26. On the general history of this period, I have relied *inter alia* on Jean Marie Mayeur and Madeleine Rebérioux, *The Third Republic from its Origins to the Great War, 1871–1914* (Cambridge: Cambridge University Press, 1984) and Theodore Zeldin, *France, 1848–1945, Volume 1, Ambition, Love and Politics* (Oxford: Clarendon Press, 1973) and *Volume 2, Intellect, Taste and Anxiety* (Oxford: Clarendon Press, 1973).

of the Bourbon pretenders, the Comte de Chambord (1820–1883). Successive Republican governments associated with figures like Jules Ferry (1832–1893), Pierre Waldeck-Rousseau (1846–1904) and Émile Combes (1835–1921)—with varying degrees of enthusiasm and severity—implemented a series of 'laic laws' which, among other actions, reduced the heavy influence of the Church in education and closed religious houses across France. This *Kulturkampf* against what Léon Gambetta (1838–1882) famously called the clerical enemy ('Clericalism? That's the enemy!') culminated in the 1905 law on the separation of Church and State.[27] As a result of this anticlericalism, more reactionary Catholics sought to identify those they saw as responsible, singling out in particular Jews and Masons, both groups who were, in general, particularly supportive of the Republic and the long-term goals of the Revolution.[28]

Aside from the very real actions of anticlerical republican politicians (some of whom were, in fact, Freemasons) there were other cultural factors which influenced the propensity of French Catholics (in particular) to believe Taxil's more outré claims. These factors included an increasing fascination with the occult and 'Satanic' which swept France over the course of the nineteenth century—something of the flipside to the resurgent interest amongst Catholics in miracles and prophecies witnessed in the contemporaneous growth in pilgrimages to the apparition sites at La Salette (1848) and increasingly at Lourdes (1858).[29] As perhaps the most significant populariser of these ideas,

27. The bibliography on this topic is extensive, see example James McMillan, "Priest hits girl": on the front line in the "war of the two Frances", in C Clark and W Kaiser, edited by *Culture Wars: Secular–Catholic Conflict in Nineteenth-Century Europe* (Cambridge: Cambridge University Press, 2003), 77–101 and Eugen Weber, *France, Fin de Siècle* (Harvard: The Belknap Press, 1986), especially 105–141. On the law of separation see Maurice Larkin, *Church and State after the Dreyfus Affair: The Separation Issue in France* (London: Macmillan, 1974).

28. See here example Richard Millman, 'Jewish Anticlericalism and the Rise of Modern French Antisemitism', in *History*, 77/250 (1992): 220–236.

29. Itself not unrelated to some of the groups, notably the Assumptionist Fathers, who spread the Taxil Hoax. See example Ruth Harris, Lourdes: Body and Spirit in the Secular Age (London: Viking, 1999); T.A. Kselman, *Miracles and Prophecies in Nineteenth-Century France* (New Brunswick: Rutgers University Press, 1983); McIntosh, *Eliphas Lévi and the French Occult Revival*, especially 157–224; and Eugene Weber, 'Religion and Superstition in Nineteenth-Century France', in *The Historical Journal*, 31/2 (1988): 399–423.

JK Huysmans, noted regarding the so-called Palladists (in whom he implicitly believed)—their (alleged) practices were *'le christianisme retourné, le catholicisme à rebours'*.[30] Indeed, long after Huysmans converted to Catholicism over the course of 1891–1892 fellow writer Jules Renard (1864–1910) still suspected him of being 'a literary Léo Taxil'.[31]

At the same time as his attacks on the Freemasons, moreover, Pope Leo XIII, arguably more than his predecessors, showed an increased interest in matters of demonology, introducing the prayers of St Michael the Archangel in 1886 and adding an additional exorcism to the *Rituale Romanum* in 1890—actions which, along with his frequent references to Satan in his writings, only fed interest in these topics.[32] Summing up this diabolical enthusiasm, the French historian René Rémond (1918–2007) noted that: 'Few periods were so receptive as this one to the fascination and mirages of Satanism, whose evocation left a sulphurous trail in the literature of the period'—though, surprisingly, Rémond does not actually mention the Taxil Hoax![33]

In addition to the Taxil Hoax, the *fin de siècle* also witnessed a series of other *affaires* which historian Eugen Weber (1925–2007) and others note gave rise to a feeling that 'the lack of respite, the persistent sense of insecurity, and [an] ambient disgust with political life' was feeding a sense of 'endless crisis'.[34] Such a period was fertile ground for conspiracy theorizing, and the Paris Bourse stock market crash (1882), fears of a right-wing coup d'état by General Georges Boulanger (1889), the Panama scandals (1892), most significant of all the Dreyfus Affair (1894–1906), each saw the apportionment of blame placed at the foot of various groups—most often the Jews or

30. Joris-Karl Huysmans, 'Préface' in Jules Bois, *Le Satanisme et la Magie* (Paris: Ernest Flammarion, 1900), xvii.
31. Quoted in Robert Baldick, *The Life of JK Huysmans* (Sawtry: Dedalus, 2005 [1955]), 252. See also here Richard Griffiths, *The Reactionary Revolution: The Catholic Revival in French Literature 1870/1914* (New York: Frederick Ungar, 1965).
32. Francis Young, *A History of Exorcism in Catholic Christianity* (London: Palgrave MacMillan, 2016), 181–207.
33. René Rémond, *The Right Wing in France: From 1815 to de Gaulle*, Second Edition, trans. James M Laux (Philadelphia: University of Pennsylvania Press, 1969), 186.
34. Weber, *France*, 114.

the Masons by the political Right and the Jesuits by the Left.[35] As Weber further noted: 'whatever else it was, the Belle Époque was a fine time for ferments, flare-ups, disorders, rampages, riots, turbulence, tumults, barricades, and bloodshed'.[36]

Finally, this period witnessed a historical high tide in both book production and press saturation in the form of what we would today call yellow journalism.[37] This occurred concurrently with the rise of the Catholic press across Europe and elsewhere (including in Australia)—most notably in France with the unprecedented popularity of the Assumptionist Fathers' 'press empire'.[38] The Assumptionist's *La Croix*, launched as a daily in 1883, was particularly successful. By 1896 *La Croix* had a daily circulation of 180,000, as well as over a hundred smaller weekly editions.[39] Far more political and belligerent than earlier French Catholic papers like *L'Univers*, *La Croix* eagerly embraced and distributed conspiracy narratives in its pages, including for a time the Taxil Hoax, achieving historical infamy and ultimately censure for its role in promoting antisemitic material both before and during the Dreyfus Affair.[40]

Combined together, each of these features of the Third Republic, helped to encourage belief in the Taxil Hoax.

Historiography of a Hoax

The serious historical study of conspiracy theories is largely a post-World War II development and has usually been undertaken

35. See example DLL Parry, 'Articulating the Third Republic by Conspiracy Theory', in *European Historical Quarterly*, 28/2 (1998): 163–188.
36. Weber, *France*, 128.
37. On the upsurge in book printing see Robert F. Byrnes, *Antisemitism in Modern France, Volume 1. The Prologue to the Dreyfus Affair* (New Brunswick: Rutgers University Press, 1950), 283.
38. On the Assumptionists see especially Ruth Harris, 'The Assumptionists and the Dreyfus Affair', in *Past and Present*, 194 (February 2007): 175–211.
39. Larkin, *Church and State after the Dreyfus Affair*, 67. Henry Chadwick, *A History of the Popes 1830–1914*, 329 suggests it had over 700,000 readers only a year later in 1897.
40. On the role of *La Croix* here see especially Harris, 'The Assumptionists and the Dreyfus Affair', especially 185. Also see Larkin, *Church and State after the Dreyfus Affair*, 65–79 and David I Kertzer, *The Popes Against the Jews: The Vatican's Role in the Rise of Modern Anti-Semitism* (New York: Vintage Books, 2001), 171–177.

alongside the study of anti-Semitism.[41] Prior to this time, as Hannah Arendt so colourfully noted, both subjects were largely the province of 'crackpots in general and the lunatic fringe in particular'.[42] While numerous writers had commented on the Taxil Hoax before this time, it was largely with post-war work on anti-Semitism in particular that the Taxil Hoax began to receive more serious attention.

The first extensive professional English-language historical overview appeared in the work of Robert F Byrnes (1917–1997), followed by brief notices appearing in the work of both Norman Cohn (1915–2007) and Léon Poliakov (1910–1997).[43] For these historians, and others later,[44] the Taxil Hoax was one particularly egregious example the type of clerical credulity and irrationality which marked the wider Judaeo-Masonic conspiracy motives common in the *fin de siècle*, as Byrnes concluded:

> The uncritical acceptance and even dissemination by so many French Catholics, especially Catholic priests, of the ridiculous charges made against the Jews and the fantastic tales concerning the role of the devil in Freemasonry demonstrate that antirationalism is the foundation of French antisemitism.[45]

Outside the study of anti-Semitism, the Taxil Hoax also came to warrant a mention in most histories of Church State relations during the Third Republic and the relationship between anticlericalism and freemasonry. Here Taxil's significance was usually downplayed, explained away, or—in the case of more apologetic popular histories—completely elided.[46] The tone in these accounts is almost

41. See example Roberts, *The Mythology of Secret Societies*, 25.
42. Hannah Arendt, *The Origins of Totalitarianism*, New Edition with Added Prefaces (New York: Harcourt, 1976), p xi.
43. Byrnes, *Antisemitism in Modern France*, 304–319. Norman Cohn, *Warrant for Genocide*, 53f. See also, Léon Poliakov, *The History of Anti-Semitism, Volume IV: Suicidal Europe, 1870–1933*, translated by George Klin (Philadelphia: University of Pennsylvania Press, 1985 [1977]), 32.
44. Notable here Marianne Closson, 'Le Diable au xixe siècle de Léo Taxil: ou les 'mille et une nuits' de la démonologie', in F Lavocat, P Kapitaniak, and M Closson, edited by *Fictions du diable: démonologie et littérature de Saint-Augustin à Léo Taxil* (Geneva: Droz, 2007), 313–332.
45. Byrnes, *Antisemitism in Modern France*, 318.
46. For various mentions see Owen Chadwick, *A History of the Popes 1830–1914*, 304; Ruth Harris, *The Man on Devil's Island: Alfred Dreyfus and the Affair that*

always somewhat embarrassed and the sober assessment of Adrien Dansette is quite representative. Dansette only alludes in passing to freemasonry giving rise to 'some violent controversies', and refers obliquely to Catholic beliefs that freemasonry was 'a secret and devilish corporation, which, under occult direction, sought to destroy Christian society'.[47] Among these historians the hoax generally features as an anecdotal curiosity in wider accounts and in Anglophone scholarship outside of specialised studies only Ruth Harris, John McManners, and Eugen Weber seem to have appreciated its wider impact and what it reveals about the hothouse environment of the Third Republic.

This muted tone is unsurprising, and it is certainly possible to overstate the hoax's significance in Church State relations.[48] As such, the most thorough accounts have appeared in the works of historians of Freemasonry and in the burgeoning area of the study of Western Esotericism—areas of scholarly interest not often overlapping with those of ecclesiastical historians. Among the latter, the hoax is considered an important episode in popular and scholarly histories of 'Satanism' or accounts of *fin de siècle* occultism. Beginning with Christopher McIntosh's important work on the French Occult Revival, the Taxil Hoax has in recent years been the subject of several exceptionally well-researched accounts among historians of Western Esotericism—most notably Massimo Introvigne and Ruben van Luijk. Even here, however, accounts can tend to be coloured by an apologetic agenda. Gareth Medway's account, for example, is clearly informed by his (very warranted) scepticism about the later 'Satanic Panic', particularly as this manifested in 1980s and 1990s Britain and elsewhere; while the brief account by Tobias Churton is marked by the

---

Divided France (London: Penguin Books, 2011), 176–178; McManners, *Church and State in France 1870–1914*, 123; Phillips, *The Church in France 1848–1907*, 322f. Weber, *France*, 35—Weber's earlier French book *Satan Franc-Maçon: la mystification de Leo Taxil* (1964) remains the most complete account of the entire affair. For an apologetic work which completely ignores the hoax, and still suggests widespread Masonic malfeasance, see especially H Daniel-Rops, *A Fight for God 1870–1939*, translated by John Warrington (New York: EP Dutton & Co, 1965).

47. Adrien Dansette, *Religious History of Modern France, Volume 2: Under the Third Republic*, translated by John Dingle (Edinburgh: Nelson, 1961), 37.

48. A point made clearly by Cubitt, 'Catholics versus Freemasons in Late Nineteenth-Century France', 121–136, 122.

author's specific esoteric interests and says almost nothing about the wider non-occult social context.[49] A similar tendency is detectable in the accounts penned by Masonic historians and apologists, for example Alec Mellor, where the episode has often (rightly!) assumed pride of place as perhaps the most patently absurd example of anti-masonic lore which has thwarted relations, and sincere mutual attempts at rapprochement, between Roman Catholics and Freemasonry well into the present.[50]

Conclusion

Perhaps only a minor episode in the types of fabrication and fanaticism symptomatic of the French *fin de siècle*, the Taxil Hoax offers an intriguing example of the political hothouse which developed in the Third Republic and the propensity for conspiracist thinking which accompanied this. As such it is unsurprising that historical accounts of this episode are often as prevalent in histories of antisemitism as of Church State relations and Western Esotericism. It is no accident that it was precisely the same figures—the 'Jew-haters' as the historian and lawyer Francis George Legge (1853–1922) labelled them—who 'formed the backbone' of the anti-Masonic movement so ready to believe Taxil's claims.[51]

While it would be historically unwise to follow writers like Norman Cohn and attempt to posthumously psychoanalyze these figures,[52] it can certainly be said that from a historical perspective the Third

49. See Tobias Churton, *Occult Paris: The Lost Magic of the Belle Époque* (Rochester: Inner Traditions, 2016), 373–6 and Gareth Medway, *The Lure of the Sinister: The Unnatural History of Satanism* (New York: New York University Press, 2001), 9–17. For a more detailed assessment from a scholar of Western Esotericism see Christopher McIntosh, *Eliphas Lévi and the French Occult Revival* (London: Rider and Company, 1972), 206–218.
50. See for example, Alec Mellor, *Our Separated Brethren: The Freemasons*, translated by BR Feinson (London: George R Harrap & Co 1961), 255–262. The most serious scholarly account of the hoax in a masonic context can be found in John Dickie's excellent recent book *The Craft* (2020).
51. F Legge, 'The Devil in Modern Occultism', in *The Contemporary Review*, 71 (1897): 694–695.
52. See example the measured critique of Cohn's use of psychoanalysis in Richard J Evans, *The Hitler Conspiracies: The Third Reich and the Paranoid Imagination* (London: Allen Lane, 2020), 13–45 especially 43.

Republic provided an ideal ecology for the growth of conspiracist ideas. In this environment it was a very small step for reactionary Catholics to take from belief in the Taxil Hoax to belief in equally nonsensical ideas like the Judaeo-Masonic complot which remains a central plank of conspiracist thinking—a point which has not been lost on more recent commentators.[53]

While we might take Taxil at his word that he was merely engaging in a harmless prank, it seems almost certain that some degree of *ressentiment* against both the Church and the Lodge lay behind his activities, and his actions almost certainly fed an already unhealthy obsession with real and imagined conspiratorial enemies already rife in the period—both among Roman Catholics and their political opponents.

The wider reaction and longer-term impact of the Taxil Hoax was not constricted to France, or indeed to Europe alone, particularly in the Anglosphere. Just as several continental European writers began to cotton on to the dubious nature of Taxil's writings in the mid-1890s, so too did a few British writers. Some of these writers, like the esotericist and autodidact antiquarian Arthur Edward Waite (1857–1942) and the lawyer and amateur historian George Francis Legge, exposed Taxil's subterfuge far earlier than many on the continent. Others, like the English Catholic apologist Fr Herbert Thurston SJ (1856–1939) were more publicly cautious, though equally incredulous.[54] Indeed, Thurston's reaction to the Taxil Hoax was to have repercussions later in his life, as he became known (and often disliked) as the 'Devil's Advocate' among English-speaking Catholics. Across the Atlantic, meanwhile, the great American political reformer and historian of the Inquisition Henry Charles Lea (1825–1909) found his comments on the matter in *Lippincott's Magazine* in 1900 not only translated into French by fellow historian Salomon Reinach (1858–1932), but also become part of Reinach's role in the public defense of Captain Dreyfus. I will examine these Anglophone writers at greater length in the second part of this article.

53. See example Closson, 'Le Diable au xixe siècle de Léo Taxil', 332 and especially Harris, *The Man on Devil's Island*, 177.

54. On Thurston's reaction see Simon Mayers, 'From the Christ-Killer to the Luciferian: The Mythologized Jew and Freemason in Late Nineteenth-and Early Twentieth Century English Catholic Discourse', in *Melilah: Manchester Journal of Jewish Studies*, 8 (2011): 31–68.

Journal of the Australian Catholic Historical Society, Volume 41/2020

'Spontaneous to Help Where a Need Called'[1] The life of Mrs JJ Clark

*Margaret Carmody and Anne Marks**

Summary

In 1874, five-year-old Margaret Agnes Power came to Adelaide from Ireland with her family. At fourteen, she became a pupil teacher and taught at Seven Hill. In 1890, she married John James Clark, a coachbuilder and they had nine children. During World War I, Margaret was a volunteer at the Cheer Up Hut. But after the War, we know very little about her life. This paper reveals her quiet contribution, those unstated, largely hidden philanthropic activities. It argues that Margaret Clark made a major contribution to social life in Adelaide motivated

Figure 1: Margaret Agnes Power c. 1888 Coloured photograph on glass. Clark Family Collection held by Margaret Speck.

---

* Margaret Carmody is an Australian women's historian, researcher and lecturer at Australian Catholic University and a great granddaughter of Margaret Agnes Clark née Power. Anne Marks is a retired teacher, a granddaughter of Margaret Agnes Clark, and highly interested in her Irish family history, their immigration and achievements. The authors acknowledge a small grant from Australian Catholic University to Margaret Carmody which enabled archival and 'treading the footsteps' research in Ireland in 2019.

1. 'The Late Mrs. J. J. Clark,' *Southern Cross* (29 November 1940). Note: Margaret Clark was always referred to as 'Mrs J. J. Clark' in the press.

by her belief in the importance of education and her Catholic faith, but most of all her understanding of how circumstances could lead to very hard times for individuals.

From Tipperary to Adelaide

Margaret Agnes Power was born in 1869 at Mohera, Annacarty, County Tipperary, Ireland where her grandfather Nicholas Power held a lease on ½ an acre[2] which supported a family of ten children and her father Cornelius Power was a labourer.[3] Margaret was five years old in 1874 when she came as an assisted passenger to South Australia with her parents, Cornelius and Sarah Power née Dwyer, her elder sisters Mary and Ellen and brother John and her younger brother Nicholas and baby sister Alice.[4] Jim and Nora were born in Adelaide.

Figure 2: Power Family 1893 Back row: Jim, Alice, Jack, Nell, Nicholas. Front row: Nora, Sarah, Cornelius, Mary, Margaret. Black and white photograph. Power Family Collection held by Anne Marks.

2. Griffith, 'Primary Valuation of Tenements. Parish of Donohill.'
3. 'Anacarty and Donohill; County of Tipperary; Diocese of Cashel and Emly. Baptisms, December 1868 to May 1869,' in Catholic Parish Registers at the NLI (Dublin: National Library of Ireland, 1869). Ordnance Survey Ireland, '1840 Os Map,' in Ordnance Survey Ireland (OSi) 19th Century Historical Maps, edited by Ordnance Survey Ireland (Dublin: UCD Library, University College Dublin, 1837–1911). Ordnance Survey of Ireland, '1889–1913 Os Map,' in Ordnance Survey Ireland (OSI) 19th Century Historical Maps, ed. Ordnance Survey Ireland (Dublin: UCD Library, University College Dublin, 1837–1911). Michael C Coleman, '"Eyes Big as Bowls with Fear and Wonder': Children's Responses to the Irish National Schools, 1850–1922', in *Proceedings of the Royal Irish Academy: Archaeology, Culture, History, Literature* 98C, no 5 (1998): 177–202. Catherine Nolan, 'The Irish Potato Famine 1846–1850.' DoChara, https://www.dochara.com/the-irish/food-history/the-irish-potato-famine-1846-1850
4. Emigration Department. Government of South Australia, 'Glenlyon 1874,' in *Passenger Lists* (Westminster UK: Archives of South Australia, 1874).

The promise of the planned society that had beckoned and their vision of life in South Australia quickly dissolved as they were confronted with the reality of heat, drought, poor transport and towns that existed merely on paper. Margaret's parents had been granted land in the drought stricken mid north of South Australia, but when they arrived and discovered there was no church and no school there, they refused to go and instead they were granted land for a market garden in Hardy Street Goodwood.

Adelaide with its plains surrounded by wooded hills was where they settled and for the next twenty two years, they lived at Goodwood. At first Cornelius worked on his market garden, he then leased it, but continued to live at Goodwood.[5] In the mid-1890s he became the 'energetic, devoted' Keeper of the Weir at Clarendon and the Inspector of Fisheries on the Onkaparinga River—both significant positions for Adelaide's water supply in the late nineteenth and early twentieth century.[6]

Figure 3: Sarah Power née Dwyer 1847–1910 Adelaide South Australia, c. 1880. Black and white photograph. Power Family Collection held by Anne Marks.

It seems that Sarah and Cornelius enjoyed living at Clarendon which with its wooded hills, rivers and streams is remarkably similar to where they had lived in Tipperary. Margaret's mother, Sarah Power was regarded as 'a very highly respected resident of Clarendon'.[7] She died in

5. John Keany, 'John James Clark (1860–1942) a Biographical Memoir', in *Clark Family History* (Adelaide, 1989).
6. 'Obituary,' *Southern Cross* (17 July 1914): 'Friendly Societies,' *The Advertiser*, 3 October 1901; 'Our Water Supply, '*The Advertiser*, 18 February 1902. 'Personal, '*The Advertiser*, 15 June 1900; 'Retiring Official, '*Daily Herald*, (29 June 1914): SA Water, 'Happy Valley Reservoir, 'SA Water. Note: The Clarendon Weir controlled the water flowing into the Happy Valley Reservoir, built between 1892–1897. edited by Gordon Young. *Onkaparinga Heritage: Historical Studies of the Onkaparinga District Council* (South Australian College of Advanced Education and South Australian Centre for Settlement Studies, 1988).
7. 'The Country,' *The Advertiser* (1 November 1910).

1910 aged seventy three years and was described as, 'well known for the many acts of charity she performed and was ever ready to give her services at the sick bedside, or for the want of a needy neighbour. This, together with possessing that piety derived only from a whole faith, won the esteem of all she came in contact with'.[8] Cornelius died in 1914 aged 72.[9]

Education

Margaret attended St Mary's Catholic primary school at Franklin Street in the City of Adelaide which had recently been taken over from the Sisters of St Joseph by the Dominican Sisters following the brief excommunication of Mary MacKillop, as documented by historian Marie Foale.[10]

At the age of fourteen years, in 1883, Margaret became a Pupil Teacher: the entry examination was based on the end of primary school examination. She was among the elite of Pupil Teachers training at the Adelaide Teachers Training College.[11]

Figure 4: Pupil Teachers at Adelaide Teachers Training College 1883. Margaret Power 6th from left in 2nd row from front—with a smile on her face, aged 14 years. (Adelaide SA: General Collection State Library of South Australia, 1883).

8. 'Obituary,' *The Southern Cross* (4 November 1910): 'Family Notices,' *The Southern Cross* (4 November 1910).
9. 'Obituary,' *The Southern Cross* (17 July 1914).
10. Marie Therese Foale, Published as The Josephite Story (Sydney & Sisters of St Joseph, 1986) Vedrana Budimir and History Trust of South Australia, 'Saint Mary's Dominican Convent and School', History Trust of South Australia: http://sahistoryhub.com.au/places/saint-marys-dominican-convent-and-school accessed on.
11. Colin Milton Thiele, *Grains of Mustard Seed: A Narrative Outline of State Education in South Australia 1875–1975* (Adelaide: Education Department South Australia, 1975).

Similar to the system in Ireland, the Pupil Teacher training was a four-year apprenticeship scheme where students combined work in schools with study and annual examinations.[12] She was appointed as the provisional teacher at Seven Hill East Primary School South Australia when she was 17.[13] She boarded with a family and rode a horse to work so she was one of the teachers described by Colin Thiele,

> [in] the tradition of the single female teacher in the bush who battled alone in a small rectangular schoolroom by day and boarded, often primitively, at a distant farmhouse by night.[14]

At this time, Mary MacKillop had established a school at Seven Hill and Fr Julian Tenison Woods was also located at Seven Hill where the Jesuits had been settled since 1851.[15] Margaret was considering entering the convent.[16] Margaret would have had contact with both Mary MacKillop and Tenison Woods while she was posted at Seven Hill.[17] This contact sowed a lifetime interest in the Jesuits and the Josephites.

Romance

Margaret married John James Clark on 24 September 1890 at St Aloysius Catholic Church at the Jesuit College Seven Hill South Australia.[18] Its gothic revival style was similar to the church Margaret

12. Anthony McGuire, 'Pupil Teachers to Junior Teachers', in *Dictionary of Educational History in Australia and New Zealand* (2013); A McGuire, "Junior Teachers (2)," (2014).
13. '*The Advertiser*, Thursday, June 17, 1886,' *South Australian Advertiser*, 17 June 1886.
14. Thiele, *Grains of Mustard Seed*, 48
15. David Strong, *Jesuits in Australia: An Ethnographic History of the Society of Jesus in Australia* (Richmond VIC: Aurora Books, 1996). 'A History of the Jesuits in Australia', Jesuits Australia: https://ignatius.sa.edu.au/uploads/docs/The_History_of_the_Jesuits_in_Australia.pdf.
16. Note: Margaret's daughter Lossie said her mother went to Seven Hill because she was thinking of entering the convent, presumably the Sisters of St Joseph.
17. Kay Whitehead, Women's 'Life-Work': Teachers in South Australia 1836–1906 (University of Adelaide, 1996). 233.
18. Ernest Gall, 'St Aloysius Roman Catholic Church Sevenhill', in *Sevenhill Collection* (Adelaide: State Library of South Australia, 1902).

Figure 5: Margaret Power c.1890 Note: engagement ring. Clark Family Collection held by Anne Marks.

had left behind at Annacarty in County Tipperary.[19] Married women were not employed by the Public Education Department[20] and so Margaret resigned from teaching.

John James Clark, known as 'J. J.' was the son of Irish immigrants Patrick Clark (1836–1865) and Ann Quinn (1837–1903) who were married at St Patrick's Church, Adelaide in 1859. John was born at Gumeracha South Australia in 1860 and died in Adelaide in 1943.[21] John had a brother, Michael, born in 1862 and twin sisters, Anne and Catherine, born in 1864. Then disaster struck when their father died at the age of twenty nine years in 1865 when JJ was only five years old and then Catherine died aged six years in 1871; the other twin, Anne, lived to the age of eighty three and there are no further records of Michael. It is not clear how the young widow Ann managed to bring up her family. John left school[22] at twelve years and worked as a farm labourer, he then was apprenticed as a wheelwright and established himself in 1888[23] as Cossey and Clark—Coach and Trolley Builders on Magill Road at St Peters.[24]

19. Peter Moore, 'McMullen Michael', Architecture Museum, University of South Australia: https://www.architectsdatabase.unisa.edu.au/arch_full.asp?Arch_ID=148. Anacarty National School, 'The History of Anacarty NS': https://www.anacartyns.ie/anacarty-ns-school-history. The Archdiocese of Cashel & Emly. 'St Brigid's Anacarty', Archbishop's House: https://cashel-emly.ie/church/anacarty/st-brigids
20. Campbell, Craig. *Adelaide High School: Inventing a State High School.* Dictionary of Educational History in Australia and New Zealand (Dehanz). 2019.
21. 'Family Notices,' *Southern Cross* 15 January 1943.
22. John Keany, 'John James Clark (1860–1942) a Biographical Memoir', in *Clark Family History* (Adelaide, 1989). Note: John attended Forreston Primary School at Gumeracha.
23. 'Advertising,' *Express and Telegraph*, (29 June 1888).
24. 'Advertising,' *Evening Journal* (13 November 1880). Note: Cossey was a blacksmith. 'Advertising,' *The Southern Cross* (3 July 1891).

At first, Margaret and JJ lived at Norwood, where there was a Jesuit parish. JJ was an active member of the Irish Catholic community, a member of the St Ignatius Society, and other Literary Societies, participating in debates and public speaking.[25] He was the first Australian-born president of the Hibernians in South Australia and he was a Justice of the Peace. It is significant that immediately he became President of Hibernians, women were admitted as full Members and Ladies' Branches were also established.[26] It is apparent that Margaret and her sister in law Anne Clark both signed the petition for women's suffrage in 1894.[27]

He was active in encouraging the St Vincent de Paul Society in relation to supporting youth.[28] He had strong views about poverty and how the community should respond.[29] He was involved in local government politics and urged to stand for Parliament. He successfully stood for election as the Labor Candidate to the Marion Council[30] and was its President.[31] Clark Avenue Glandore is named after him.[32]

Family life

After their marriage in 1890, Margaret and JJ proceeded to have nine children: Mary Kathleen (1891–1970), known as 'Kitty' was a

25. 'A Trip to Clare,' *The Southern Cross* (1 February 1901); 'St. Ignatius' Literary Society,' *The Southern Cross* (26 April 1895); 'Fare Anomalies,' *Register* (8 August 1928); 'Purely Personal,' *Southern Cross* (21 July 1916); 'H.A.C.B. Society,' *The Southern Cross*, 24 August 1900. 'Hibernian Benefit Society News,' *The Southern Cross* (8 January 1943).
26. 'H.A.C.B. Society,' *The Southern Cross* (13 October 1899); 'Purely Personal,' *Southern Cross* (16 March 1900).
27. 'The Alphabetical Index to the Women's Suffrage Petition of 1894', editor Parliament House South Australia (Adelaide: Research and Access Services: State Records, 1894).
28. 'Presentation to Mr. Molloy and Family,' *The Southern Cross* (9 February 1912).
29. 'Correspondence,' *The Advertiser* (25 May 1906).
30. 'General News'; 'Unley Corporation.'
31. 'Marion,' *Observer* (15 June 1918); 'Marion District Council,' *The Advertiser* (20 May 1914); 'Marion District Council,' *The Advertiser* (21 December 1915); 'Marion District Council,' *Express and Telegraph* (21 July 1915); 'District Council Elections,' *Express and Telegraph* (6 July 1914).
32. David Charles Morley, *The Glandore Story from Hulk to Haven: A Story Built around the History of the Site of the Glandore Community Centre* (Glandore SA: Glandore Community Centre, 1995).

Figure 6: J. J. Clark 1899. Herald

primary school teacher; Cornelius (1892–1942), known as 'Neil' and John Leo (1894–1958), known as 'Leo' were coach builders and both served in World War I.[33] Aloysius (1895–79), known as 'Louis' was a cabinet maker; Marguerite Ann (1897–1974), known as 'Rita' went to the 'academically based' Advanced School for Girls[34] and was a secretary.[35] Malachi Marcus (1901–73), known as 'Marcus' was an electrician, Kevin Ronald (1906–84) was a salesman, Laurentia Nora Eileen (1909–2001), known as 'Lossie' ran a fashion and haberdashery store at Edwardstown; John Francis (1911–1943), known as 'Jack' was a tradesman. JJ and his four adult sons formed Clark Company Limited in 1926. They manufactured motor bodies, railway carriages, wagons, vehicles, and 'conveyances of all kinds'.[36]

Work and Social life

In 1896, St Thomas Catholic Primary School Goodwood was opened with most of the students from the Orphanage, and the first teacher

33. Australian War Memorial, 'John Leo Clark', AWM: https://www.awm.gov.au/collection/R2298001accessed on. Note: Neil Clark seems to have served in the Merchant Navy from information in letters from his sister Kitty. Mary Kathleen Clark, 'Letter to Cornelius Patrick Clark 24 May 1918', in *Keany Family Papers* (Adelaide, 1918); 'Letter to Cornelius Partick Clark 5 August 1918', in *Keany Family Papers* (Adelaide, 1918).
34. Corrine Ball, 'Australia's First State High School for Girls', Migration Museum, https://migration.history.sa.gov.au/blog/australias-first-state-high-school-for-girls/accessed on. Campbell, Adelaide High School: Inventing a State High School'; Thiele, *Grains of Mustard Seed.*
35. Note: Rita was the secretary of author Simpson Newland. Simpson Newland, *Paving the Way: A Romance of the Australian Bush* (London: Gay and Hancock, 1919).
36. 'Trade, Finance, and Mining', *Register*, (30 November 1926).

was Margaret Clark.[37] Margaret had four children under five years, including a four-month-old baby. Fortunately, the Catholic Education System employed married women, for the 1990s depressed economy would have affected the business of Cossey and Clark.[38] However, soon after, Margaret and JJ were able to purchase 388 South Terrace, now named Cross Road, Clarence Gardens and build their home. It was a large bluestone villa surrounded by verandas, some enclosed, on three acres.

Figure 7: Margaret & Anne Clark in the Garden at 388 Cross Rd Clarence Gardens SA c. 1928. Black and white photograph. Clark Family Collection held by Anne Marks.

There was a productive garden with vegetables, flowers, an orchard and a tennis court and numerous outhouses, sheds and stables. Her grandson John Keany described it as, 'a small boy's paradise. It abounded in trees and various interesting features [including] a mouldering hansom cab and an old windmill'.[39]

From when they moved to their new home, JJ's sister Anne Clark who was a dressmaker, lived with the family.[40] With Anne's assistance, Margaret was able to bring up a large family, contribute to the family income and engage in community activities.

Supporting the Community

Margaret was an active supporter of various Community and Catholic Charities such as the St Vincent de Paul's Orphanage at Goodwood

37. 'The Late Mrs. JJ Clark,' *The Southern Cross*, 29 November 1940; St Thomas School and Preschool Goodwood, 'Our History', St Thomas School and Preschool Goodwood: https://www.stg.catholic.edu.au/about-us/our-history/accessed on.
38. Bryan Fitz-Gibbon and Marianne Gizycki, 'Rdp 2001-07: A History of Last-Resort Lending and Other Support for Troubled Financial Institutions in Australia. 6. The 1890s Depression', ed. Reserve Bank of Australia (Sydney: RBA, 2001).
39. John Keany, John James Clark (1860–1942) a Biographical Memoir', in *Clark Family History* (Adelaide:1989).
40. Speck, 'Interview'.

and the Brighton Catholic Parish, helping to raise funds for them.[41] She donated money and her time in the service of others which according to historian Shurlee Swain was typical of philanthropic women at the end of the nineteenth century.[42] There are records of her contributions to the fetes.[43] Sometimes Margaret and JJ were both involved.[44]

Margaret used her teaching skills and organised events to raise money for the Orphanage, such as the concert at the Edwardstown Institute in 1913 to aid the Orphanage.[45] She was part of the 'willing band of ladies, who have been working for weeks to make the fete a success'.[46] On another occasion, she is listed as donating 5/- to the cake stall and goods to other stalls.[47] She was part of that group of well-educated South Australian women who used their knowledge and skills, as described by researcher Helen Jones, 'leading to an enrichment of society'.[48]

Irish But not Isolated

It is important to note that Irish Catholics in South Australia were a very small group, constituting no more than 10 per cent of nineteenth century immigrants. This relatively small population resulted in the Irish being invisible in a number of ways: their narratives are not the dominant narratives in the foundation of the state. Their Catholicism

---

41. Karen George and Gary George, 'St Vincent de Paul Orphanage (1866–1975)', Find & Connect: https://www.findandconnect.gov.au/ref/sa/biogs/SE00049b.htm. Note: The St Vincent de Paul Orphanage relocated to 181 Goodwood Road Goodwood in 1888, on the other side of Brownhill Creek from the Power family market garden. The Orphanage was staffed by the Sisters of St Joseph until 1889, then by the Sisters of Mercy from 1890.
42. Shurlee Swain, 'From Philanthropy to Social Entrepreneurship', in *Diversity in Leadership* edited by Joy Damousi, Kim Rubenstein, and Mary Tomsic (Canberra: Australian National University Press, 2014), 189
43. 'St. Vincent de Paul's Orphanage,' *The Southern Cross* (28 January 1916): 'Brighton Catholic Fete,' *Mail*, 21 November 1925.
44. 'Fetes and Fairs,' *Register* (22 November 1912).
45. 'St. Vincent de Paul's Orphanage Fete,' *The Southern Cross* (8 February 1918); 'Goodwood Orphanage,' *The Southern Cross* (7 November 1913).
46. 'Goodwood Orphanage.'
47. 'St. Vincent de Paul Orphanage, Goodwood,' *Southern Cross*, (13 December 1912).
48. Jones, 'Women's Education in South Australia: Institutional and Social Developments, 1875–1915'.

was unpopular in the dissident context of the colony's attitudes to religion, which were predominantly Anglo-Scottish Protestant, resulting in a lack of representation in historical records. However, they were Irish but not isolated.[49]

Margaret had a wide circle of friends, which was typical of Irish immigrants living in Adelaide: this is evident from the published lists of attendees at functions and weddings she went to.[50] It is worth remembering that the Jesuits in South Australia, who established Seven Hill, ran the Catholic Parish in Norwood and the St Ignatius Literary Society, were responsible to Austria until 1900 when they amalgamated with other Australian Jesuits and became responsible to Ireland.[51] Thus the South Australian Hibernians included members of many different nationalities, Poles, Austrians, Germans, Irish and Australians.[52] Irish people in Adelaide did not form into a separate group as in Sydney and Melbourne, and it is evident that JJ played a conciliatory role in South Australia between the various Irish Catholic Groups and the Irish National Federation.[53] Margaret and her husband associated with the leaders of the community through JJ's various positions in public life and their extended family.[54] Two of their sons married two daughters of Michael McAuley the pastoralist from the mid north of South Australia.[55] They had friends of all faiths: two of their daughters married protestants, both with German origins.[56] This is an example of the diffusing of the Irish in society.[57]

---

49. Eric Richards, 'Irish Life and Progress in Colonial South Australia,' in *Irish Historical Studies,* 27 (1991): 107
50. 'Miss Dorothy Kingston's Pupils' Concert,' *Mail* (29 August 1914).
51. Strong, *Jesuits in Australia,* 2–3, 8.
52. 'A Trip to Clare'.
53. 'I.N. Federation,' *The Southern Cross* (24 January 1896); 'St. Patrick's Day. Meeting in St. Francis Xavier's Hall,' *The Southern Cross* (7 February 1896).
54. 'Weddings,' *The Advertiser* (5 August 1927).
55. 'Obituary Michael James McAuley, Unley Park,' *The Southern Cross* (6 April 1934); 'Mr. Michael McAuley,' *Chronicle* (12 April 1934): 'Obituary,' *The Advertiser* (14 April 1934).
56. Mary Kathleen Clark, 'Letter to Cornelius Patrick Clark 5 August 1918', In Keany Family Papers. Adelaide, 1918 3. Note: In 1920 Kitty Married William Christian Keany who had changed his name from Kuhne and in 1937 Lossie married Gordon John Metters, son of Alfred Metters, Baptist Minister and Ottolie Stremple. 'Advertising,' *The Advertiser* (19 August 1918).
57. Janine McEgan, 'Irish Graves of South Australia's Mid-North, 1850–1899: An Examination of Cultural Significance' (Flinders Unniversity, 2017).

Cheer Up Hut

World War I has been identified as a key point for women to become involved in the public sphere.[58] The Cheer-Up Hut was established by philanthropic ladies in Adelaide to provide comfort and entertainment for soldiers on leave during the war.[59] Margaret was a voluntary worker for the Cheer-Up Hut and Honorary Secretary of Adelaide's 11th Field Ambulance Comforts Club.[60]

Margaret's children lamented their mother's dedication to charitable work, fearing she was wearing herself out, as in family letters written during World War I:

> Mamma has not been well lately. She's had influenza, suffering also from too much patriotic work. Australia Day was a very big function & Mamma and her [team] of workers XI F. A. [Field Ambulance] Comforts Club took charge of the Afternoon Tea at the Exhibition Building.
> Yesterday she had the second annual meeting of the Comforts Club & they presented her with a very handsome Cake Stand. Of course, she works very hard, but it is nice to be recognised.[61]

The driving force behind Margaret's engagement in this voluntary work was the experience of her eldest sons Leo, who was an Ambulance Driver,[62] and Neil, who was a merchant seaman, along with her two brothers Jack and Jim who served in the AIF.[63]

---

58. Swain, 'From Philanthropy to Social Entrepreneurship', 192.
59. Brett Williamson, 'South Australia's Cheer up Hut Volunteers Remembered for War Service', (ABC Radio Adelaide, 2016). Gordon Walker, *Cheer up Hut* (Adelaide SA, 1919). *The Cheer-up Hut: Burra Hall*, 1918. Photograph (B&W print), 8 cm x 13.1 cm. State Library of South Australia.
60. Catherine Speck, *Painting Ghosts: Australian Women Artists in Wartime* (Melbourne: Craftsman House, 2004), 53.
61. Clark, 'Letter to Cornelius Patrick Clark 5 August 1918.' 4.
62. Australian War Memorial, 'John Leo Clark'; Australian Military Forces, 'Clark John Leo', in *Australian Imperial Force World War I* (Canberra: National Archives of Australia, 1916).
63. Mary Kathleen Clark, 'Letter to Cornelius Patrick Clark 24 May 1918'; 'Letter to Cornelius Patrick Clark 5 August 1918', Australian Military Forces, 'Power John Thomas', in *Australian Imperial Force World War I* (Canberra: National Archives of Australia, 1916). 'Power James', in *Australian Imperial Force World War I* (Canberra: National Archives of Australia, 1915). 'C.B.C. Boys at the Front,' *The Southern Cross* (9 November 1917).

Mystery

After the War, the Cheer Up Hut was disbanded,[64] but Margaret seems to have continued her voluntary work during the 20s, however, the nature of that work has been a mystery. We have two pieces of information. According to her granddaughter Margaret Speck, Margaret 'would get dressed up and go into town most days and no one in the family knew where she went or what she did'.[65] According to her youngest daughter Lossie, after her elder siblings had left home, there would often be women and their children staying temporarily on the enclosed verandas of their home, 'It was always a full house'.[66]

It seems most likely that Margaret continued her charitable work with the St Joseph's House of Providence on West Terrace in the City of Adelaide, where homeless people were provided with meals.[67]

In addition to free meals and shelter for the aged, a major activity of the Josephites at the Providence was providing refuge to 'helpless' women, many of whom had met the sisters while they were in gaol, as detailed by Foale.[68] They also ran a refuge specifically for unmarried mothers at Fullarton which received no government subsidy.[69] The attitude that infused these institutions is summed up in the statement by Archbishop O'Reily, 'Charity takes its most effective form when it strives to help the suffering who are helpless to help themselves'.[70] This attitude was in direct contrast to the prevailing ideas about caring for 'worthy [married] women' and the 'deserving poor' and the government's provision of care for the 'undeserving' at the Destitute Asylum.[71]

---

64. 'Formation of the Cheer-Up Society', Veterans SA. Note: The Cheer-Up Hut was disbanded on 24 December 1919.
65. Speck, 'Interview'.
66. Laurentia Metters, conversation with Anne Marks 1990.
67. Jude Elton, 'West Terrace at the Turn of the Century', History Trust of South Australia, http://sahistoryhub.com.au/places/west-terrace/accessed on.
68. Foale, *The Sisters of St Joseph: Their Foundation and Early History, 1866–1893*. Foale, 'The Providence 1868–1972'.
69. Karen George and Gary George, 'St Joseph's Refuge (1868-c. 2001)', Commonwealth of Australia.
70. 'Fullarton Refuge: Archbishop's Progress Report,' *Southern Cross* (12 May 1905).
71. Gary George and Karen George, 'Queen's Home (1902–1939)', Commonwealth of Australia: https://www.findandconnect.gov.au/ref/sa/biogs/SE01198b.htm. Karen George and Gary George, 'Destitute Asylum (1851-c. 1917)', ibid: https://www.findandconnect.gov.au/ref/sa/biogs/SE00062b.htm/accessed on. 'A Thematic Heritage Study on Australia's Benevolent and Other Care Institutions—Thematic Study', edited by Australian Heritage Council (Canberra: Commonwealth of Australia, 2016).

The Providence could take twenty women but often there was an overflow with as many as thirty looking for shelter before the extensions built in 1929.[72] At such times, various people quietly offered their homes to these women, according to Foale.[73] An explanation for the women and children who stayed at 388 Cross Road was that Margaret Clark was one of those people who quietly offered their homes. The temporary accommodation and food came at a cost, and with considerable risks, yet she and JJ were prepared to take those risks.

In many ways, Margaret fits into the mould of the typical philanthropic lady in late 19th and early 20th centuries, as described by Swain.[74] She had the freedom to engage in such activities due to her husband's enterprise and her own shrewd investment in real estate.[75] Like other South Australian women who had the benefit of higher education, she was part of what Jones describes as 'the development of a community of interest in literature, the arts and general social questions'.[76] However, in other ways, she does not fit this mould at all because she was professionally qualified, she had a very large family and she only rarely held executive positions in the charities she supported and even more rarely received any acknowledgement of her work.[77] Typical of late nineteenth century philanthropic women, and like her own mother, her praise came after her death at the age of seventy in 1940.[78]

Conclusion

What emerges about the life of Margaret Clark is the sense of practical charity, of meaningful activity, not seeking attention or honour, not holding high profile office bearer positions, just doing

72. 'St. Joseph's Providence,' *The Southern Cross* (19 April 1929).
73. Marie Therese Foale, *Providence: 125 Years of Josephite Aged Care, 1868–1993* (Adelaide SA: Sisters of St Joseph Flora McDonald Lodge Aged Care Services, 1993).
74. Shurlee Lesley Swain, 'The Victorian Charity Network in the 1890s' (University of Melbourne, 1976).
75. Speck, 'Interview by Margaret Carmody and Anne Marks'.
76. Jones, 'Women's Education in South Australia: Institutional and Social Developments, 1875–1915', 318.
77. Clark, 'Letter to Cornelius Patrick Clark 5 August 1918'.
78. Swain, 'From Philanthropy to Social Entrepreneurship', 191. 'The Late Mrs. JJ Clark.' 'Obituary.'

the hard work—cheerfully. She did not adhere to the concept of the 'deserving poor', nor did she campaign for social change. She did believe in the Australian value of a fair go for everyone, especially the most vulnerable in society and her enclosed verandas were a welcome refuge for many.

Overwhelmingly, when we consider the life of Mrs JJ Clark, Margaret Agnes Clark née Power, there is an understanding that people could be in very difficult circumstances through no fault of their own. This non-judgemental attitude reflects her Irish origins, her experience of the 1890s depression and the knowledge of how difficult life was for JJ as a child. She understood that individuals could be adversely affected by powerful forces beyond their control. Margaret's Christian faith inspired her to work for those in need, reflecting the ideas of Mary MacKillop, 'never see a need without doing something about it'.[79] As stated in her obituary, 'Spontaneous to help where sickness or need called, the late Mrs. Clark endeared herself to many by her cheerful and competent manner'.[80]

Through her hard work and dedication to helping those less fortunate than herself, Margaret was a leader, she was a driving force, in the support of the Goodwood Orphanage, in the Cheer-Up Hut during the Great War and in her practical generosity towards women considered to be 'helpless' during the 1920s. She was one of those quiet achievers, those 'silent workers' whose hard work among the poor and the needy helped to create a more caring society in early twentieth century Adelaide.

---

79. Sisters of Saint Joseph of the Sacred Heart, 'Introduction', 'Sisters of Saint Joseph': https://www.sosj.org.au/our-foundress-mary-mackillop/legacy/introduction/ accessed on.
80. 'The Late Mrs. J. J. Clark.'

John Sheehy: 'An Irishman and a Sterling Catholic'[1]

*Anne-Maree Whitaker**

John Sheehy, 1898
(Freeman's Journal)

In November 1921 a gathering of Catholic clergy and Irish committeemen assembled in St Patrick's, Church Hill, Sydney, to honour John Sheehy for 'splendid services to the Irish cause.' Dr Maurice Joseph O'Reilly, rector of St John's College within the University of Sydney, presided while other speakers included the parish priests of Rozelle, Waterloo and Chatswood, the President of the Catholic Federation and the Deputy President of the Hibernian Society. A 'handsome cheque' was presented to Sheehy by the chairman, who described him as 'an uncompromising Irishman, whose influence could clearly be traced in Sydney opinion on the Irish question.' Dr O'Reilly went on to state that 'the INA, under the leadership of John Sheehy, has been the soundest upholder of the Irish spirit in Australia.'[2] Sheehy had just completed five years as President of the Irish National Association, a term spanning the

* Anne-Maree Whitaker is a professional historian with a special interest in Australia's Irish and Catholic history. She was a Councillor of the Australian Catholic Historical Society from 1995 to 2005.

1. 'Presentation to Mr John Sheehy', *Freeman's Journal*, (10 November 1921): 22.
2. 'Presentation to Mr John Sheehy', *Freeman's Journal*, (10 November 1921): 22.

most tumultuous period of Irish history. Coincidentally he had also turned sixty earlier that year.

John Sheehy was baptised in Ballingarry, County Limerick, on 17 January 1861. He was the son of John Sheehy and his wife Margaret (née Storin).[3] He was educated at St Munchin's diocesan college in Limerick City, and entered St Patrick's College Maynooth to train for the priesthood. Sheehy took his matriculation examination on 10 September 1880 and entered with advanced standing into the second-year course. However he left Maynooth due to ill health, and instead trained as a solicitor. He later claimed that he qualified and practised in Dublin for some years, even describing himself as 'Irish solicitor' on his marriage certificate.[4] However the annual Irish Law Directories which should show his date of admission and business address do not include him in the period 1886–1889.[5] It is possible he served as an articled clerk but did not complete his qualification.

Sheehy's mother died on 1 April 1883 and his father on 22 March 1890, leaving an estate valued at 278 pounds. Sheehy senior was described in his will as a shopkeeper and postmaster.[6] Before his father died John junior had already emigrated. He travelled as a saloon passenger on the *Orient*, leaving London on 5 July 1889 and arriving in Sydney after 'an unusually quick passage' on 20 August, with stops at Gibraltar, Naples, Port Said, Colombo, Albany and Melbourne.[7]

After two years settling in to his new home, Sheehy's first public role was in the William O'Brien branch of the Irish National Foresters

3. Baptisms, Ballingarry Parish Register, microfilm no 02421/02, Catholic Parish Registers, National Library of Ireland, https://registers.nli.ie/
4. 'The Democratic Party in the Fight', *Catholic Press* (9 March 1922), 19; *pers comm*, Anna Porter, Archivist, St Patrick's College Maynooth, 2 November 2020; NSW Registry of Births Deaths and Marriages, marriage certificate 263/1896.
5. Pers comm, Linda Dolan, Administration Assistant, Law Society of Ireland, 31 October 2020.
6. Margaret Sheehy, death registration district of Castletown, union of Croom, entry 206, 1 April 1883, Group Registration ID 6814077; John Sheehy, death registration district of Castletown, union of Croom, entry 389, 22 March 1890, Group Registration ID 6712641; both from https://civilrecords.irishgenealogy.ie/. Probate details from 'Calendar of Wills and Administrations 1858–1922', National Archives of Ireland, http://www.willcalendars.nationalarchives.ie/
7. Shipping news, *Daily Telegraph* (21 August 1889): 7.

when he was elected to the position of Woodward in December 1891.[8] The Irish National Foresters were founded in 1877 as a friendly society providing health and unemployment insurance for their members. In return for a weekly subscription, a member of the INF off work owing to illness would receive a weekly allowance and payment for medical treatment. A funeral grant would also be paid when a member or his wife died.[9]

The Foresters were among the best known friendly societies in Ireland during the nineteenth and early twentieth centuries. In their heyday they had branches throughout Ireland and the Irish diaspora; the most prominent Irish political, religious and civic figures were members, and their banners and regalia added colour to major public processions and demonstrations. They were also closely associated with Irish nationalism.[10] At first the Australian version of the INF only required members to be Irish by birth or descent, but in 1903 the constitution was amended to stipulate that members must be Catholic leading to a rapid growth in membership.[11]

The INF expanded from Melbourne to Sydney following a visit from Melbourne delegates in June 1891, and by the end of the year five branches had been formed. Sheehy recalled that the first meeting of the William O'Brien branch was held at Garrett's Hotel (Market Street, Sydney), chaired by Chief Ranger Brother James Peter Kavanagh. Subsequently meetings were held at the Shamrock Club (George Street), then the former Oddfellows' building in Castlereagh Street, and eventually settled down at St Benedict's (Broadway) where they remained until at least the 1930s. The first Secretary of the branch was Michael Langan, but Sheehy soon succeeded him and continued as branch secretary for eleven years. Sheehy also recalled a letter of encouragement from William O'Brien, journalist and Irish nationalist, after whom the branch was named.[12]

In April 1892 a further visit from Melbourne resulted in the formation of a NSW state executive of which Sheehy was elected general secretary on a salary of 30 pounds a year. Since the INF had

8. *Sydney Morning Herald* (9 January 1892): 9.
9. Joe Fodey, 'The Creation of the Irish National Foresters Benefit Society, 1877', in *History Ireland,* 27/2 (March/April 2019): 24–26.
10. Fodey, 'The Creation of the Irish National Foresters Benefit Society, 1877', 24.
11. 'Irish National Foresters', *Freeman's Journal* (6 April 1933): 15.
12. 'Irish National Foresters', *Freeman's Journal* (6 April 1933): 15.

expanded from Victoria to NSW in 1891 the William O'Brien branch had enrolled 100 members and collected over 100 pounds. The other NSW branches were John Mitchel (Redfern), Daniel O'Connell (Newtown), Robert Emmet (Balmain) and William Bede Dalley (Wickham).[13]

As a recent immigrant, the thirty-year-old Sheehy's involvement in the Foresters enabled him to establish links within the Irish community which would stand him in good stead for decades. He was an enthusiastic worker for the cause, receiving the presentation of a meerschaum pipe in 1894 for introducing the most new members to the branch.[14] The following year he travelled to Orange to assist in the formation of a new branch, and was entertained at a dinner at which the proceedings were 'of an enthusiastic nature'. The toast of the evening, 'The Guest', was 'suitably responded to by Mr Sheehy, who pointed out the advantage of becoming a member of the order in a lucid manner'.[15]

Sheehy's next public role was as secretary of the Michael Davitt tour committee in 1895. Davitt was a legendary figure among Irish nationalists. Active in the Fenian rising of 1867 he was subsequently imprisoned in England from 1870 to 1877. In 1879 he founded the Land League in his native County Mayo, and this movement spread rapidly across Ireland. He was elected MP for County Meath in 1882 but was disqualified because he was once more in prison. He was returned to parliament for North Meath in 1892 and North East Cork in 1893.[16] Davitt had a long-standing interest in Australia and embarked on his visit with the dual aims of augmenting his personal finances and studying the seven Australasian colonies (including New Zealand) which were regarded as social laboratories. He filled six diaries with notes and on his return to Ireland published a 470-page account, *Life and Progress in Australasia.*[17]

13. 'The Irish Foresters in Sydney', *Freeman's Journal*, (23 April 1892): 16; 'Irish National Foresters', *Catholic Press* (24 October 1935): 30.
14. 'Irish National Foresters', *Evening News* (17 July 1894): 7.
15. 'Irish National Foresters, Orange', *Australian Star* (29 October 1895): 8.
16. D George Boyce, 'Davitt, Michael (1846–1906)', in *Oxford Dictionary of National Biography*, http://www.oxforddnb.com/accessed on edition to provide.
17. Carla King, '"I am doing fairly well in the lecturing line": Michael Davitt and Australia 1895', in *Australasian Journal of Irish Studies*, 12 (2012): 25–27.

While Davitt had been travelling around South Australia and Victoria, organising in NSW did not begin until May 1895 when an 'executive committee representing the various Irish societies' was formed. As its secretary Sheehy wrote to country towns throughout the state on 17 May, urging the formation of Davitt Committees to organise lecture venues, advertising, accommodation and so on. Others on the committee were Francis Bede Freehill, Thomas Joseph McCabe, Patrick O'Loughlin, William Hogan and John Woods.[18] Davitt's lectures were aimed at a broad audience and were based around three themes. The first was 'Parliamentary photographs' comprising thumbnail sketches of various British and Irish politicians such as Gladstone, Joseph Chamberlain, John Dillon and Justin McCarthy. The second topic was 'the trend of the labour movement in Great Britain', while the third was the current position of the Irish Home Rule movement.[19]

When Davitt arrived in Sydney on 6 July he was met by a crowd of 10,000 including members of parliament, mayors and clergy. He was then taken by a procession of brass bands and fraternal societies through the city to his accommodation at the Grosvenor Hotel where he addressed an enthusiastic crowd from the hotel balcony.[20] After a visit to Queensland he returned to New South Wales in August and spoke in country centres including Maitland, Newcastle, Goulburn, Bathurst, Orange, Yass, Wagga Wagga and Albury. During this leg of his tour a general election was called in Britain and his fundraising switched from the personal to the political. Over 3000 pounds was sent back to London to assist the Irish Parliamentary Party's campaign, and Davitt was elected MP for South Mayo in his absence.[21]

Sheehy's personal circumstances changed in January 1896 with his marriage at St Benedict's Broadway to twenty seven-year-old Margaret Clinton. She was the daughter of James and Mary Clinton, immigrants from Dublin.[22] Sheehy not only acquired a spouse but also a family of in-laws including her brother William who also became active in Irish causes. The first of their children, James Paul, was born

18. 'Mr Michael Davitt', *Gundagai Times* (24 May 1895): 3.
19. King, 'Michael Davitt and Australia 1895', 30–31.
20. 'Davitt in Sydney', *Freeman's Journal* (13 July 1895): 6.
21. King, 'Michael Davitt and Australia 1895', 30; 'Mr Davitt's Visit', *Barrier Miner* (20 September 1895): 2.
22. NSW Registry of Births Deaths and Marriages, marriage certificate 263/1896.

in April 1897 and his birth certificate shows his father's occupation as 'clerk solicitor's office'.[23]

Sheehy's attention returned to his role as general secretary of the Irish National Foresters with the organisation of the society's first banquet in September 1897. It was attended by around 200 members of the several branches based in Sydney and was judged to be 'most successful'.[24] Along with toasts and musical items there were a number of speakers, including Sheehy. He focused on the commemoration of the centenary of the 1798 Rebellion the following year, and said he hoped the suggestions made that evening would be acted upon. Sheehy stated that 'he would be keenly disappointed if, in addition to a worthy patriotic demonstration, they did not erect a fitting monument over the remains of Michael Dwyer'. He continued: 'it might be necessary to remove the remains of Michael Dwyer and those of his wife from the old Catholic cemetery in Devonshire Street to (say) the Waverley Cemetery'. These details could be settled later but all he asked was that 'the proposal to do honour to the men of '98 should not end at that banquet'.[25]

Michael Dwyer was a United Irishman and local leader in Wicklow during the 1798 Rebellion. After fighting at the battle of Arklow, he was promoted 'captain' on 24 June. Dwyer killed at least one Welsh cavalryman in an ambush at Ballyellis on 30 June. In mid-July, as the rebellion waned, he joined the militant rump commanded by Joseph Holt, which rejected amnesty terms, hoping for military assistance from France. Actions later in 1798 established Dwyer's reputation as a dynamic rebel leader. A core group attached to him kept fighting after Holt surrendered in November 1798 and Dwyer's group evaded capture for at least five years and were therefore seasoned guerrilla fighters. He was sent as a free settler to New South Wales in 1806 and settled in the Liverpool area south-west of Sydney where he died in 1825.[26]

---

23. NSW Registry of Births Deaths and Marriages, birth certificate 9266/1897.
24. 'The Irish National Foresters', *Freeman's Journal* (4 September 1897): 17–18.
25. 'Sydney and the "Ninety-Eight" Celebration: a monument to Michael Dwyer', *Freeman's Journal* (4 September 1897): 15.
26. Ruan O'Donnell, 'Dwyer, Michael (1772–1825)', *Australian Dictionary of Biography*, http://adb.anu.edu.au/biography/dwyer-michael-12896/text23301

The seed sown by Sheehy's speech grew astonishingly quickly. Dr Charles MacCarthy, who was present at the banquet, was inspired to pledge a donation of five pounds towards the project, only to find himself within a few months chairing the organising committee. Sheehy's proposal to move the remains of Dwyer and his wife to Waverley Cemetery in Sydney's Eastern suburbs resulted in the largest centenary event for the 1798 Rebellion and the finest Irish Republican monument in the world. Despite his own role as chairman of the committee and designer of the memorial, MacCarthy was careful to give credit where it was due: 'the success of the procession and of everything connected with the movement was due, not to him, but to the secretary, Mr John Sheehy'.[27]

After a frantic few weeks, when the committee organised the exhumation, purchase of a new gravesite and construction of a tomb to lie underneath the proposed memorial, the centenary ceremonies began on 20 May 1898 when the Dwyer vault in Devonshire Street was unsealed. The remains of Michael Dwyer and his wife Mary were placed into a large cedar casket and removed to St Mary's Cathedral on the night of 21 May. After 11 am high mass on Sunday 22nd the procession set off to Waverley, ten kilometres away. The cathedral was packed and there were reportedly 50,000 people crammed into College Street and Hyde Park to witness the occasion, while the whole crowd was estimated at 200,000.[28]

The procession was led by around 200 citizens including members of parliament, mayors and representatives of country and interstate 1798 committees. They were followed by regalia-clad members of the Australasian Holy Catholic Guild (500 persons), the Hibernian Australasian Catholic Benefit Society (600) and the Irish National Foresters (400). Next came the coffin on a glass-sided hearse drawn by six horses, and flanked by ten pall bearers including Dr MacCarthy, John Sheehy, and the committee's treasurer John Woods. When the procession turned into Oxford Street it was found to be just as crowded, and for most of the journey to Waverley Cemetery the cortege 'made its way through two dense lines of spectators',

27. Ruan O'Donnell, 'Irish-Australia and the 1798 Centenary in Sydney', in *Echoes of Irish Australia: Rebellion to Republic* edited by Jeff Brownrigg, *et al*, (Galong NSW: St Clement's Retreat and Conference Centre, 2007), 2; 'The Ninety-Eight Commemoration', *Freeman's Journal* (4 June 1898): 15.
28. O'Donnell, 'Irish-Australia and the 1798 Centenary in Sydney', 6–8.

with the front of the procession arriving at 4 pm, two hours after leaving the cathedral. Further ceremonies continued at the cemetery, including the interment of the coffin and the laying of the memorial's foundation stone. Waverley parish priest Patrick Bede Kennedy OSF and around twenty other priests recited the burial prayers before Dr MacCarthy delivered an oration.[29]

Sheehy's proposal for a Celtic cross over Dwyer's grave rapidly developed into a much more elaborate monument. Architectural tenders were called in February 1898 and in April architects Sheerin and Hennessy signed a contract with stonemasons Ross and Bowman to undertake the construction. The design included a base thirty feet wide and twenty four feet deep surmounted by a Celtic cross rising to thirty feet. The main material is white Carrara marble, and the enclosed area has a floor embellished with mosaics including round towers and thatched cottages, a harp and shamrocks. The front wall is surmounted by two bronze Irish wolfhounds and there are also bas relief sculptures executed by Dr MacCarthy depicting 1798 heroes Michael Dwyer, Wolfe Tone, Lord Edward Fitzgerald, Father John Murphy, Henry Joy McCracken and Robert Emmet. Two rectangular panels depict the arrest of Lord Edward and the Battle of Oulart, while there are inscriptions in Gaelic, Ogham and English. The monument was completed and unveiled in April 1900 for a final cost of 2,600 pounds.[30]

John and Margaret Sheehy's family continued to grow through the 1890s and 1900s. Sadly, the two sons named after their father failed to survive childhood, John William (born and died 1898) and John Anthony (1901–1905). Their first daughter, Margaret Mary Madeleine, was born in 1899 and named after her two grandmothers. She was followed by Gerald William (1903), Roger Benedict (1905), Evelyn Catherine (1906) and Sheila Beatrice (1910). Another happy family event was the marriage of Margaret's orphaned niece Eileen Fitzgerald in 1908 when she was given away by John Sheehy.[31] Less welcome news was the death of Margaret's parents Mary Clinton in 1905 and James Clinton in 1909.[32] Although the Irish political scene had quietened down Sheehy was kept busy with parish activities at

29. 'Who Fears to Speak of '98?', *Freeman's Journal* (28 May 1898): 6.
30. O'Donnell, 'Irish-Australia and the 1798 Centenary', 6, 10.
31. 'Social Items', *Freeman's Journal* (2 April 1908): 29.
32. *Sydney Morning Herald* (12 September 1905): 10 and 29 May 1909: 24.

St Benedict's and committees such as the Hospital Sunday United Charities Appeal and the St Patrick's Day committee.[33] He stood down as General Secretary of the NSW Foresters in 1900 but remained secretary of the William O'Brien branch for a further three years.

The period of Irish history from 1912 to 1922 began with the signing of the Ulster Covenant and ended with civil war and the partition of the island. The events which took place in Ireland and worldwide, including the 1916 Easter Rising and the First World War, made this an era of change, conflict and great social upheaval. Watching from Australia, Irishmen such as John Sheehy responded in the time-honoured fashion by organising committees and campaigns, conducting fundraising and eventually commemorating defeats and victories. There was also much debate locally, focusing on the conscription referenda of 1916 and 1917.

In July 1915 the Irish National Association was established in Sydney with the formal aims 'to assist Ireland to achieve her national destiny and to foster an Irish spirit amongst the Irish portion of the community'.[34] One of the earliest members was Dr Patrick Tuomey, assistant priest at St Benedict's Broadway, who joined the INA in November 1915 and was soon elected to its executive committee. He wrote a sternly-worded letter to Archbishop Kelly in June 1916 in response to his public criticisms of the organisation, and as a result was transferred seventy miles out of Sydney to Mittagong. He went further in 1918 when he was fined thirty pounds for a 'disloyal' speech. As his obituary noted: 'His fame became Australia wide in the anti-conscription campaigns and the controversies aroused by Easter Week in 1916'.[35]

Sheehy soon joined the INA and by January 1917 was acting president before being confirmed in the position in July. One of his first acts was to host a formal presentation to Dr Tuomey before his departure for his country parish. The occasion was the INA half-yearly meeting and included in the presentation was 'a cheque for a substantial amount'. Sheehy made 'eulogistic references to the services Dr Tuomey had rendered the association by his interesting

33. 'All About People', *Catholic Press* (30 October 1941): 2.

34. 'Irish National Association, Sydney', *Freeman's Journal* (5 August 1915): 21.

35. Patrick O'Farrell, 'Archbishop Kelly and the Irish Question', in *Journal of the Australian Catholic Historical Society*, 4/3 (1974): 4–6; 'Remarkable Irish Priest Mourned', *Catholic Weekly* (24 February 1955).

and instructive lectures in Irish history and patriotism'. In responding, Dr Tuomey made 'a characteristic speech, in which Irish humour, Irish vigour and Irish determination were happily blended'.[36] He later received an equally enthusiastic tribute from his former parish of St Benedict's.[37]

Presentation to Dr Tuomey by INA President John Sheehy, 29 January 1917 (National Library of Australia)

One of Archbishop Kelly's other actions to try to counter the rise of groups such as the INA was the formation in early 1917 of the Irish National Executive, a coalition of Catholic and Irish organisations such as the Hibernians and the Foresters chaired by himself.[38] As time passed and the Archbishop's views mellowed, Sheehy and others joined the meetings in St Mary's Cathedral presbytery. Sheehy's own political views were no secret: 'he had been reared among Fenians in Ireland, and he could not help being a sincere Sinn Féiner'. The Fenian Rising of 1867 took place when Sheehy was 6 years of age, and planned actions in Limerick included attacks on the police barracks in Ardagh, Bruff and Kilteely. Although the surname Sheehy does not feature among those arrested it is likely his teachers and other childhood role models would have been at least sympathetic to the cause.[39]

In June 1918 the acting Prime Minister William Watt announced that seven members of the Irish Republican Brotherhood had been arrested in raids on premises in Sydney, Melbourne and Brisbane and interned in Darlinghurst Gaol in Sydney. Those arrested in Sydney were Albert Dryer, William McGuinness, Edmund McSweeny and Michael McGing. In the lead-up to this development on 25 March 1918 military and civilian forces had raided the homes of John

36. 'Irish National Association of NSW', *Catholic Press* (8 February 1917): 21.
37. 'A Popular Priest. Dr Tuomey', *Catholic Press* (22 February 1917): 26.
38. O'Farrell, 'Archbishop Kelly and the Irish Question', 8.
39. 'Presentation to Mr John Sheehy', *Freeman's Journal* (10 November 1921): 22; Robert Herbert, 'The Fenian Movement in Limerick', *Limerick Leader* newspaper, 25 June 1949 (reprinted 17 April 2010: 18).

Sheehy, INA secretary Albert Dryer and his mother Mary Weber, and William Muir and taken books, letters and other documents. The INA offices were raided in May and membership records seized, leading to more raids the following day. Following the arrests there was a public enquiry, and fundraising and protest meetings were organised. Sheehy and other office-bearers who had not been interned led the campaigning, and when six of the seven men were released in December after the armistice Sheehy was one of the first to greet them at the prison gate. In March 1919 he hosted a celebration at St Patrick's Hall which was addressed by Dr Tuomey amid 'scenes of extraordinary enthusiasm'.[40]

Events in Ireland through 1919 and 1920 made almost daily news in Australia. For much of 1919, Irish Republican Army activity involved capturing weaponry and freeing republican prisoners, while the Dáil or parliament elected in 1918 set about erecting a parallel state. In September 1919, the British government outlawed the Dáil and Sinn Féin and the conflict intensified. The IRA began ambushing police and British Army patrols, attacking their barracks and forcing isolated barracks to be abandoned. The British government sent further recruits from Britain—the Black and Tans—who became notorious for ill-discipline and reprisal attacks on civilians. In mid-1920 Sinn Féin won local government elections across most of Ireland and took over functions of government from the state such as tax collection and law enforcement.[41]

In August 1920 the Lord Mayor of Cork, Terence MacSwiney, was arrested and sentenced to two years in prison for possessing seditious documents, and immediately went on hunger strike. Early in October 1920 Sheehy, along with Patrick Scott Cleary of the Catholic Federation, paid a visit to the Lord Mayor of Sydney William Patrick Fitzgerald requesting him to convene a public meeting in support of MacSwiney. Fitzgerald was not inclined to assist and stated that the Town Hall was booked out until December. On being asked to forward a protest to the British Prime Minister he replied that: 'the reports from Ireland were very much exaggerated, and, anyhow,

40. Witness statement of Albert Thomas Dryer, WS1526, Bureau of Military History, Ireland; 'The Irish-Australian Internees', *Catholic Press* (13 March 1919): 20.
41. John Dorney, 'The Irish War of Independence: a brief overview', The Irish Story, https://www.theirishstory.com/2012/09/18/the-irish-war-of-independence-a-brief-overview/#.X6tphfMzbIU.

we were too far away from the scene of action to make an effective protest'.[42] MacSwiney died on 25 October and Sheehy sent a telegram to his widow Muriel stating: 'Terence's martyrdom will achieve his dearest wish, which will be your greatest consolation under God'.[43]

In January 1921 Sydney was entertained by the spectacle of a steamship moored in Rose Bay with an Irish activist banned from landing in Australia. Osmond Esmonde was a twenty four-year-old somewhat foppish figure with a monocle, bowtie and pencil moustache, but he was also an envoy from Sinn Féin leader Eamon de Valera. Esmonde had travelled from Canada via New Zealand where he had also been refused admission. Trapped in Sydney Harbour by a shipping strike, Esmonde became something of a tourist attraction as well-wishers ventured out by boat to take gifts and cheer the visitor.[44] In late January the INA chartered a ferry to carry a reported 900 supporters out to serenade Esmonde with a pipe band and massed singing of patriotic songs. After Esmonde made an impromptu speech across the water, John Sheehy 'hoisted, amidst great cheering, a large yellow, white, and green flag, in a position where the glare of the electric lights made it stand out very prominently'.[45]

While Sydneysiders had been distracted by this sideshow, Esmonde's fellow envoy Katherine Hughes slipped into Sydney on a different ship with little fanfare. Hughes was a fourty four-year-old Canadian writer who had spent the preceding year touring Canada to set up Self-Determination for Ireland League branches, succeeding in recruiting 20,000 members in a few months. De Valera had agreed that Hughes and Esmonde should undertake similar action in Australia, with Esmonde assigned to undertake a speaking tour while Hughes concentrated on organisation. The Self-Determination for Ireland League was an initiative by de Valera to create a broad-based support movement which could appeal to both moderate supporters of Home Rule and more radical Republicans. By the time Katherine Hughes departed Australia in July she left behind 369 branches of the League with over 30,000 members.[46]

42. 'Lord Mayor McSwiney', *Catholic Press* (4 November 1920): 27.
43. 'Cables of Sympathy', *Freeman's Journal* (28 October 1920): 20.
44. Shane Lynn, 'Osmond Esmonde's Dominion Odyssey: Irish Nationalism in the British Empire 1920–21', in *Australasian Journal of Irish Studies,* 14 (2014): 69–90.
45. 'Mr Grattan Esmonde Serenaded', *Catholic Press* (3 February 1921): 25.
46. Lynn, 'Osmond Esmonde's Dominion Odyssey', 71, 75.

The first branch was founded in Sydney with a meeting in the Hippodrome in February 1921. The main speaker was Dr Maurice O'Reilly of St John's College, who congratulated the 'vast and tumultuously enthusiastic gathering' on their attendance at just two days' notice, noting there was an overflow of 10,000 outside the venue. O'Reilly invoked the men of Anzac who went to fight for the self-determination of Belgium even though they were not themselves Belgian. He quoted the Archbishop of Canterbury and Sydney's own Archbishop Kelly in support of the cause of self-determination for Ireland, and concluded by invoking the spirit of Eureka: 'The soldiers killed 30 diggers, and captured 135, and consequently they won, but they lost all the same'.[47]

Sheehy, who was on the organising committee but not an office-bearer, made a stirring contribution to the evening's rhetoric:

> Britain had done everything to vilify Ireland. Consequently, the Australian people did not know the truth about Ireland. It would, therefore, be necessary for us to organise against the vile propaganda which is promulgated every day in the daily press, a propaganda of truth that will tell the people something of what they ought to know about the conditions in Ireland. We hear it stated by men such as Lloyd George and Greenwood, that the Irish Republican Army, the noblest band and most fearless body that ever God put on earth, is nothing but a band of assassins. There were no assassins in the Irish Republican Army. That army was established on a moral basis. If one wanted to look for assassins one would find them dressed in the British uniforms.[48]

The Sydney meeting was widely reported throughout Australia, and within six weeks nearly seventy branches were established. In Sydney branches had formed in Ashfield, Woollahra, Redfern, Lewisham, Rozelle and Kogarah, while NSW country towns included Port Macquarie, Wauchope, Cowra, Goulburn, Merriwa, Casino, Glen Innes, Yass, Cootamundra and Bega. Fundraising was an important component of the League's activities, and its NSW Treasurer Dr

47. 'Great Irish Self-Determination Meeting In Sydney', *Catholic Press* (3 March 1921): 19.
48. 'Great Irish Self-Determination Meeting In Sydney', *Catholic Press* (3 March 1921): 19.

O'Reilly reported on monies received while also appealing for further donations. While the Australian press was dominated by pro-British views, he explained, access to funds would enable the League to print its own 'short and pithy expositions of the Irish situation'.[49]

Dr O'Reilly was a Vincentian priest and former president of St Stanislaus' College in Bathurst, now rector of St John's College. He was a noted controversialist in public debates on Catholic issues, such as education policy and Empire Day.[50] When it was decided to make a presentation to John Sheehy for 'his splendid service to the Irish cause for more than thirty years' O'Reilly presided at the function in the Southern Cross hall in Elizabeth Street. Monsignors John Patrick Moynagh and Joseph Collins, Father Thomas Barry, and Messrs Patrick Scott Cleary and Daniel Joseph Walsh also 'spoke in eulogy of Mr Sheehy as an Irishman and a sterling Catholic'. The vote of thanks to the chair was moved by the Attorney-General Edward Aloysius McTiernan and seconded by Dr Cyril Joseph Fallon. A 'handsome cheque' was presented to Sheehy and musical items rounded out the evening.[51]

Among his many other community activities Sheehy had been an active member of the Catholic Federation since at least 1915. The Federation was founded to advocate the political interests of the Catholic Church, and at its height had over 100,000 members in NSW. He had been president of the St Benedict's branch of the Federation and also served on the state executive. In early 1922 he nominated for the Democratic Party, the Federation's political arm, in the NSW state election for the seat of Balmain. Described as 'one of the most popular Irishmen in New South Wales', Sheehy's Irish and Catholic community credentials were spelt out in his publicity. His daughter Madeleine had taken a year off from her medical studies at the University of Sydney to support his campaign, but when the polls closed in March he failed to win a seat.[52]

49. 'Self-Determination for Ireland', *Freeman's Journal* (21 April 1921): 27.
50. John Wilkinson, 'Father Maurice O'Reilly: a controversial priest', in *Journal of the Australian Catholic Historical Society*, 7/3 (1983): 3–23.
51. 'Presentation to Mr John Sheehy', *Freeman's Journal* (10 November 1921): 22.
52. Jeff Kildea, 'Troubled Times: an overview of the history of the Catholic Federation of NSW', in *Journal of the Australian Catholic Historical Society*, 23 (2002): 9, 17–19; 'The Democratic Party in the Fight: notes and news', *Catholic Press* (9 March 1922): 19.

Late 1922 saw Sheehy's last act as president of the INA, a position he had held for nearly six years. The occasion was a welcome to the new Coadjutor Archbishop Michael Sheehan, a noted Gaelic scholar. It was held in the Southern Cross hall, home of the Knights of the Southern Cross, and all speeches were in Gaelic (with translations helpfully supplied to the press). Led by Father Michael Ryan for the Gaelic League, the next speaker was John's eldest daughter Madeleine representing the women's group Cumann na mBan. John rounded off the presentations with a warm welcome: 'You come to us not as a stranger, but as one of our own. Your monumental labours for faith and fatherland have made the Irish people at home and abroad your debtor. Wherever an Irish heart beats you are loved and revered.'[53] Following this function Sheehy tendered his resignation due to ill health and Edmund McSweeny took over the role of INA president.

The next ten years saw the deaths of a number of Sheehy's close colleagues and friends, beginning with John Woods in March 1924. Both were from Limerick and throughout the 1890s they had served respectively as secretary and treasurer first to the William O'Brien branch of the INF from 1891, then on the Michael Davitt tour committee in 1895 and finally on the 1798 Memorial committee from 1897 to 1900. Thereafter their paths diverged. Woods built up a successful wine and spirit dealership, was awarded a knighthood of St Sylvester in 1920 and left an estate of 56,000 pounds with generous legacies to Catholic charities including the Cathedral building fund, orphanages and the Mater hospital. He was also a director of the *Catholic Press* newspaper and treasurer of the Cathedral building fund.[54] Sheehy represented the INA at Woods's funeral along with Christopher Boland and Edmund McSweeny. Unlike Woods his decades of service had not resulted in material reward. Sheehy lived in rental homes all his life and died intestate, declaring that 'as he did not have any assets there was no need for him to make a will'.[55]

The 1920s also saw a modification to the 1798 Memorial with the installation of a railing fence across the front of the memorial

53. 'Archbishop Sheehan Welcomed by Irish National Association', *Catholic Press* (23 November 1922): 18.
54. 'The Late Mr John Woods KSS', *Catholic Press* (20 March 1924): 23; 'John Woods's Will', *Catholic Press* (24 April 1924): 25.
55. Affidavit of Evelyn Catherine Dalton, probate packet John Storin Sheehy, 4/702429, NSW Archives and Records.

1798 Memorial, Waverley Cemetery, before the addition of the fence in 1927 (MAAS)

effectively privatising access to the platform which functioned as a stage or quasi-sanctuary. Fundraising began in 1926 and the completed fence was unveiled by Archbishop Kelly on New Year's Eve 1927. Sheehy does not seem to have been involved in this project as his name was not mentioned in reports of the organising committee nor the unveiling.[56]

In February 1929 came news of the death of Edmund McSweeny, which Sheehy described as severing 'a comradeship of 40 years'. Sheehy called a meeting along with J Woods, probably John's brother Jeremiah, to discuss erecting a memorial over McSweeny's grave. The meeting elected Dr Patrick Tuomey as president of the committee with Sheehy as vice-president and Woods as treasurer. The memorial was somewhat extravagantly described as 'the most beautiful Celtic Cross in Waverley Cemetery' which is replete with such monuments.

56. Jonathan M Wooding, '"It was in Human Nature to Love One's Native Land and Make Sacrifices for it": Monumental Commemorations and Corporeal Relics in 1920s Irish-Australia', in *History Australia*, 4/2 (2007): 39.8–39.15.

Sheehy's speech at the unveiling later that year reflected on his friendship with Ned McSweeny and his long involvement in Irish community affairs.[57]

He began by stating that nothing could prevent him from being there that day, to witness the magnificent demonstration of love and affection for 'as good an Irishman as there is already in Waverley Cemetery'. Mentioning others such as William Walsh, Dr MacCarthy, John Woods, Eugene Ryan and John Joseph McGough, he described them as 'sentinels guarding the '98 Monument' and added that 'there is nobody whose spirit is capable of keeping a more vigilant eye on that monument than Ned McSweeny'. In conclusion he pointed out the lines in Gaelic on McSweeny's monument, which had been supplied by Archbishop Sheehan and translated as: 'Gael in heart, Gael in deed, Gael that flinched not in the hour of need; Thy shield be upon his soul, O Patrick of the Gael.'[58]

The next death was even closer to John Sheehy, when in 1932 his brother-in-law William Clinton passed away. Clinton had lived with the Sheehys for a number of years, and described himself on the electoral roll as a book collector. His obituary stated that 'he was the possessor of a remarkable library including much rare Australiana' and 'his knowledge of old Sydney was extensive'.[59]

In 1933 Sheehy had the opportunity to meet old friends and review the events of fourty years earlier when he was invited to a reunion of the INF, billed as 'Back to William O'Brien Branch Night'. The gathering was held at St Benedict's and included a talk on the early history of the INF by Sheehy's successor as general secretary Thomas Edwin Avery. Sheehy himself was 'honoured and pleased' to be invited to unveil the framed dispensation from Ireland authorising the establishment of a subsidiary executive in NSW back in 1892. Sheehy gave an outline of the early history of the branch, and noted that the occasion brought back many pleasant memories, and he was pleased to meet old friends like Brothers Curry, Dempsey, McGuire, W Cawley and others.[60]

---

57. 'Edmund McSweeny Memorial', *Catholic Press* (31 October 1929): 20; 'Late Mr Edmund McSweeny', *Catholic Press* (7 March 1929): 19; 'Late Edmund McSweeny Proposed Memorial', *Catholic Press* (7 March 1929): 32; 'A Worthy Patriot', *Catholic Press*, (17 October 1929): 21.
58. 'Edmund McSweeny Memorial', *Catholic Press* (31 October 1929): 20.
59. 'Mr William Clinton', *Sydney Morning Herald* (4 May 1932): 12.
60. '"Back to William O'Brien" Night', *Freeman's Journal* (30 March 1933): 19; 'Irish National Foresters', *Freeman's Journal* (6 April 1933): 15.

He recounted that the dispensation and a letter of approval from the late Cardinal Moran hung in the INF's meeting room in the Shamrock Club, and when the premises were damaged by a fire at the adjacent Lawler's bedding factory in 1894 they were the only items from the meeting room which were saved. Unveiling an honour board of Chief Rangers, Sheehy read out the names and 'recalled many incidents associated with those with whom he had been acquainted'.[61]

In January 1941 the John Mitchel branch of the INF congratulated Sheehy on his 80th birthday, but by then his days were drawing to a close.[62] Sheehy died on 7 October 1941 at his residence, 10 Kingston Street, Haberfield. His death certificate noted the cause as myocarditis and senility which he had suffered for three to four years.[63] After being responsible for two notable Celtic cross memorials in Waverley Cemetery, Sheehy himself was buried in a modest grave with a plain cross in Rookwood Cemetery with his father-in-law and brother-in-law James and William Clinton.[64]

---

61. 'Irish National Foresters', *Freeman's Journal* (6 April 1933):15.
62. 'Irish National Foresters', *Catholic Press* (6 February 1941): 31.
63. NSW Registry of Births Deaths and Marriages, death certificate 23106/1941.
64. Rookwood Catholic Cemetery, Section Grave Mortuary 2, Area C, Grave 896. Margaret Sheehy was added to the grave on her death in 1944.

Journal of the Australian Catholic Historical Society, Volume 41/2020

A Higher Loyalty? A Case Study of Anti-Catholicism and Section 44 of the Australian Constitution

*Benjamin Wilkie**

The immediate post-war period was a time of expansion for the Catholic Church in Australia. In the middle of the 1950s, ninety three new Catholic churches, two new hospitals, four new orphanages, and nearly fourty boys' and girls' high schools had been built; Catholic primary school enrolments grew by over 30,000 pupils, and high school enrolments had grown by around five thousand students; eighty new priests were ordained, and 163 women became nuns in those years.[1] A former Anglican Archbishop of Sydney, Sir Marcus Loane, described the 1950s as 'a decade of spiritual renewal' for Catholics in Australia.[2]

A renewed presence in Australian religious life, however, and high-profile interventions in contemporary issues, opened new entry points for sectarian polemic shaped by local affairs. Benjamin Edwards notes that interdenominational relations in the postwar decade were marked by Protestant co-operation and Catholic isolation.[3] As Edwards has argued, nevertheless, although sectarian polemic in the 1950s 'was sometimes triggered by contemporaneous local contingencies, it was framed within the traditional sectarian discursive context.'[4] That is to say, while the sectarianism of 1950s

* Dr Ben Wilkie is a historian with diverse interests in Scottish and Australian history.

1. *Catholic Weekly*, (17 January 1957): 1.
2. Quoted in Stuart Piggin, 'Towards a Bicentennial History of Australian Evangelicalism,' in *Journal of Religious History*, 15/1 (1988): 30.
3. Benjamin Edwards, 'Vatican II and the Dying Gasps of Australian Sectarianism', in *Journal of the Australian Catholic Historical Society*, 33 (2012): 115.
4. Benjamin Edwards, 'Proddy-Dogs, Cattleticks and Ecumaniacs: Aspects of Sectarianism in New South Wales, 1945–1981', PhD thesis (Sydney: University of New South Wales, 2007), 121.

Australia was shaped by local and sometimes new concerns, polemic drew on old ideas and language.

One element of anti-Catholic discourse that was sustained and appropriated for Australia was the assertion, as Edwards describes it, 'that Catholics cannot be loyal subjects of sovereign states because they owe a higher loyalty to the pope, a foreign temporal power'.[5] Indeed, when British governance first came to Australia, it brought the old prejudices with it. Mere days after the First Fleet arrived in January 1788, on February 13, Arthur Phillip pledged allegiance to the King in the presence of the new colony's judge-advocate. After first announcing that 'I do believe that there is not any Transubstantiation in the Sacrament of the Lord's Supper or in the Elements of Bread and Wine at or after the Consecration thereof by any Person whatsoever', Phillip 'acknowledged and declared George III to be the only lawful and undoubted sovereign of this realm, and that he abjured allegiance to the descendants of the person who pretended to be the Prince of Wales during the reign of James II'. Alas, Bonnie Prince Charlie—exiled leader of the Scottish Jacobite cause—would die in Rome on January 31, 1788.[6]

The notion was, perhaps, most infamously articulated in the words of British Prime Minister William Gladstone in 1874, writing in response to Pope Pius IX's *Syllabus of Errors*: 'No one can now become [Rome's] convert without removing his moral and mental freedom, and placing his civil loyalty and duty at the mercy of another'.[7] About seventy five years later in Australia, this sentiment was raised again in a unique and high-profile manner with the suggestion that lay Catholics were, due to their faith, still beholden to a sovereign and foreign power and thus incapable of proper allegiance to Australia.

In August 1950, *The Argus* in Melbourne informed readers that a High Court judge had ruled on 'the question of whether a Roman Catholic could be a member of Parliament'. One Henry William

5. Edwards, 'Proddy-Dogs, Cattleticks and Ecumaniacs', 26.
6. CMH Clark, *A History of Australia*, Volume I (Melbourne, Melbourne University Press: 1963), 89. See also Benjamin Wilkie, 'Treacherous objects: A Jacobite Compass in Australia?', in *History Workshop Online*, 19 June 2016: http://www.historyworkshop.org.uk/treacherous-objects-a-jacobite-compass-in-australia/ accessed on
7. WE Gladstone, *The Vatican Decrees in their bearing on Civil Allegiance: A Political Expostulation* (London: John Murray, 1874), 6.

Crittenden had run as an independent candidate for the electorate of Kingsford Smith in the 1949 Federal election. He was unsuccessful. Crittenden's successful opponent was Gordon Anderson, a railway worker and unionist who had served four terms as the Labor Mayor of the Waverley Municipal Council in the eastern suburbs of Sydney. *The Argus* announced that, some months later in January 1950, Crittenden had challenged Anderson's nomination and election. 'He claims that the Commonwealth Constitution bars Anderson from being a member of the House of Representatives', it said. 'Crittenden submits that the Roman Catholic Church is an integral part of a world-wide political regime headed by the Pope, as sovereign pontiff and ruler of a foreign power'.[8]

The grounds for Anderson's election to be made void, thought Crittenden, were laid down in Section 44 of the Australian Constitution: any person who 'is under any acknowledgment of allegiance, obedience, or adherence to a foreign power, or is a subject or a citizen or entitled to the rights or privileges of a subject or a citizen of a foreign power . . . shall be incapable of being chosen or of sitting as a senator or a member of the House of Representatives.'[9] This article briefly examines the mid-twentieth century context and background of the case, details some of content of the accusation levelled at Anderson and, by extension, all Catholics in Australia, and outlines the eventual judgement that Catholics could, in fact, run for office in Australia.[10] Although sectarianism in postwar Australia was muted in comparison to earlier decades, it was not entirely absent from public discourse.

The 1949 election campaign in the New South Wales electorate of Kingsford Smith had, by some accounts, presaged Crittenden's more formalised attacks on the rights of Catholics in Australia. When it reported on the petition in January 1950, *Truth*, a newspaper known for scandal and gossip, suggested that there had been a 'flood of anti-Roman Catholic propagandist literature in the division during the campaign'. It indicated that 'Feelings of deep indignation had been aroused in the Roman Catholic community in Kingsford Smith, and the cause of certain Liberal candidates, who are Protestants and who

8. 'Challenge to Catholics in Parliament', *Argus* (15 August 1950): 3.
9. 'Challenge to Catholics in Parliament', *Argus* (15 August 1950): 3; *Australian Constitution* s 44(i).
10. Thanks are due to Gray Connolly for commenting on a draft of this article.

are alleged to have been responsible for the propaganda, is believed to have suffered materially in consequence'.[11] Crittenden in particular had a track record for sectarian polemic.

Crittenden was described as 'the moving spirit in a plan to form a new political party' in 1943, to go under the name of British-Australian Union, to combat the 'blatantly anti-British Irish fifth of Australia . . . it was anti-trade unionists; anti-labor governments; anti-Communists, anti-party governments, and anti-religious denominational schools'.[12] Later, in 1947, he attempted to establish his own newspaper, which would be called the *Monitor*. It would 'endeavour to preserve a high moral tone from the British-Australian viewpoint while ruthlessly challenging any and all attempts by minorities to further prejudice or destroy our British heritage of freedom and equal opportunity'.[13]

His viewpoint would become more openly sectarian. Writing for the virulently anti-Catholic publication, *The Rock*, in May 1950, Crittenden levelled criticism at the popular Catholic apologist and writer, Leslie Rumble, exposing a swath of religious, ethnic, and class prejudices. He described Rumble's title—doctor—as 'unacceptable' because it 'would prejudice the dignity of less pretentious witch-doctors of other more primitive branches of pagan theology'.[14] Rumble was a convert to Catholicism from Anglicanism, and Crittenden said it was 'difficult for me to accept that you were trained for the Anglican ministry in the English traditions of decency, as you still permit your readers to believe. It seems that St Ligouri's [*sic*] villainous "Moral Theology" is hardly the textbook for transforming congenitally handicapped Irish students into gentlemen'.[15] Catholicism was a perfectly balanced compound of polytheistic paganism and Machiavellian politics . . . the hybridised product of the union of early Christianity with still earlier paganisms, he also wrote. Touching on the Gladstonian fears for civil allegiance, Crittenden said that Catholicism—a 'foul racial-religious-political combination'—had corrupted all our British institutions in Australia; poisoned our National soul; and, from its present domination, now threatens our

11. *Truth*, 29 January 1950, 5.
12. 'What, Again?', *Smith's Weekly* (5 April 1947), 16.
13. 'What, Again?', *Smith's Weekly* (5 April 1947), 16.
14. 'Stand Up Father Rumble', *The Rock* (13 August 1950).
15. 'Stand Up Father Rumble', *The Rock* (13 August 1950).

entire future as a great State.[16] This was the sectarian background from which emerged the suggestion that Catholics could not, under Section 44 of the nation's constitution, be eligible for public office in Australia.

In the petition presented to the courts, Crittenden alleged that 'Gordon Anderson is not capable of being chosen or of sitting as a Member of the House of Representatives he being under acknowledgement of adherence, obedience and/or allegiance to a foreign power within the meaning of Section 44 of the Commonwealth Constitution.'[17]

> Elaborating on the accusation, Crittenden said that Anderson 'was, at the time of his nomination and election, a professed member of the Roman Catholic Church. As such he, as in the case of all members of that Church in all countries, is under 'acknowledgement of Adherence, Obedience or Allegiance to a Foreign Power'—the Papal State. He is therefore incapable of being chosen or of sitting as a Member of The House of Representatives'.[18]

Crittenden believed that his case was bolstered by the fact that "the sovereign status of the Vatican was restored through the signing of the Lateran Treaty of 1929 by Mussolini and Pope Pius XI."[19]

Sir Wilfred Fullagar was the High Court judge—sitting as a Court of Disputed Returns under the Commonwealth Electoral Act—who would hand down the final judgment on Crittenden's petition. An erudite Melbourne lawyer with a staunchly Presbyterian outlook—and therefore, perhaps, having some understanding of religious minorities in a predominantly Anglican nation—Fullagar was described by his friend, the judge Sir Owen Dixon, as a man who 'had combined, with a remarkable legal erudition, great resources of scholarship. His judgments commanded the admiration of lawyers, not only for their penetration, their soundness and their correctness, but for the exposition of legal principles in an almost unequalled

---

16. 'Stand Up Father Rumble', *The Rock* (13 August 1950).
17. *Crittenden v Anderson* High Court (Fullagar J) 23 August 1950. Available online at http://eresources.hcourt.gov.au/historical/showbyHandle/1/16205/accessed on
18. *Crittenden v Anderson* High Court (Fullagar J) 23 August 1950.
19. *Truth* (29 January 1950), 5.

English style'.[20] He was appointed to the High Court of Australia on 8 February 1950, and the question of Catholics and the Australian Constitution would be one of his early cases.

Fullagar clarified Crittenden's accusations. He wrote that 'the petitioner made it quite clear to me that he did not allege that the respondent had entered into any individual or particular acknowledgement of adherence, obedience or allegiance to what he describes as the Papal State'.[21] Which is to say, Crittenden's argument was not that Anderson had specifically and explicitly, as an individual, sworn any allegiance to a foreign power. Instead, explained Justice Fullagar, Crittenden thought that 'merely by virtue of being a professed member of the Roman Catholic Church, the respondent owes allegiance to a foreign power.' Fullagar continues to summarise the full implications of the argument for the relationship between Catholics and the Australian state: 'What [Crittenden] is saying is no more and no less than that every member of [the Catholic Church] is the subject of a foreign power and for that reason incapable of becoming or being a member of either House of the Parliament of the Commonwealth'.[22]

The petition was widely covered in Australia's major capital city and regional newspapers. The nation's Catholic press, especially, took an interest. Shortly after the petition was delivered in January, Adelaide's Catholic newspaper, the *Southern Cross*, editorialised on the matter: 'There is a grave misconception here due to the fact that Mr. Crittenden fails to distinguish between temporal authority and spiritual authority—a mistake that could only be made in a very materialistic age. Is that a distinction Catholics make just to get out of a difficulty? Of course not'.

> The *Southern Cross* continued to explain: 'Every Anglican in South Australia recognises [Thomas Playford, Premier of South Australia] as holding temporal and Bishop Robin spiritual authority over them. Every Australian Catholic hails

20. RL Sharwood, 'Fullagar, Sir Wilfred Kelsham (1892–1961)', in *Australian Dictionary of Biography*, National Centre of Biography, Australian National University: http://adb.anu.edu.au/biography/fullagar-sir-wilfred-kelsham-10258/text18123/
21. *Crittenden v Anderson* High Court (Fullagar J) 23 August 1950.
22. *Crittenden v Anderson* High Court (Fullagar J) 23 August 1950.

> the King as his temporal ruler, the Pope as his spiritual ruler. The Pope has temporal authority, too—but not over us. He has spiritual authority over all Catholics throughout the world; temporal authority only over the citizens of the Vatican State. The Australian Catholic, or any Catholic not a citizen of the Vatican State, owes no allegiance to the Pope as civil ruler. The fact that there is a Vatican State at all is non-essential and comparatively unimportant. It does not belong to the essence of the Papacy'.[23]

Fullagar's own judgment and opinion of Crittenden's argument was clear and unambiguous: 'It is obvious, in my opinion, that no such major premiss [sic] can be supported.' What Crittenden was attempting to argue, thought Fullagar, was rather transparent, and spoke to old bigotries. The judge contended that the sovereignty of the Vatican was irrelevant to the question. He said that 'the root of the matter . . . lies in the fact that the petitioner really seeks to revive a point of view which was abandoned in England in 1829', referring legislative changes that allowed Catholics to sit and vote as a member of either house of parliament in the United Kingdom. Fullagar said that 'our own Constitution was, of course, not enacted by men ignorant or unmindful of history' and noted that the Australian Constitution determines that 'no religious test shall be required as qualification for any office or public trust under the Commonwealth . . . it is, in my opinion, sec. 116, and not sec. 44(i) of our Constitution which is relevant when the right of a member of any religious body to sit in Parliament is challenged on the ground of his religion'.[24]

> Fullagar continues: "One may observe, as a matter of law, that every person born in Australia, into whatever religion he may be born and whatever religion he may embrace, is according to the law of this country (which is the only relevant law) a British subject owing allegiance to His Majesty, and of that allegiance he cannot rid himself except in certain prescribed ways. One may observe, as a matter of fact, that many thousands of Catholics have fought in the armed forces of this country in recent wars."[25]

---

23. 'Loyalty to the Vatican', *The Southern Cross* (3 February 1950), 6.
24. *Crittenden v Anderson* High Court (Fullagar J) 23 August 1950.
25. *Crittenden v Anderson* High Court (Fullagar J) 23 August 1950.

That Fullagar pointed towards Section 116 of the Australian Constitution in defence of the nation's Catholics was apt. Half a century earlier, in the lead up to the Federation of the Australian colonies in 1901, Catholics had been ambiguous about the project, not least because the rhetoric surrounding Federation was distinctly British and imperial. Although he was a supporter, when Patrick Francis Cardinal Moran was informed that only the Anglican Primate would be allowed to read prayers and give blessings at the inauguration ceremonies, he led the Church in Australia in a boycott of Federation celebrations. Very few Catholics had participated in the preceding federal conventions that would decide the shape of the new Commonwealth. Only three of fifty delegates at the first convention in 1897 were Catholic: Patrick McMahon Glynn, Richard O'Connor (described as 'one lone Catholic in a sea of Protestants'), and Matthew Clarke. It was Glynn who, as one writer puts it, 'is popularly remembered, if remembered at all, as the man who put God into the Australian Constitution'.[26] With the support of Victorian Presbyterians, Glynn convinced the final convention in Melbourne to insert the phrase 'humbly relying on the blessing of Almighty God' into the preamble of the Constitution. Most importantly for those Catholics who would later face questions about their faith and allegiance to a foreign power, Glynn had the convention insert Section 116 into the Australian Constitution: 'the Commonwealth could not legislate to establish any religion, to impose any religious observance, to prohibit free exercise of any religion, or to impose any religious test for holding Commonwealth office'.[27]

In the end, Crittenden's accusations were dismissed. In his judgment, Justice Fullagar determined that the arguments put forward were 'quite untenable', that they were not sufficient grounds for declaring the Anderson's election void, and that 'the petition shows on its face that it has no prospect for success, and that it is vexatious and oppressive in the relevant sense.' The proceedings were 'for ever stayed'. So unimpressed was Fullagar that instead of ordering Crittenden to pay fixed costs as was often the case, he crossed out the relevant phrases in his judgment and thereby opened the applicant

26. Tony Cahill, 'Catholics and Australian Federation', in *Journal of the Australian Catholic Historical Society*, 22 (2001): 9–30, at 27.
27. Cahill, 'Catholics and Australian Federation', 17.

to whatever costs Anderson had incurred defending himself.[28] The judgment was published in full on the front page of Sydney's *Catholic Weekly* newspaper, which proudly declared: 'Catholic M. H. R. Wins Case: Religion No Bar To Election, Judge Declares'.[29]

As the editors of the *Southern Cross* in Adelaide had predicted in February 1950 as news of Crittenden's petition first emerged: 'No Australian Catholic is under any act of acknowledgement, allegiance, or obedience or adherence to the Vatican State, or is a subject or citizen entitled to the rights or privileges of a subject or citizen of the Vatican State.'[30] As Fullagar had recognised, however, that point was irrelevant: the framers of the Australian Constitution had, fifty years earlier, defended believers against discrimination when it came to the question of public office. Gordon Anderson held the seat of Kingsford Smith until his eventual retirement in 1958.

28. *Crittenden v Anderson* High Court (Fullagar J) 23 August 1950.
29. *Catholic Weekly* (31 August 1950) 1.
30. 'Loyalty to the Vatican', *The Southern Cross* (3 February 1950): 6.

Journal of the Australian Catholic Historical Society, Volume 41/2020

Les Murray's Sacramental Poetics

*Stephen McInerney**

I want to begin by situating Les Murray's sacramental poetics—that is to say, Murray's sense of himself as a sacramental poet—in the context of the history of attempts to relate poetry and sacrament, which in turn is part of a trend that relates literature and religion (or that sees literature as having assumed the role of religion).

In the late nineteenth and early twentieth century, as Terry Eagleton and others have persuasively argued, the rise of English Literature as a prominent discipline first in 'Mechanics' Institutes, working men's colleges and extension learning circuits' (23), and later in universities and at schools, not only related to the slow but steady demise of Classics as a central discipline, but—more importantly—to the decline of religion. As Eagleton writes:

If one were asked to provide a single explanation for the growth of English studies in the later nineteenth century, one could do worse than reply: 'the failure of religion'. By the mid-Victorian period, this traditionally reliable, immensely powerful ideological form was in deep trouble. It was no longer winning the hearts and minds of the masses, and under the twin impacts of scientific discovery and social change its previous unquestioned dominance was in danger of evaporating. . . . Fortunately, however, another, remarkably similar discourse lay to hand: English literature. George Gordon, early Professor of English Literature at Oxford, commented in his inaugural lecture that 'England is sick, and . . . English literature must save it. The

* Stephen McInerney is Deputy Director of the Ramsay Centre for Western Civilisation. This is an updated version of Chapter 4 of his book, *The Enclosure of An Open Mystery: Sacrament and Incarnation in the Poetry of Gerard Manley Hopkins, David Jones and Les Murray* (Oxford: Peter Lang, 2012).

Churches (as I understand) having failed, and social remedies being slow, English Literature has now a triple function: still, I suppose, to delight and instruct us, but also, and above all, to save our souls and heal the State'. Gordon's words were spoken in our century, but they find a resonance everywhere in Victorian England . . . As religion progressively ceases to provide the social 'cement', affective values and basic mythologies by which a socially turbulent class-society can be wielded together, 'English' is constructed as a subject to carry this ideological burden from the Victorian period onwards.[1]

Even if, like Peter Barry, 'I do not accept the simplistic view that the founders of English were motivated merely by a desire for ideological control",[2] nonetheless there is much to be said for Eagleton's analysis. One can certainly trace from the mid-nineteenth-century through to the mid-twentieth-century, a tendency in the first instance to see an analogy between religion and poetry, and then, over time, the gradual demotion of religion in favour of poetry, where poetry (and imaginative literature more generally) is said to assume the role formerly held by religion, and takes on the properties of religion in communicating moral truths and timeless realities, so much so that it comes to be described in sacramental, liturgical and theological terms. So, for example, in the peroration to his *Lectures on Poetry* delivered in the first half of the nineteenth century, John Keble, the Anglican poet and priest, declared, 'Poetry lends religion her wealth of symbols and similes; religion restores them again to poetry, clothed with so splendid a radiance that they appear to be no longer symbols, but to partake (I might almost say) of the nature of sacraments'.[3] Almost fifty years later, Matthew Arnold argued that since the 'fact' had failed it, the strongest part of religion was the 'unconscious poetry' of its rites and rituals.[4] A hundred years later still, the English novelist and philosopher Iris Murdoch declared that art and poetry fill the void left by sacraments and prayer in an 'unreligious age'.[5] Yet, while Murdoch was paradoxically equating art and sacrament at the very same time

1. Terry Eagleton, *Literary Theory* (Minneapolis: University of Minneapolis Press, 2008), 20–21.
2. Peter Barry, *Beginning Theory* (Manchester: Manchester University Press, 2009), 14.
3. John Keble, *Lectures on Poetry: 1832–1841* (Bristol: Thoemmes Press, 2003), 481.
4. Matthew Arnold, *Essays in Criticism* (Second Series) (London: MacMillan, 1903), 1.
5. Iris Murdoch, *The Fire and the Sun* (Oxford: Clarendon Press, 1977), 76.

as she was sounding the death-knell of religion, the Catholic painter and poet David Jones was coming to the end of a career that had been devoted to reconnecting art with its ancient roots in sacramental practice. Persuaded by Jacques Maritain's extraordinary claim that 'the Eucharistic sacrifice [is] at the heart of poetry',[6] Jones related art to the sacramental life with a sophistication and depth that exceeded any before him. For Jones, the sacraments themselves were a form of craftsmanship by which the work of human hands became an incarnation of the Divine. Jones first relates the Eucharist to painting. As the body and blood of Christ are said to exist under the 'species' of bread and wine respectively, so a painted object or scene really exists 'under the species of paint', and 'as through and by the Son, all creation came into existence and is by that same agency redeemed, so we, who are co-heirs with the Son, extend, in a way, creative and redeeming influences upon the dead works of nature, when we fashion material to our heart's desire'.[7] In his major work, *The Anathemata*, poetry too is subsumed into the Eucharistic sacrifice, where the poet working at his poem is compared with the priest at the altar, "making this thing other."[8]

Contemporary literary criticism has also borne witness to the increased awareness of the relationship between poetry and the sacraments, giving rise to something of a minor genre in critical discourse.[9] This is particularly noticeable in Hopkins scholarship where some extraordinary claims have been made about Hopkins' intentions for his poetry. Maria Lichtmann, for example, has argued,

6. Jacques Maritain, *Art and Scholasticism* and *The Frontiers of Poetry*, translated by Joseph W Evans (Notre Dame, Indiana: University of Notre Dame Press, 1974), 132.
7. David Jones, *The Dying Gaul and Other Writings* (London: Faber and Faber, 1978), 287.
8. David Jones, *The Anathemata: Fragments of an Attempted Writing* (London: Faber and Faber, 1972), 49.
9. See, for example, *Christ: The Sacramental Word–Incarnation, Sacrament and Poetry* edited by David Brown and Anne Loades (London: Society for Promoting Christian Knowledge, 1996); Theresa DiPasquale, *Literature and Sacrament: The Sacred and the Secular in John Donne* (Cambridge: James Clarke & Co., 2001); Eleanor McNees, *Eucharistic Poetry* (Lewisburg, PA: Bucknell University Press, 1992); Kathleen Norris, 'A Word Made Flesh: Incarnational Language and the Writer,' in *The Incarnation: An Interdisciplinary Symposium on the Incarnation of the Son of God*, edited by Stephen T Davis, *et.al* (Oxford: Oxford University Press, 2002), 303–12.

'The poem, for Hopkins, is the Body of Christ. It is the Eucharist in the sense of bearing the motionless, lifeless Real Presence of Christ, of acting with sacramental, transforming instress on the reader as Hopkins has himself instressed nature'.[10] Eleanor McNees is equally daring (and equally vague) in her claim that Hopkins 'crafts a poem as a kind of Mass in which all words work to voice the one Word–Christ. The successful poem enacts the Eucharistic process. . . . The moment of sacrifice is the culmination of real presence in the reader'.[11] Margaret R Ellsberg, meanwhile, has argued that, for Hopkins, poetry "is the sacrament of flesh, word and spirit charged by their interpenetration with each other'.[12]

More recently, connections between art and sacrament have been brought to a new point of fusion in the poetry of Les Murray, who argues that the 'sacramental is the body, it's the mystery of embodiment [and] words form a body called a poem'.[13]

Murray stresses the mystical similarities between poetry and religion:

> Religions are poems. They concert
> our daylight and dreaming mind, our
> emotions, instinct, breath and native gesture
> into the only whole thinking: poetry.[14]

Yet Murray goes further, advancing an idea of the poet as a priest, an offerer of sacrifice. His view of the poet as priest links him with Jones. Unlike Jones, however, Murray does not stress the relationship between the 're-presentation' of Christ's sacrifice in the Mass as the *representation* of a 'thing' under another 'species' (paint, clay, or language). For Murray, the poet is rather a hierophant, a speaker for the tribe who offers 'unbloody' sacrifices. With respect to his own

10. Maria Lichtmann, 'The Incarnational Aesthetic of Gerard Manley Hopkins,' in *Religion and Literature*, 23/1 (1991): 44.
11. Eleanor McNees, *Eucharistic Poetry: The Search for Presence in the Writings of John Donne, Gerard Manley Hopkins, Dylan Thomas and Geoffrey Hill* (Lewisburg, PA: Bucknell University Press, 1992), 77.
12. Margaret R Ellsberg, *Created to Praise: The Language of Gerard Manley Hopkins* (Oxford: Oxford University Press, 1987), 45.
13. William Scammell, 'Les Murray in Conversation,' in *PN Review* 25/2 (1998): 31.
14. Les Murray, 'Poetry and Religion,' in *Collected Poems: 1961–2002* (Potts Point: Duffy and Snellgrove, 2002), 265.

work, he has spoken in specifically Christological terms: 'This quasi-priestly work of poetry is Christ, for me; it's His life as I can live it by my efforts'.[15]

Like both Hopkins and Jones before him, each of whom also converted to Roman Catholicism in his early twenties, after his reception into the Roman Catholic Church in 1964, the young poet was spiritually and intellectually riveted by the Church's principal ritual:

I identified with the Eucharist. I thought, yes, yes, the absolute transformation of ordinary elements into the divine. I know about that. It didn't strike me as unlikely, and it opened such illimitable prospects of life. Most secular mythologies seem to be anxious to close the possibilities of life down and delimit them. This one opened out.[16]

The tenor of this statement closely resembles that of another that Murray made in an interview in 1998, where he addressed a more ideological reason for his conversion. As though in response to the critic who once aligned a dimension of his work (and, by implication, his religion and politics) with 'pinched unadorned belligerence and dogma',[17] he stated, 'My politics are anti-totalitarian. That's why I became a Catholic. It's for everybody. It may have a low opinion of sinners, but it's equally low of all. You're warned not to be proud, but also assured that you're of infinite worth'.[18]

If it was an attraction to the Eucharist and to the inclusiveness of Catholicism that drew Murray to that faith, it was the work of the poet-priest Hopkins which principally 'turned [him] on to poetry'[19] and opened to him a dimension of the craft which, many years later, he would link with the Eucharist. After reading Hopkins, 'bang, I suddenly discovered this language with a live electric current through it–you know, powerful stuff. I'd been casting around for an art form for a year or so. I'd gradually been moving away from military fantasies . . . I discovered that poetry was about presence'.[20]

---

15. Quoted in Peter F Alexander, *Les Murray: A Life in Progress* (Melbourne: Oxford University Press, 2000), 155.
16. Missy Daniel, 'Poetry is Presence: An Interview with Les Murray,' in *Commonweal,* 119/10 (1992): 10.
17. Gig Ryan, 'And the Fetid Air and Gritty', *Heat* 5 (1997): 199.
18. Scammell, 'Les Murray in Conversation,' 36.
19. Daniel, 'Poetry is Presence,' 10.
20. 'Poetry is Presence,' 10.

Certainly, if poetry is about 'presence' so is the Eucharist, and if the Eucharist is about the transformation of the ordinary into the divine, so too is poetry concerned with the interaction between the everyday and the absolute. As Kevin Hart has noted, Murray 'sometimes follows what he calls 'an incarnational logic' in which, as Christ is both God and man, a poem is about the holy and the ordinary at once.'[21] Similarly, if the Eucharist stands against 'secular mythologies' that 'close the possibilities of life down,' so too is poetry (in what Murray calls the 'celebratory mode') characterized by a 'refusal of alienation and a species of humility' which 'doesn't presume to understand the world, at least never reductively, and so leaves it open and expansive, with unforeclosed potentials.'[22] Yet while a poem may be open to 'unforeclosed potentials,' it is also 'a very contained thing that holds down these tremendous energies.'[23]

The 'tremendous energies' Murray refers to represent two opposed forces in his work–divine presence, on the one hand, and the need for blood sacrifice on the other:

> Wait on! Human sacrifice? Surely that's an archaic horror that survives only very marginally in a few Third World groups that anthropologists write about? Surely the holocausts of this century in what we call 'our' civilization can only be called human sacrifices in a very metaphoric sort of way? Surely there's a distinction to be made here between the literal and the metaphorical? My answer is, there may be, but I don't know of one water-tight enough to prevent the blood from seeping through it.[24]

A poem, for Murray, transforms the desire for sacrifice into a 'presence' as Christ on the Cross is simultaneously the victim of the sacrifice and the offerer of His presence. A poem holds down both 'energies' within itself:

A poem which stays within the realm of literature completes the trinity of forebrain consciousness, dream wisdom and bodily sympathy–of reason, dream and the dance, really–without needing

21. Kevin Hart, "Interest' in Les A. Murray,' in *Australian Literary Studies,* 14/2 (1989): 158.
22. Les Murray, *A Working Forest: Selected Prose* (Potts Point: Duffy and Snellgrove, 1997), 360.
23. Scammell, 'Les Murray in Conversation,' 31.
24. Murray, *A Working Forest,* 131–32.

to embody itself in actual suffering or action, and without the need to demand blood sacrifice from us. It is thus like Christ's Crucifixion, both effectual and vicarious.[25]

Elsewhere the simile is reversed:

> Jesus is like a literal poem, taking these terrible energies that sacrifice people–looking for significance, to underline and stimulate it, by giving it sacrifice. He's saying, that's a superceded principle, I've taken that upon myself, it's all in here, refer to this figure, it's contained. I'm always looking for the containment of human sacrifice.[26]

Believing that a desire for human sacrifice and 'significance' underpins human activity to varying degrees, Murray sets up an opposition between a resolved work of art, such as a poem, and disembodied "idols" which 'demand' blood sacrifice 'to embody' themselves.[27] The need for sacrifice, as such, is either resolved in ritual or art, or actual human sacrifice. Murray aims to craft a poem which is a contemplative site, the point into which human blood-lust is transformed into 'a never-murderous skim/distilled', and thus to show how it shares in a Eucharistic identity in the sense that it incarnates a presence which feeds the human desire for sacrifice and therefore, potentially, prevents such sacrifice through catharsis.[28] In this way it is both 'effectual and vicarious'. If poetry symbolises for the poet the completion of his youthful journey away from 'military fantasies' (and marks a rejection of them), so the Eucharist, as part of what he calls 'The Iliad of peace',[29] stands against and resolves the 'human sacrifice . . . at the heart of literature',[30] along with the innate need to offer blood sacrifices that military fantasies represent.

Murray's first collection of verse, *The Ilex Tree*, was published jointly with his friend Geoffrey Lehmann in 1965. Murray's contribution to the small collection contains poems that evoke the world of rural farmers and timber workers and celebrate the freshness

25. *A Working Forest*, 321–22.
26. Scammell, 'Les Murray in Conversation,' 31.
27. See, for example, Murray, 'The Instrument,' in *Collected Poems*, 458.
28. 'The Instrument,' 458.
29. 'Animal Nativity,' in *Collected Poems*, 374.
30. Les Murray, *The Boys Who Stole the Funeral* (Sydney: Angus and Robertson, 1980), 29.

and regenerative powers of the natural world. 'Spring Hail',[31] a poem clearly influenced by Hopkins' 'Spring' and Dylan Thomas' 'Fern Hill', delights in its natural setting where the numinous permeates the physical landscape—"Fresh minted hills/smoked, and the heavens swirled and blew away'—and where the experience of 'spring hail' evokes an atmosphere of reverent awe before the mystery of God's creation, such that the occasion of the poem becomes (through a pun on 'hail') at one with the speaker's response of praise. It strikes a note that has reverberated throughout Murray's career, one that can be heard resoundingly in his second collection, *The Weatherboard Cathedral* (1969), whose title suggests the nature of Murray's project: to craft from his humble origins something beautiful for God, 'the transformation of ordinary elements into the divine', a Cathedral in weatherboard. In Murray's vision, the natural world is made 'vivid' by the Incarnation,[32] re-manifesting Christ's presence in creation so that it can always be turned to for spiritual nourishment:

The things I write about are mainly religious or metaphysical–I am concerned with relations between human time and eternity at the odd points where they meet and illuminate each other, example where matter becomes immortal, or spirit enters time 'for a season'. (It happens.) This heirophanic [hierophantic] thinking works both ways of course: calling on men to witness the world of spirit and, almost, calling on that world to witness us. Like Octavia Paz said in a poem I once translated: the Mass is "an incarnate pause between this and timeless time". Joints and junctions like that, arising in the oddest places, are my meat.[33]

In 'Once in a Lifetime, Snow', the poet offers an example of eternity entering time 'for a season', and it is interesting to note the response of the farmer to this occurrence. He eats the snow as he recognizes its numinous significance:

A man of farm and fact
he stared to see
the facts of weather raised
to a mystery

31. *Collected Poems*, 8.
32. 'Animal Nativity', in *Collected Poems*, 374.
33. Quoted in Alexander, *Les Murray*, 91.

white on the world he knew
and all he owned.
Snow? Here? he mused I see.
High time I learned . . .

perceiving this much, he scuffed
his slippered feet
and scooped a handful up
to taste, and eat

in memory of the fact
that even he
might not have seen the end
of reality . . .[34]

The numinous snow, a fact of weather 'raised to a mystery,' assumes by analogy some of the qualities of the Eucharist where the bread and wine are raised to the mystery of Christ's body and blood in 'memory' of Christ's passion. The farmer's response is similarly Eucharistic: he tastes and eats the snow 'in memory of the fact' that reality exceeds the limits of material existence (anticipating the poet's description of the Incarnation as the making 'Godhead a fact').[35] Eating the numinous snow is the means by which the farmer physically responds to the spiritual dimension of what has taken place; he incorporates it into himself both to 'taste' and savour the experience as well as its significance. While the phrase "in memory of the fact" recalls Christ's words 'Do this in memory of me,' 'Taste, and eat' also echoes part of the Eucharistic words of institution—'Take and eat'—and recalls the scriptural injunction, 'O taste, and see that the Lord is sweet.'[36] These connections are quite deliberate. By exceeding the limitations of 'reality' as understood by the farmer, the event hints at all the spiritual dimensions hitherto ignored by him–the unforeclosed potentials of the natural world. Eating the snow is the means by which that which had previously been beyond the imagination of the farmer–that which had been external to his vision–is incorporated into his imagination without being exhausted by it.

34. Murray, *Collected Poems*, 23.
35. *Collected Poems*, 537.
36. Ps 33:8.

The *Weatherboard Cathedral* reveals the many-sidedness of Murray's sacramental poetic. As well as depicting a world saturated with God's presence (a dimension of Murray's work that reached its apotheosis in the 1992 collection *Translations from the Natural World*), it also shows how the sacramental enlarges to embrace the sacrificial aspects of the human and animal kingdoms. What Bernadette Ward has said of Hopkins applies equally to Murray: 'to look for the intellectual core of his work is to move . . . well beyond a mere generalized feeling about something spiritually nourishing in the beauty of the world. Sacramentality is sacrificial, having to do with loss as well as joy; it perceives God's action in scenes not at all attractive to the senses'.[37] In poems like 'Blood' and 'The Abomination', Murray uncovers the need for sacrifice at the heart of the animal kingdom. In "Blood," the speaker describes himself walking

> back up the trail of crowding flies,
> back to the knife which pours deep blood, and frees
> sun, fence and hill, each to its holy place . . .
> And notes:
> A world I thought sky-lost by leaning ships
> in the depth of our life–I'm in that world once more.
> Looking down, we praise for its firm flesh
> the creature killed according to the Law.

The pig killed according to the 'Law' is an imperfect type of the true sacrifice, held aloft to the sun in a manner that recalls the elevation of the Host in the Mass. Like the snow in 'Once in a Lifetime, Snow', this meat will be eaten, and the idea of 'eating' in response to revelatory moments, as a means of reinforcing a sense of communion among individuals and the spiritual world, figures strongly in Murray's sacramental vision. It becomes a prominent theme in *Poems Against Economics* (1972), his third collection. 'Towards the Imminent Days' celebrates the sacrament of marriage,[38] the union of lovers which 'will heal the twentieth century'. Set in a landscape of houses and 'loved fields, all wearing away into Heaven', it delights also in the earthy, hearty rituals of a country wedding: champagne and chicken suppers, whiskey, pumpkins, and 'poddy calves', as the animal, human, and divine realms–

37. Bernadette Ward, *World as Word: Philosophical Theology in Gerard Manley Hopkins* (Washington, DC: Catholic University of America Press, 2002), 131–32.
38. Murray, *Collected Poems*, 37.

flesh, intellect, and spirit–interconnect in a consciously incarnational celebration of love. More darkly, *Poems Against Economics* questions the obverse drive in humanity, the need to make war, in 'Lament for the Country Soldiers'.[39] 'Vindaloo in Merthyr Tydfil',[40] by contrast, takes a humorous view of a mystical experience resulting from the eating of a hot curry (reverently mocking the then-fashionable glances to the Hindu East of many western intellectuals). 'Walking to the Cattle Place',[41] meanwhile, a major sequence of fifteen poems, fuses the central ideas of the collection as it engages with the genuine connections–of language and cattle–between Indian and European civilizations.

In Murray's work, natural food frequently parallels supernatural food, most famously in 'The Broad Bean Sermon'[42] from *Lunch and Counter Lunch* (1974), his fourth collection. In this poem, the poet explores another one of the 'oddest places'—which is, at the same time, one of the most 'ordinary'—where natural fecundity discloses its own inexhaustibility and invites the poet to explore the variety of its minutiae. As the title suggests, the poem is concerned with the way in which the natural world can become an unassuming voice preaching a 'sermon'. The title is partly ironic, for the first image the poet uses to describe the broad beans is that of 'a slack church parade/without belief, saying *trespass against us* in unison'. This image illustrates the way in which, at first glance, the broad beans are a mass of seemingly indistinguishable vegetation—yet the ensuing succession of metaphors and similes belies this impression, as the poet is drawn deeper and deeper into the world that holds his attention, and deeper and deeper into his own imaginative and linguistic resources. In the second stanza, the broad beans are still discussed as a collective, while in the third the poet describes the world above 'a thin bean forest'. From the fourth stanza until the conclusion, however, the poem explores the relationship between the universal 'you' of the poem who goes to pick the beans and the inexhaustible diversity of the beans themselves. This plenitude keeps disclosing more and more variety and difference, which both the bean picker and poet seek to rein in. The rapid succession of compound images is typical of Murray at his exuberant best:

39. *Collected Poems*, 43.
40. *Collected Poems*, 54.
41. *Collected Poems*, 55.
42. *Collected Poems*, 112.

At every hour of daylight
appear more that you missed: ripe, knobbly ones, fleshy-sided,
thin-straight, thin-crescent, frown-shaped, bird-shouldered,
boat-keeled ones,
beans knuckled and single-bulged, minute green dolphins at
suck.[43]

Lunch and Counter Lunch was followed by *Ethnic Radio* (1977) and *The Boys Who Stole the Funeral* (1980), the first of Murray's two verse novels. The Eucharist, described by the poet as 'food that solves the world',[44] stands at the heart of this work, which describes an unlikely incident in which two friends, Kevin Forbutt and Cameron Reeby, sensing that Forbutt's uncle will not receive a proper funeral, steal his body. The crime propels a series of adventures during which the protagonists confront their own inadequacies and approach spiritual enlightenment, recognizing the sacred in the everyday realities of work, family, and nature. Sacrifice, again, is the dominant theme: human sacrifice–which takes the form of war, murder, abortion, and ritualized attacks on individuals–is explicitly set against God's sacrifice ('The true god/gives his flesh and blood. Idols demand yours off you'[45]). In one key episode, the boys pick up a hitchhiker who elaborates what is later referred to as 'his blood theology':

It was all resolved once: this is My Body, My Blood.
It's coming unsolved now.[46]

The work argues, imaginatively and forcefully, that it is not possible to ignore Christ's sacrifice without reverting to more ancient, pagan forms of sacrifice, even if these are disguised in the modern age (in the case of abortion, for example) under the veil of 'progress'. As Murray writes elsewhere, paraphrasing Chesterton: 'who lose belief in God will not only believe/in anything. They will bring blood offerings to it'.[47]

43. *Collected Poems*, 112.
44. *The Boys Who Stole the Funeral*, 35.
45. *The Boys Who Stole the Funeral*, 44. These lines reappear in 'The Muddy Trench' at the end of the 2002 Australian edition of the *Collected Poems*, and in 'Church,' a poem dedicated to the memory of Joseph Brodsky, in Murray's collection, *The Biplane Houses* (2006). Their reappearance suggests their centrality to Murray's vision.
46. *The Boys Who Stole the Funeral*, 9.
47. 'The Craze Field,' in *Collected Poems*, 161.

The question of 'sacrifice' looms large in Murray's second verse novel, *Fredy Neptune* (1998). *Fredy Neptune* tells the tale of Fredy Boettcher, a German-Australian sailor who, after witnessing the genocide of Armenian women at the hands of Turkish nationalists in 1917, loses feeling in his body, only to recover it when he learns to forgive his enemies. It is the poet's grand, Homeric exploration of the Enlightenment's disembodiment of humanity and the Christian alternative–the reception of a body (analogous to the reception of the Eucharist) which makes a person whole. The work forms a key part of Murray's career-long attempt to make sense of the relationship between poetry, religion, and ideology, and to find meaningful distinctions between artistic, religious, and political efforts to map experience. By an analogy evident throughout the work, the acceptance of Christ and the regaining of the body are linked with poetry, while totalitarian ideologies are linked with disembodied 'poems' (which stand to true poetry as idols stand to the true God) that seek to close people inside them.

After 265 pages of poetic narrative divided into five books of dense eight line stanzas; after having described his journeys through the Middle East, Asia, North America, Europe and Australia, through two world wars and the Great Depression; after having saved the lives of numerous people either from accidents or from murderous regimes; after having worked in circuses, a 'strong man' asylum, on Hollywood films, on boats, an airship, for corrupt politicians, for Banjo Paterson and Lawrence of Arabia; after having dined with Marlene Dietrich and spoken with Charlie Chaplin; after having been in more adventures than any comic book character and—finally—after having recovered his sensate flesh, Fred concludes his story thus:

nothing

would bring my null-body back. It was gone forever.
The limelight goes off me with it. We went on living:
Joe got married next year, which filled his dimples with grins.
Lou went to high school. I backed Norrie when I'd make extra cash
and some people picked I was different. *Not up in your point-shoes,*
Fred? as Ron asked me, getting back into his, after the war.
Later on we travelled—I paid to sleep!—and people died
of old age. But there's too much in life: you can't describe it.
(*FN*, 265).

As the theologian Michael G Michael pointed out to me in a conversation about this passage, the last line echoes the final words of John's Gospel: 'Jesus did many things; if one were to write them down one by one, the whole world, I believe, could not contain the books one would write about them'.[48] It is interesting to recall here Murray's words on the 'celebratory mode in poetry', characterised by a 'refusal of alienation and a species of humility' which 'doesn't presume to understand the world, at least never reductively, and so leaves it open and expansive, with unforeclosed potentials'.[49] By deferring to silence, Fred defers to the example of the great apostle of the Incarnation. The work enacts the restoration of Fred's body, making it present, but it is the presence of individual mystery restored to wholeness and completeness and therefore, paradoxically, to that which is unforeclosed—contained but not reducible to its confinement in language.

Like the farmer in "Once in a Lifetime, Snow", Fred realises that reality exceeds the limits even of his incredible experience. The text—which has become his 'body', the book called *Fredy Neptune* without which we could not know him and through which he exists—contains but does not limit the existence it maps, any more than the books of Scripture or the sacraments can limit the life of God. God remains an ungraspable trace and yet he mediates his life through the textual, concrete and particular facts of material existence. Art—whether this book or any other—is inexhaustible because life is inexhaustible. This does not mean that the text has no relationship to life, or that the text has no existence outside of itself, for as Murray writes elsewhere: 'nothing's true that figures in words only' ('Poetry and Religion', *CP*, 265). On the contrary it confirms such existence because it confirms that it derives its life *from* outside of itself, from grace, and mediates that life to (as it receives it through) the reader's touch.

Fred's humility before the enormity of life and of human existence, his *apophatic* refusal to totalise by summary and generalisation, sets him apart from the purveyors of racial and class theory depicted in the book, whose poems 'burn women'. What distinguishes Fred's response to illness from those who become murderers for a cause,

48. JN 21: 25. In conversation at Tory's Hotel, Kiama, December 2004.
49. *A Working Forest*, 360.

is Christ. Christ as God is the law against closure, the guarantee of diversity and the protector of individual integrity and worth. Fred acquires the internal authority of the Logos by agreeing to accept his body, thus becoming a true individual. With his body back, he is no longer like a disembodied and abstract concept. The centre, as Murray has said, is where any living thing is, and Fred becomes a centre by becoming a fully living thing. The centre of the world can no longer be understood exclusively as a geographical place (home, the city, or a Nation); rather it becomes the personal integrity of the individual, actualised in the combined workings of the dreaming and rational minds embodied in time and space. A key part of Fred's learning to pray with a single heart is learning that he is not beneath being a 'centre' of the universe, nor beneath being a concrete realisation of God's 'poem' that makes the centre complete and present at every point, including the periphery.

Throughout the work Fred always acknowledges and protects the rights of others to their place in life—writing them, as it were, into his own book of life. Unlike the Communists' red book and Hitler's *Mein Kampf* (which is described as 'his dead body . . . that he'd enclosed my people in', *FN,* 207), Fredy Neptune, both character and book, is alive—*his* once "dead body" resurrected by God's grace. When Fred receives his body back and becomes fully himself, the silence that soon follows reveals that it is the very open-ended-ness of the work (representing Fred's humility) that places it within the divine economy articulated during one of his theological discussions:

> At speed after there I asked Iowa: *What about it? God saving us?*—It's a promise . . . Buy it, and nobody's a failure. No one's book is closed. (*FN,* 158)

The book is finished but not 'closed' for 'like any poem, it must be inexhaustible and complete', as Murray writes in 'Poetry and Religion'. And God, as Murray writes in the same poem, is the law against its closure, the one who cannot ultimately be quantified by the univocal urge to transform the other into the self. He is thus, in Christ, the only answer, the only point of resolution who can be found everywhere. In accepting this, Fred places the eucharistic sacrifice at the heart of his poem, a sacrifice that *is* human with the crucial difference that it is also divine.

Murray's images of sacrifice, his theory of the importance of the body for an understanding of the whole person, and his explorations of all the places where God is "caught, not imprisoned," have extended the possibilities of a sacramental poetic by showing how aesthetics embraces ethics. What Tom D'Evelyn said of *Fredy Neptune* in the *Providence Sunday Journal* applies to Murray's work as a whole: '[it] embodies the hope of a human order in an inhuman and disordered time'.[50]

50. Quoted on back cover of Les Murray, *Fredy Neptune* (New York: Farrar, Straus and Giroux, 1999).

Journal of the Australian Catholic Historical Society, Volume 41/2020

David Coffey: Theologian of Spirit

Paul Crittenden[*]

David Coffey would sometimes say of a theologian that he or she was a historian of the subject, not a real theologian. What he had in mind was someone who thought that there was nothing more to say in theology, that it came to an end, let's say, when the Council of Trent closed in 1563, or with the definition of papal infallibility at the first Vatican Council. His own conception of the theologian's task is to take Scripture and tradition as the essential reference points, but always with a view to going forward, contributing in some measure to the development of doctrine and understanding. This was manifest in his first book, *Grace: The Gift of the Holy Spirit* and has remained characteristic of his many books and journal articles.[1] He recognised nonetheless that theology has an inbuilt historical character. For in going beyond what might be established about God by reason, its primary focus concerns God's presence in history as recorded in the Bible. From Genesis to Revelation, the Bible itself is a collection of documents with a history, many of which take the form of (putative) histories. So, theology, based in Scripture, has a history embodied in the development of doctrine, a history marked by a chequered

---

* Paul Crittendon is Emeritus Professor of Philosophy at the University of Sydney. He is the author of *Learning to be Moral: Philosophical Thoughts About Moral Development* (Atlantic Highlands, NJ: Humanities Press International, 1990); *Changing Orders; Scenes of Clerical and Academic Life* (Blackheath, NSW: Bradl & Schlesinger, 2008); *Sartre in Search of Ethics* (Newcastle upon Tyne: Cambridge Scholars, 2009); *Reason, Will and Emotion: Defending the Greek Tradition against Triune Consciousness* (New York: Palgrave Macmillan, 2012); and *Life Hereafter: The Rise and Decline of a Tradition* (New York: Palgrave Macmillan, 2020).

1. *Grace: The Gift of the Holy Spirit* (Sydney: Catholic Institute of Sydney, 1979); revised edition (Milwaukee: Marquette University Press, 2011).

story of scholarship and achievement along with schisms, heresies, disputes, bitter conflict, even war, tied up with the imperative for orthodox doctrine.

In seeking to address David's significance as a theologian, I propose to consider his contribution to several topics in their historical setting, focussed in each case on the Holy Spirit. The first concerns Spirit Christology. The second is the '*Filioque*' controversy, a cause of longstanding division concerning the Spirit between Greek and Latin Christianity. I will then comment on recent discussion of 'Third Article Theology', concerning the role of the Holy Spirit in salvation history. Before that, however, I should say a word about David Coffey himself.

Already in his schooldays, David had an acknowledged talent for music, mathematics, logical thinking, and quiet achievement generally. As a seminary student in the 1950s he was among the first to study in the newly established Faculty of Theology at Manly where he completed a doctorate in 1960. In a Rome-approved Faculty staffed by Rome-educated professors, the curriculum proceeded strictly on Roman lines. A different world opened up when he went abroad for two years of post-doctoral study in the Catholic Faculty of Theology at the University of Munich, under the guidance of Professors Michael Schmaus and Karl Rahner. This was in 1964 as the Second Vatican Council was approaching its end. Back in Sydney in 1967, he resumed what was to be a long career of teaching and research in the Catholic Institute of Sydney (in which the Manly Faculty was now incorporated). In time he took on—reluctantly, perhaps, but efficiently—the administrative roles of Dean and then President in the years that gave rise to the Sydney College of Divinity. Finally he was appointed in 1995 to a Chair in Systematic Theology at Marquette University, Milwaukee. There he spent a happy and productive decade before retiring as Professor Emeritus in 2006 and returning to Sydney.

The Munich years were critical in Coffey's theological formation, for they provided the basis for his continuing dialogue with Karl Rahner's theology. That connection involves the endorsement of Rahner's thought in many respects, but not without constructive criticism and commonly in ways that take Rahnerian ideas to a further level. David's published work is scholarly and demanding, not something to be dealt with in 'Readers' Digest' fashion. He is a 'theologians' theologian', which is to say that he doesn't write for the general reader, although he hopes that others might communicate his ideas more widely. A short survey of his thought can't delve very deeply, but must suffice in present circumstances.

Spirit and Word Christology

The Councils of Nicaea (325) and Constantinople (381) were concerned to clarify trinitarian doctrine. Subsequently, the Council of Chalcedon (451) proclaimed that Jesus Christ was truly God and truly human, begotten from the Father from eternity, born in time from the Virgin Mary. This teaching, with its emphasis on God the Son coming down to earth and taking human form, has constituted the primary expression of the Incarnation and the core of Christology ever since. Resting on the metaphor of descent from heaven, the doctrine is aptly described as a descending Christology focussed on the divinity of Christ—not over against his humanity, but in a way that has tended to overshadow it. The biblical witness lies primarily in John 1:14, a text that is not as clear as might appear in its common interpretation, 'The Word became flesh and lived among us'. This yields the alternative term Word (or Logos) Christology, the Word being God the Son. In troubled and disputed times in which belief impacted on the political order (and vice versa), the achievement of Chalcedon was of immense significance. But the price of the achievement meant that a complementary approach to Christology was ignored and subsequently forgotten for fifteen hundred years. Here the direction moves from the human side in being focussed on the elevation of the sacred humanity of Jesus to divine sonship. This was an approach taken in the School of Alexandria, culminating with Cyril of Alexandria (died 444). In this case the biblical basis was found in the Synoptic Gospels in their attention to the role of the Holy Spirit at the conception of Jesus and his baptism. The primary text is Luke 1:26–38. The relevant metaphor in this case is ascent—the elevation of the humanity of Jesus to divine sonship. Coffey summarises this ascending Christology as follows:

> The paradigm of all grace is Jesus Christ . . . The union of divinity and humanity in him must be understood as the elevation of the sacred humanity to divine Sonship, so that

> it is precisely in his humanity that Jesus is the Son of God. This elevation was brought about through the bestowal, by the Father, of the Holy Spirit as Spirit of Sonship, on Jesus in the act which at the same time created his humanity, sanctified it and united it in person with the pre-existent divine Son.[2]

The man Jesus came into existence in the act of anointing. The anointing by the Spirit is identical with his coming into being, hence identical with the incarnation of the Son of God.

Ascending Christology, as indicated, has its basis in the Synoptic gospels and complements the descending Christology of John's Gospel. With its focus on the anointing of Jesus by the Holy Spirit, it is now commonly called Spirit Christology. Taken together the two approaches provide a more profound expression of the teaching of Chalcedon that Jesus Christ was truly human and truly divine. Why was this complementary aspect of Christology overlooked at Chalcedon? Cyril of Alexandria, a leading thinker in giving systematic form to the Greek theology of the Trinity and the Incarnation, would have had the authority to argue the case for ascending Christology. But he had died seven years before the Council. One likely factor in the neglect of the approach was concern that attention to the elevation of the humanity of Jesus might be confused with earlier theories of adoptionism (the view that Jesus was not truly divine, but Son of God 'by adoption'). Another was the seemingly clear teaching of the Johannine *Logos* (Word) and its resonance with the rich concept of *Logos* in Hellenistic culture. For the next fifteen hundred years incarnation as descent constituted the full extent of Christology.

In bringing Spirit and Word Christology together, originally in his book *Grace: The Gift of the Holy Spirit*, Coffey was able to provide a fully coherent and simplified account of the fragmented Catholic doctrine of grace as unified around the anointing of the Holy Spirit. This anointing took place in Christ substantially and uniquely in the 'grace of union'; and it takes place in a dependent and secondary way in all human beings who share in his sonship. Ascending Christology culminates in the created grace of union, that is, the fully graced human nature of Jesus, in readiness for, but not attaining, the transcendence of the Incarnation itself. For that, what is needed is

2. David Coffey, *Grace: The Gift of the Holy Spirit* (Sydney: Catholic Institute of Sydney, 1979); revised edition (Milwaukee: Marquette University Press, 2011)

the descending Christology of Chalcedon, the divine nature joined with human nature. This complementary approach to Christology also led to the recovery from the distant past of a congruent account of the Trinity in which the Holy Spirit is conceived as the mutual love of the Father and the Son. But the trinitarian connection with Spirit Christology, essential as it is, and utterly central as it is to Coffey's theology, is a complex and complicating consideration—so I will set it aside to comment briefly on the significance of the recent recovery of Ascending or Spirit Christology.

The major consideration is that the grace of the Incarnation can be seen more clearly as historical in character in human terms, as unfolding and developing over time on the familiar pattern of human life in which the subject moves from birth to maturity to death. Coffey expresses this developmental dimension of Christ's divinity as follows:

> Even though the divine Sonship was bestowed on Jesus at the beginning of his life, it needed his history and his death for him to realize fully in his humanity the reality of the Son of God.[3]

The divine sonship of Jesus began in the first moment of his existence with the bestowal of the Holy Spirit, but its complete realization was a gradual process that reached its fulness only in his death. Beginning at his conception, the grace of the Holy Spirit filled each stage of his life. This leads Coffey to speak, by way of analogy, of the 'incarnation' of the Holy Spirit—'not in the sense of divine being incarnate in human being as in the Incarnation properly so called, but as divine love incarnate in human love, the love of Jesus'[4]

Thus:

> Parallel to the progressive actualization of the divine Sonship, there was a progressive actualization of the Holy Spirit in Jesus' transcendental love of the Father.[5]

---

3. David Coffey, *Grace: The Gift of the Holy Spirit*, 1979, 152; 2011, 87.
4. David Coffey, 'The Holy Spirit as the Mutual Love of the Father and the Son', in *Theological Studies*, 51 (1990): 193–229.
5. David Coffey, 'The "Incarnation" of the Holy Spirit in Christ', in *Theological Studies*, 45 (1984): 466–480.

His mission of preaching and healing after the years of obscurity in Nazareth reached its fulness in his death, the ultimate and supreme expression of his Spirit-filled love for humankind and of God the Father. For in Karl Rahner's words 'explicit love of neighbour is the primary act of the love of God'. In the full realization of his humanity in death, Christ was constituted as mediator between God and humankind with authority to send the Holy Spirit, the Spirit of divine love, upon the Church and the world. Jesus Christ, the Son of God made man, constitutes the heart of Christianity, but the guiding expression of divine love and the guiding power of human history towards its fulfilment is the proper mission of the Holy Spirit. That will be a subject for brief consideration later.

The *Filioque* Controversy between East and West

The second topic concerns the 'Filioque' controversy that arose between the Greek and Latin Church. Along with the Western Patristic tradition associated especially with Augustine, David Coffey's early research took him to the Eastern (Greek) Fathers, notably Athanasius and Cyril of Alexandria, also the Cappadocians—Basil of Caesarea, Gregory Nazianzus, and Gregory of Nyssa, a galaxy of theologians (and saints) around the time of the first Council of Constantinople (381). His interest in the *Filioque* topic appears and re-appears in his publications over the years. Here I will refer mainly to his article 'The Roman "Clarification" of the Filioque'.[6]

The Council of Nicaea (325) affirmed belief in God the Father and the Son in clear terms, but said nothing more of the Spirit than, 'We believe in the Holy Spirit'. This terseness reflected a longstanding degree of uncertainty and disagreement about the divinity of the Holy Spirit. Indeed, a vocal group of bishops had emerged known as 'Opponents of the Spirit' (*Pneumatomachians*) because they treated the Spirit as a lesser power, not truly God. Faced with this situation the first Council of Constantinople (381) affirmed the divinity of the Spirit with the Father and the Son in the familiar Creed somewhat misleadingly called the 'Nicene Creed':

6. David Coffey, 'The Roman "Clarification" of the Filioque', in *International Journal of Systematic Theology*, 5 (2003): 3–21.

> And we believe in the Holy Spirit, the Lord and Giver of Life, who *proceeds from the Father*, who together with the Father and the Son is worshipped and glorified, who has spoken through the prophets. (Emphasis added.)

The pope sent representatives to the Council, but it took some time before the West accepted the doctrinal decisions of the Council of Constantinople as universally binding. Meanwhile, a conciliar agreement emerged in the following century that the short Nicene Creed, expanded at Constantinople, should not be altered except by an ecumenical Council. According to the Creed, the Spirit proceeds from the Father. A generation or so after the first Council of Constantinople, however, Augustine in the West wrote a long treatise on the Trinity in which he proposed that the Holy Spirit proceeds from the Father and from the Son, principally from the Father, but by a double procession as from a single principle. This set the basis for an eventual separation between East and West: in keeping with the Nicene-Constantinopolitan Creed, the East affirmed that the Spirit proceeds from the Father alone; following Augustine, the West came to affirm that the Spirit proceeds from the Father and the Son (*ex Patre Filioque*). (Augustine makes no reference in this context to the Council of Constantinople or the Greek Fathers.)

For the next two hundred years the Creed remained unchanged. But at a local Synod of bishops in Toledo in 589, a resolution decided to amend it to say that the Spirit proceeds 'from the Father and the Son' (*Filioque* in Latin). In time this formula spread from Spain to France and Germany and the issue became a cause of increasing tension as Church and State powers in the West exerted pressure on the East to conform. Charlemagne, the Emperor of the Romans, took up the cause with particular enthusiasm in looking to extend his authority in the East. Even so, Pope Leo III rejected his demand for the universal adoption of the *Filioque* early in the ninth century. Two hundred years later Rome changed its mind when Benedict VIII, a Pope known for his military initiatives and political interests, formally approved the addition of the *Filioque* to the Creed at the request of Emperor Henry II in 1014. The decisive break came forty years later, occasioned critically by the ham-fisted diplomacy of Cardinal Humbert whom Pope Leo IX had sent to Constantinople to negotiate a settlement. The mission came to nought when Humbert burst into the Cathedral of Hagia Sophia in 1054 and placed a papal excommunication of the Patriarch, Michael Cerularius, on the high altar. A week later, the Patriarch responded by anathematising the pope.

In summary, the East was committed to the original Constantinopolitan Creed as expressing the belief that the Spirit proceeds from the Father alone (*monopatrism*), as against the later teaching in the West of a double procession, from Father and Son acting as a single principle. Over the centuries, the Greek Patriarchs, Michael Photius in particular, had set out their objections to the addition of the *Filioque*, arguing that its theological basis was open to question and objecting to it as an interpolation made without reference to a general Council. They recognised nonetheless the necessity for a relation between Son and Spirit within the Trinity—proposing for instance that the Spirit proceeds from the Father (alone) but through the Son as mediator or that the Spirit is 'of the Son' but not 'from the Son', or that the Spirit proceeds from the Father and reposes on the Son. Following the schism of 1054, the Greek commitment to the ultimacy of the Father alone as cause of the Son and equally of the Spirit, was pitted against the Latin insistence that reunion could proceed only if the Byzantine Church would affirm the *Filioque*.

The first major attempt at reunion was at the Second Council of Lyon (1274). Here the Greek delegates were told that the double procession of the Holy Spirit 'is the unchangeable and true doctrine of the orthodox Fathers and Doctors, both Latin and Greek'. The Greeks, not unfamiliar with the Greek Fathers and Doctors, were not impressed. The next and last major attempt at reunion was at the Council of Florence (1439) where it seemed that all had been resolved. In the Bull of Union with the Greeks, the Council affirmed the double procession of the Spirit, 'from the Father and the Son' and declared that this was satisfied by the Eastern formula 'from the Father through the Son'. Anxious to receive help from the West with the rising threat of Ottoman forces, the Greek representatives agreed. The bells rang, the heavens were called on to rejoice, but when the Eastern bishops returned home, the faithful would have none of it. In any case everything changed soon afterwards with the fall of Constantinople and the Byzantine Empire in 1453.

For any significant development beyond Florence, one must move forward more than five hundred years to the Second Vatican

Council. Delegates from the Orthodox Churches attended the Council, and at its end in 1965 Pope Paul VI and Athenagoras I, Patriarch of Constantinople, lifted the respective excommunications of 1054. Numerous meetings have followed in the past half-century, but without the prospect of achieving agreement. Perhaps the most promising development arose with a visit to Rome by Bartholomew I, Patriarch of Constantinople, in 1995. On the occasion Pope John Paul II requested a 'clarification' of the *Filioque* doctrine with a view to bringing out its harmony with the Creed of Nicene-Constantinople—'the Father as the source of the whole Trinity, the one origin both of the Son and the Holy Spirit'. In response, the Pontifical Council for Promoting Christian Unity produced a document, 'The Greek and Latin Traditions regarding the Procession of the Holy Spirit', published in the English language version of *L'Osservatore Romano,* 20 September 1995.

In a general comment on the dispute, David Coffey observes that, without looking closely, the contending formulations, *'from the Father and the Son'* and *'from the Father through the Son'* might be counted as no more than a terminological difference, not grounds for a major disagreement. Considered more closely, he suggests, they are different but related in that the 'through the Son' formula was a significant step towards the development of the 'and from the Son' formula in the West. The Roman Clarification, he comments, is ecumenically sensitive, an attempt to argue that the two traditions are complementary, specifically that the 'Filioque' does not contradict the Eastern view. This shows up in an initial affirmation of the monarchy of the Father as the ultimate source (cause) of the Holy Spirit and of the Son in keeping with the Creed of Constantinople. But the Roman Clarification repeats the questionable Florence claim that in employing the formula 'through the Son', the Eastern Fathers attributed an instrumental role to the Son akin to the '*Filioque*', yielding a difference in emphasis rather than content. Coffey questions this ready assimilation of East with West, in part because the document makes no reference to the decree issued at the Council of Florence. The Clarification is well-intentioned, he suggests, but it appears to play down the full force of the *Filioque*, presumably to make it more palatable to the Orthodox.

The Catholic teaching at Florence affirms that the 'Holy Spirit is eternally from the Father and the Son and has his essence and subsistent being at once from the Father and the Son, and he proceeds eternally from both as from one principle and one spiration'. (Talk of the inner being of the divine Trinity inevitably relies on metaphors.) The decree further declares that this is what the Eastern Fathers tended towards in saying that 'the Holy Spirit proceeds from the Father through the Son'. As the theologian Yves Congar observes, Florence interpreted the Eastern 'through the Son' in the light of the Western *Filioque*—from which he concludes that 'Florence was too great a victory for the Latins and the papacy for it to be a full Council of union'.[7] Or as Coffey puts it, 'Florence represented nothing less than the capitulation to the West on the part of the East at a time when the East was under intense political pressure to come to an agreement'.[8]

What is Coffey's proposed resolution to the schism? Florence was an ecumenical Council, which means that its doctrinal teaching cannot be revoked. In any case, the 'Filioque' has long been a major theological tradition in trinitarian doctrine in the West. Nonetheless, he considers that the Florentine declaration was one-sided and wrong in equating the Greek 'through the Son' with the *Filioque*. The formulas are not equivalent. But, as indicated, they are complementary in that the one is subsumed in the other. Now, union between East and West does not require that the parties say the same thing: 'it suffices that each be convinced that the formula of the other does not contradict its own and that both are biblically legitimate'. For the West, the importance of the *Filioque* rests on two considerations: that in Scripture the Holy Spirit is confessed as the Spirit of the Son as well as the Spirit of the Father; and that this manifests itself in a correspondence between the Trinity revealed at work in the world and internal relations in the eternal Trinity. At the same time, the one operation in the double procession involves two levels: the Spirit proceeds principally from the Father as ultimate principle or origin and from the Son on the basis of a power communicated by the Father. In this way, the *Filioque* acknowledges the monarchy of the Father albeit not as professed by the Greek, Byzantine, or Orthodox Churches over the centuries.

7. Yves Congar, *I Believe in the Holy Spirit*, volume 3 (New York: Herder and Herder, 1997), 187.
8. Coffey, 'The Roman "Clarification" of the Filioque', 10.

In looking for a way forward, Coffey proposes that 'although the two faith professions are not identical in content, they are not necessarily exclusive, and there is room for each in the one *communio* or *koinwnia*'.[9] This was the way it was before the Synod of Toledo (589) and even up to the schism of 1054. Communion allows for 'legitimate diversity of expression *within* one faith'.[10] An agreement on these lines would not resolve a complex history of misunderstanding, separation, and genuine differences in belief, religious practices, and conceptions of papal primacy. But it would be a considerable development in its own right and of great value for all concerned.

The Proper Mission of the Holy Spirit

On the model of the Holy Spirit in the life of Christ, Coffey explores the Spirit's mission in the Church and the unfolding course of salvation-history. That the Spirit has a proper mission in relation to Christ and the world is of special significance, he notes, in Orthodox theology and faith. In its absence, Western theology lacks 'a firm basis for the development of fruitful dialogue with the East'.[11] In a wider context, this absence also reflects a long-established reluctance to recognise the continuing validity of God's covenant with the Jewish people, and the presence of the Spirit in world religions, and in the lives of people of good will everywhere.

The reluctance to recognise a proper mission for the Spirit has a history going back to early debates about the Trinity, especially the Western emphasis on divine unity first in advance of the trinity of persons as against the Eastern focus on the three distinct persons in advance of showing how they share one divine nature. That God the Son has a proper mission as the Word made flesh was clear. And the ultimacy of God the Father as cause or principle within the godhead is also clear. That aside, the prevailing general principle in the West is that divine activity in the world is common to all three persons as united in the one nature. The Holy Spirit was there with Father and Son at creation and the incarnation, but essentially as sharing

9. Coffey, 'The Roman "Clarification" of the Filioque', 21.
10. Coffey, 'The Roman "Clarification" of the Filioque', 12.
11. David Coffey, 'A Proper Mission of the Holy Spirit', in *Theological Studies*, 47 (1986): 227.

the divine nature. The Latin reluctance to acknowledge a proper mission for the Spirit may have been linked with a growing suspicion of excessive charismatic-type phenomena originally manifested at Pentecost. This concern may have increased in the Middle Ages when the mystic Joachim of Fiore envisaged a trinitarian conception of history, marked by an age of God the Father, a second age of God the Son incarnate, and finally a third age of the Holy Spirit to be inaugurated, he predicted, in 1260. The Church intervened well in advance at the fourth Lateran Council (1215) and condemned his views as heretical and, for good measure, insane.

Joachim's prophecy of a third age of the Spirit did not eventuate. But the recovery of Spirit Christology in the twentieth century has helped to reshape the central doctrines of Christianity. Late in his life Karl Rahner spoke prophetically of the possible emergence of a new universal theology related to the Spirit:

> Taking account of the universal salvific will of God and in legitimate respect for all the major world religions outside of Christianity, this approach may perhaps make a pneumatology, a teaching of the inmost, divinizing gift of grace for all human beings (as an offer to their freedom), the fundamental point of departure for its entire theology, and then attempt at this point . . . to gain a real and radical understanding of Christology. For a theology of this kind what is needed is attention to scriptural passages which extol the universal salvific will of God, which let the Spirit speak through all the prophets and make known that the Spirit has been poured out on all flesh ('Jesus Christ in the Non-Christian Religions.[12]

This prospect has taken shape in Spirit Christology or more broadly in what is called 'Third Article Theology', that is, theology related to the third article of the Creed, belief in the Holy Spirit.

In Coffey's account, the title by which the Spirit has a proper mission is not linked with the phenomena or practices associated with modern Pentecostalist-type movements. It has its basis firmly in Christ's Spirit-filled love of neighbour as the pattern of Christian

12. Karl Rahner, *Theological Investigations*, volume 17 (London: Darton, Longman & Todd, 1981), 39–50, 17.

life, for which the ultimate ground lies in the Father's love for the Son in the Trinity in bestowing the Spirit of love on the Son eternally. The Holy Spirit enters the plan of salvation definitively through his personal action at the beginning of Jesus' life, constituting him Son of God. The Spirit then enters upon his proper mission to the world in being sent by the risen Christ, having become 'incarnate' in Jesus' love of God and neighbour. In this context Coffey adopts Rahner's term 'the Spirit of Christ as entelechy' where entelechy means 'directive principle'. This is the Spirit who was active in creation, in prophecy, and throughout Christ's mission, and who moves the world thereafter in its grace-filled return to God. Given the salvific will of God, the Spirit, present in Christ in a supreme and unique form, is open in a secondary manner to every human being through grace. In Coffey's words,

> In the person of Jesus the Holy Spirit as entelechy is completed and perfected as outpoured Spirit. The Holy Spirit relives this personal history [in Christ] to varying degrees in the life of every human being. All are affected by the Spirit of Christ as entelechy guiding them to salvation.[13]

This is universal in reach, for where there is love of neighbour there is love of God, and where there is love of God, there is the Spirit of Christ.

I have written elsewhere that Coffey's theology is daring in many respects yet closely argued and closely grounded in scripture and the patristic and scholastic traditions as well as modern thought. It is also fundamentally constructive. Above all his Spirit Christology, beginning in his seminal book on grace, yields a reshaping and enlargement of traditional theology, an illuminating synthesis of the main areas of theological inquiry. Taking Pneumatology and Christology as the starting point, there follows a theology of the Trinity, a theology of grace, a theology of the Church, a theology of world religions, and an eschatology embracing all human beings and the history of the world. David Coffey is a theologian of international significance in his time.

---

13. David Coffey, 'A Trinitarian Response', in *Theological Studies*, 69 (2008): 864.

The Reverend Emeritus Professor David Michael Coffey: Selected References

Books

Grace: The Gift of the Holy Spirit (Sydney: CIS, 1979); revised edition (Milwaukee: Marquette University Press, 2011)

Deus Trinitas: The Doctrine of the Triune God (New York: Oxford University Press, 1999)

'Did You Receive the Holy Spirit When You Believed?' Some Basic Questions for Pneumatology (Milwaukee: Marquette University Press, 2005)

Journal Articles

'The Teaching of the Constantinopolitan Creed on the Holy Spirit', in *Issues for the Australian Church,* edited by Neil Brown (Sydney: CIS, 1982), 65–75

'The "Incarnation" of the Holy Spirit in Christ', in *Theological Studies,* 45 (1984): 466–80

'A Proper Mission of the Holy Spirit', in *Theological Studies,* 47 (1986): 227–50

'The Holy Spirit as the Mutual Love of the Father and the Son', in *Theological Studies,* 51 (1990): 193–229

'The Spirit of Christ as Entelechy', in *Philosophy and Theology* 10 (2001): 363–98

'The Roman "Clarification" of the Filioque', in *International Journal of Systematic Theology,* 5 (2003): 3–21

'A Trinitarian Response', in *Theological Studies,* 69 (2008): 852–74

'The Method of Third Article Theology', *Third Article Theology,* edited by Myk Habets (Minneapolis: Fortress Press, 2016), 21–36

Journal of the Australian Catholic Historical Society, Volume 41/2020

Celebrating a Quiet Revolution: A Practical Response to Vatican 2: Celebrating the Life and Achievements of the Institute of Counselling—Archdiocese of Sydney

*Ron Perry, Bryan Gray and Alison Turner**

Ron Perry:

It is fifty years since the first courses of the Institute of Counselling, Archdiocese of Sydney began. It is certainly worth celebrating.

Fr Ed Campion, well known here, named the Institute as **one of the significant achievements of the Archdiocese of Sydney** after the Second Vatican Council. That is an important and perhaps surprising statement from such a significant historian.

The late Dr David Bollen is a core figure. A prize-winning historian, he researched both the objective and the subjective history of the Institute, producing an extraordinary book.[1] David is also symbolic of so many contributors to this quiet revolution—contributors characterised by GENEROSITY. There was another feature in so many contributors—a belief that what was being done was also valuable and exciting.

David became interested in the story and found himself so intrigued that he did lengthy research—unpaid but extraordinarily detailed and, as we will keep saying, both objective and subjective.

Like many quiet revolutions, it was not specifically intended as a revolution . . . it became one in the context (the time in the Church and in society) in which it came into being and flourished.

---

* Ronald Perry was Founding Director of the ICS and Psychologist; Bryan Gray was Consultant Psychologist and long-term lecturer (ICS); Alison Turner was Second Director (ICS) and Counselling Psychologist. This is the edited text of talks given to the Australian Catholic Historical Society on 15 November 2020.

1. David Bollen, *Opening Up: A history of the Institute of Counselling* (Melbourne: John Garratt Publishing, 2009).

I am going to describe some of the beginnings. Bryan will help us search out some of why it was revolutionary—in a quiet way!!—and Alison will describe some of the later factors and events which have led to its disappearance.

It DID start from the Sydney Archdiocesan Pastoral Council—a body which was in itself an outcome of Vatican 2. This particular resolution started with a letter to that Pastoral Council from social worker Valda Ferns working then at Caritas, a psychiatric arm of St Vincent's Hospital.

She was concerned that adolescents with emotional difficulties were being hospitalised with disturbed adults as there was nowhere else for them. The suggestion was that the Church set up an institution for disturbed adolescents.

Her question was taken up at the Pastoral Council where Mary Lewis, a leading social worker at the Catholic Family Welfare Bureau, a colleague and friend of Valda Ferns, was a member.

The idea was investigated but it was judged impractical for the Church to set up a psychiatric institution. However Mary Lewis took up an alternative but related need. She was counselling a lot of adolescents. She was also involved with helping leading people in the Catholic Education system (mostly Religious Sisters and Brothers at that time) to assist the adolescents she was counselling. She was also involved in assisting people involved in both formation and service (ministry) in the Religious Orders. She could therefore underline a then current need—for key people both those involved in education and those involved in religious formation to have a better understanding of human development and counselling.

I keep referring to the social context of the times . . . the need for counselling was being recognised and accepted more broadly . . . In the Protestant Churches, counselling and therapy were sometimes being taken up instead of traditional ministry. Almost all of the original students at the Institute were religious or priests and the study was seen as enriching to their ministry as well as necessary.

The concept of a training program was explored and accepted by the Pastoral Council. The project was handed over to the Catholic Family Welfare Bureau to carry forward. The team there knew or were in contact with many of the leading professionals in related fields in Sydney. This meant that those involved with developing the course were experienced, informed and thoughtful practitioners themselves. It also meant that they could access leading practitioners and lecturers from various services and Universities in Sydney.

As we celebrate the revolution that the Institute was able to become, we have to acknowledge that it occurred in a social context as well as a Church context.

I was actually studying in Rome while the Vatican Council was proceeding . . . I could and did read an English translation of the Vat 2 document **The church in the modern world** before it was presented, argued about and the final version was approved and passed.

The way the Church spoke was changing—you could think more broadly—you could think of talking to the modern world!! In a way this was revolutionary. However talking to the modern world would not necessarily be universally straightforward.

My next experience was at a Jesuit-led program designed to study the documents of Vatican 2 in preparation for teaching them and using them in ministry and Church formation. There were missionaries there from all over the world. The new ideas and questions were exciting but also challenging for all of us. Some of the stories were very poignant.

There were three priests there from an African country. Two were keen young priests; the other a quite senior Monsignor. After a time, the Monsignor was not attending classes. We asked the younger priests what was happening. Well, they said, he comes from an animist culture. He was able to put that culture aside and learn the scholastic philosophy and theology we were taught but it is too hard for him now to try to put that aside and learn all this new thinking.

I think that story underlines what was happening in many places but often not admitted or dealt with. The 'freedom' to question was certainly inspiring but we could forget that letting go of previous 'certainties' could be at least unsettling and sometimes quite disturbing. I doubt if this was much understood or addressed. It did occur at the same time as society itself was questioning many other 'certainties' in terms of structures, sexual mores and other institutions.

The Institute did not have to deal with these questions directly but training in counselling meant that people had to learn to listen to and accept different experiences—including different reactions to the modern world. The Institute had to be prepared to hear and hold a variety of experiences and reactions without offering immediate and comprehensive answers. The African Bishop's response indicates some of what might occur.

At this same program, I was introduced to the strange experience called 'group work' which was then achieving recognition in various training programs, both secular and religious.

You sat in a group, the 'leader' gave very little direction and you talked about what was interesting, concerning, disturbing in your personal experience (which at that time could include all the changes resulting from the documents of the Council).

The members of these groups experienced lots of uncertainty, lots of anxiety, lots of developing openness to the experiences of other people. Overall generally there was movement from an anxious situation to a mutually supportive group of people.

Interestingly for the planning of the Institute of Counselling, group work was beginning to be seen as an essential component of training in counselling and therapy. Bryan will explore some examples of how central that learning could be.

It can seem strange to say it fifty years on, but that acceptance of human experience and the questions that come from that acceptance was a significant part of the quiet revolution.

Back in Australia the place of and need for counselling and informed counsellors was beginning to be felt. Christian Brother Mark Egan from the United States toured Australia explaining counselling and its place.

So with the help of those clinicians at Catholic Family Welfare we developed a course. At first it consisted of lectures and this 'new' entity—group work.

Partly because of the wide reach of the Catholic Family Welfare Bureau clinicians, the Institute students were usually treated to inspiring specialised lecturers whose input helped make the course attractive and energising.

With regard to the group work, it is sufficient here to say that it accepted the conviction that in learning counselling you had to listen to a variety of personal experiences. Less obviously but also central, you also had to take account of your own personal experiences, difficulties and limitations. Learning counselling was more than being lectured at and learning what was said. In a way this too was revolutionary.

Quite important in the group work were the residential week-ends which offered an intensity as well as a support.

The next task for the Institute would be to keep up with the dramatic learning that was going on in the profession. So we soon learnt to incorporate 'counselling skills' into the Institute curriculum. Di Carmody was one of our most consistent and creative contributors in that area. She and so many others led the training with that energy and generosity I have already underlined.

If there was a quiet revolution, it depended so largely on that wonderful gift from so many people. They were all learning too and they experienced and promoted the excitement that made so much worthwhile.

In naming generosity I need to mention the Religious Orders. The Marist Brothers, the Christian Brothers, the North Sydney Mercy Sisters all assisted by making learning and administrative spaces available.

It is not possible to acknowledge contributors individually. There were Board members, lecturers, group leaders, administrators, librarians, office workers, caterers and other helpers. There was so much talent and leadership so much generosity and excitement that accompanied the learning. The quiet revolution attracted a lot of thoughtful, talented generous people.

As David Bollen points out in his history, the clientele at first was almost entirely from religious orders and the clergy, later Catholic lay people . We never excluded others but it was some time before the Institute learners were a broader group. We often had Bishops bless the end of year ceremonies. It was an archdiocesan institution.

Before I finish, some simple stories about the learning:

I met an ex-student one morning at an oval in Willoughby. Her statement was: 'I am not afraid of anything any more after surviving those groups'!

Some of the learning was painful even if profound.

A tradie came to see me once—probably sent by his wife who was doing the course. His statement was 'I don't understand how one person doing a course can affect a whole family'!

And just recently I was talking to a colleague who had been a long-time lecturer and who was recalling attending an end of year ceremony where the qualifications gained (a Graduate Certificate in this case I think) were being given. He remembered seeing a woman and her daughter being photographed with the attending Bishop. He said 'The look on the daughter admiring her mother ('Good on you Mum' was implied) was so delightful. Many who attended, women especially, had not had the chance to do formal study and this daughter was so pleased both for her mother and for her qualification.

I have briefly noted some of the beginnings of the Institute and some of the contextual issues that were present at that time.

We are celebrating so much learning, so many challenges, so much generosity, so much impact on people's lives and even on institutions.

I have suggested previously that the Institute in some ways rode the waves of the time—waves that were rolling in society as well as in the Church. For many it became a useful surf-board for those times as well as an enriching training in counselling.

Bryan Gray:

Introduction:

Three Strands of the Institute of Counselling Course

1. Lectures which exposed students to established ideas in the field of counselling.
2. Skills Training which taught key practices in listening and responding in counselling.
3. Experiential Group Work which gave students the opportunity to learn from their own experience in a group whose Primary Task was to increase their awareness of group dynamics and the challenge of taking up their own authority as a group member.

Three sets of interrelated factors underpinned this experience:

1. Personal: The individual . . . the other . . . the group
2. Modalities: Cognition, Emotion and Behaviour.
3. Tenses: Past, Present, Future.

Four selected times in the life of the experiential group will illustrate how becoming attentive to these interactions increases this self and group awareness. The Group Facilitator's role and the focus on the Primary Task of learning from this experience will be illustrated in four 'scenes' taken from a group experience.

Scene 1.

When the group met, as the Facilitator I told the group that the Primary Task of the exercise was to become aware of what was happening in the group and its relation to themselves as members.

Silence!

One group member began crying. Group members immediately focused on her 'problem'.

I said, 'I wonder if anyone else is anxious about working with me'.

This was my attempt to 'hold' the group which had just been born and to relate to the group members in the very earliest moments of the group life.

The group member stopped crying. She never cried again in the life of the group.

Gradually, members of the group tentatively began to express something of how they felt about working with me. They began to see how they shared in some way their concerns about working with me as the Facilitator.

Scene 2.

Further in the group's life a member reported to the group about a very disturbing dream he'd had.

"I set out to go somewhere in a foreign country. I has no idea where I was, where I was going or what I was looking for. Fleeting by-passers didn't notice me. I couldn't speak their language and was overwhelmed by being the outsider and foreigner. I kept trying to clarify where I was going, but to no avail. I woke up feeling very disturbed."

The group became very involved in interpreting the dream.

I listened to these discussions and then drew the group's attention to the Primary Task by saying: "could this be something like you are experiencing in this group with me?"

The discussion that opened up helped the members see how they could access their group experience by 'associating' other dreams, images and metaphors with the member's dream.

This second "scene" illustrated how reflection on a member's experience can lead increased sharing, enhancing and active membership.

Scene 3.

About midpoint in the group's life members seemed to be sharing in circular comments, observations and discussions. I thought that the group was beginning to feel frustrated and mildly depressed.

I wondered what might be limiting the sense of exploration which had become part of the culture for the group to this point. I tentatively formed an hypothesis that they were collectively anxious about what would happen in the group if they took more authority to introduce secretly held ideas and observations.

I put my question to the group.

A different type of silence ensued.

Over some weeks members expressed their concern about the possibility of disharmony, argument and rejection if they used their own authorisation as a member. Some went further and questioned whether I would 'leave it to them to solve any problems', implying that I would abandon my role and them!

Over some weeks the question of taking 'personal authority' in group membership began to be explored leading to some suggesting that each person had the opportunity to learn how to voice their opinions on this group and in other groups of which they were a member. (E.g. family, work, Church).

This critical phase in the group experience raised themes of envy, jealousy and emotions that silenced ideas being articulated and explored.

Scene 4.

The last session of the group's life began with several members keen to talk about various moments of significance to them. These included being bewildered but not knowing how to connect with others in the group, gratitude to other members for their support, learning how make membership connections in ways they hadn't know about before, expressions of sadness that they would miss them and the meetings, surprise at how the journey had unfolded and how to say 'goodbye'.

I observed and noted that there was no mention of 'regrets'.

They took up the observation.

Some even said that they thought that I should have been more active and involved.

I noted with them that they were talking as if 'learning time' ended with the group's lifetime.

The final part of the last session opened up questions about continuing experiential learning.

Final Comment.

To the extent that some transformative learning occurred during this group experience, one could wonder how this flowed on into members' lives in their families, work groups and Church membership. Imagine the outcome of using personal authority as a group member.

Alison Turner:
So, what happened? How did it come about that this unique and wonderful Institute, described so eloquently by Ron and Bryan, no longer exists?

It's going to be difficult to write about the Institute, without mentioning quite a lot of people. While the Institute's life as an entity lasted forty-three years, 1970–2013, it was the people who worked within it that gave it life. As David Bollen aptly noted in *Opening Up* 'people did not so much work for the Institute, as comprise it.'

I became Director in 2006; it was 'an in-house succession' to use David Bollen's description. I had been assisting Margaret McGovern with the preparation of the voluminous documentation required for possible Higher Education Board (HEB) accreditation, which we attained in late 2003, the same year Marg died. I was fortunate: the foundations and scaffolding of the Institute were in great shape, its reputation solid and respected thanks to Ron's stewardship. The Institute was certainly a trail blazer within the history of counselling in Australia. In that sense, continuing from that solid base made my job easy.

By the time I became Director we were based in a federation house named The Cottage on the campus of the Australian Catholic University (ACU) in Strathfield. Ron had managed to get a three-year lease and we were gearing up for another HEB accreditation process in 2006. We also applied and attained Government assistance through Fee Help, a student loan scheme for Post Graduate Students, plus we applied for and gained Charity status, so we were swamped with paperwork that year, as well as getting on with our usual business of teaching. It was a heady time.

In 2006 we were accredited with HEB for five years, which gave us some breathing space to get on with the core business of running our courses. We underwent a few transitions in those five years, with some long time Institute people moving on. However, the heart and soul of the Institute continued to beat strongly. Patrick and Barbara Lewis stepped into the breach on several occasions and were a great support. By this time the student requirement for professionally recognised degrees had increased significantly. Therefore, at the next HEB accreditation in 2012 apart from reaccrediting the Institute's original courses there was the addition of a new master's course with specialty units in drug and alcohol counselling, child and adolescent counselling and bereavement counselling.

During all three accreditation processes the Institute managed to maintain its mode of teaching, which by University standards was heavy on hours and labour intensive. There was a large component of experiential group work encompassing counselling skills and, most importantly, personal development (a vital component of counsellor education) via our interaction groups. Our courses had many more hours than the HEB allowed, especially compared to the many courses that were now sprouting up in competition. However, the HEB accepted our rationale and despite jumping through a few hoops and making small concessions we continued to retain the unique identity and substance of our courses. No mean feat.

Fully qualified Psychologists and Psychotherapists were employed to run the interaction groups on their own. We had always had two group facilitators, however now that casual staff with professional qualifications were being paid market rate renumeration, the budget could not stretch to more than one facilitator. The same applied to the skills groups. We were massaging where we could whilst ensuring the quality of the courses was retained.

This is all the good news, but I still haven't told you what happened. We were sailing along well when we were approached by ACU to undertake the possibility of an amalgamation. They were keen to have counselling courses added to their curriculum offerings. The Institute of Counselling Board was keen to explore this option as it had been discussed as a possibility over the years at Board level. We were on the ACU campus, a ready-made product with an excellent reputation and part of the Catholic family. What could possibly go wrong?

This is a good time to mention that I am eternally grateful to Erin White for helping us find David Bollen. David was an academic, an historian, and an award-winning author, having won the NSW Premiers Literary Award for local history with his book *Up on the Hill*, a history of St Patrick's College Goulburn.[2] What a find! The Institute

2. David Bollen, *Up on the Hill: A History of St Patrick's College, Goulburn* (Sydney: UNSW Press, 2008).

of Counselling History Committee comprised of Ron Perry, Bryan Gray, Erin White, Ken Paul, Michael Costigan and me. Thank God for that committee and the fact our history was recorded so brilliantly and expertly by David, just in the nick of time. *Opening Up: A history of the Institute of Counselling*, was published in 2009.

Back to what happened. Ann Mulheron and I met with the hierarchy of ACU many times over the course of a year, firstly to explore the options and eventually to negotiate a Memorandum of Agreement. Those meetings went very well. In particular our main non-negotiable was to retain our mode of teaching. The group work was our signature tune and a vital and core part of our courses. We questioned how our course could be viable within a University semester system and the consequent budgetary constraints. We were assured that our requirements could be accommodated and a detailed agreement that included specific funding arrangements for the group work was formulated. The Institute of Counselling Board met with the powers that be at ACU and an agreement was signed off in 2012. The Institute was welcomed into the ACU family. At the time I likened it to a first cousin, related but one step removed, from a different family but close enough to give us a suitable home. A ceremony was held on campus to commemorate the event and the task began of transitioning students into ACU.

The transition was fairly seamless, with no disruption to the students' course work or progression. However, behind the scenes, within a few short months, the wheels were beginning to fall off. The first thing to go was the provision of a meal for the lecturers. This had been a ritual since 1970. I understood there would be some culling of extras to assist with budgeting, so I adopted the view that change needed to happen, and I adapted to those changes, although sometimes reluctantly, one, by one, by one. The course hours needed to be culled to fit into University semesters, whereas the HEB had not required that of us. The group work was constantly under threat. I would be contacted by the finance department, which was based in Brisbane, on a regular basis and asked, 'Why are we paying five lecturers instead of one for fifty students?' Another long explanation would ensue. The enormous national system of ACU did not seem to have a way of cross fertilising its information and my explanations became a revolving repetitive pattern.

As the changes kept coming it felt like each week there was another battle to fight in regard to honouring the Memorandum of Agreement, which by this time was beginning to look like a distant memory. Towards the end of that first year I was invited to breakfast with the person in charge of several faculties at the time. During that breakfast a paper was pushed across the table towards me 'Alison you need to fix this'. The paper contained the budget for the Institute over the last six months. 'But we have an agreement!' I exclaimed. The response was, 'I know you will understand, this cannot continue'.

This was unexpected, stressful and heartbreaking, and I was not inclined to try and understand. The premise of embarking on this future pathway was for the Institute to live on in a system where it was not overly dependent on the Director and the courses could continue in perpetuity. However, the system we were encountering was large and cumbersome. ACU was a national University and they wanted complete uniformity across campuses in all states. How on earth were they going to replicate the Institute across the cities of Australia? This was a system under stress, and we would be the collateral damage.

There was no longer an Institute Board or Academic Committee, we had dropped our HEB accreditation, our Registration as a Training Organisation and our Charity status. The Institute was no longer an entity in the legal sense. There was only me and Ann Mulheron in terms of permanent academic staff. I decided to get a group of the old guard together and hold a meeting to talk over what was happening and the decision I had come to. I needed a group. There were about twelve of us squeezed into a circle in the board room that night, amongst them, Ron Perry, Bryan Gray, Erin White, Patrick Lewis, Lorraine Rose, David Leary, Mal and Di McKissock, Ann Mulheron and me. I voiced to the group that I feared if the Institute remained within ACU that it would no longer resemble itself in any shape or form. We would exist in name only; I could not bear the thought. I wanted to withdraw the Institute from ACU. It felt surreal. How could this be happening?

As Bryan mentioned, Universities are not favourable to experiential learning; to use Bryan's words they are in the business of teaching students what other people think. We also taught theory, but in counselling work it's also vital to know your own mind and to have the personal authority and creativity to respond to intense and difficult emotional situations with some authenticity, not with rote theoretical phrases. Learning from experience is a cornerstone of counselling training and our courses excelled at it.

In hindsight, maybe we should have tried foster care before the full adoption, but regardless the fit was not good, the cousin had been harmed, and further damage was imminent, so removal was the safest option.

So, the Institute did not die, it finished while well and truly alive, with a full complement of students, and financially viable. Due to the fact that there was no longer an Institute in the sense of it being a registered entity, I liaised with ACU to have the Institute's financial reserves donated to The National Centre for Childhood Grief (NCCG). They provide a free service to children and adolescents who have experienced a significant death. $170,000 was transferred to the NCCG on behalf of the IC. The current Clinical Director of the NCCG, Dr Liz Mann is a graduate of the Institute, which was a heart-warming thought amongst the personal distress of this situation.

As a supervisor to other counsellors, I see the reverberations of the Institute's learning in those who live out its ethos in their counselling work. Interestingly, my PhD thesis was titled Mutuality in the Therapeutic Relationship. I don't think I have mentioned yet that I was a student at the Institute. I did all three courses and I learnt more about human relationships and mutuality at the Institute than in any other area of study. Despite the fact the Institute no longer exists in its physical form, it lives on in the hearts and minds of all those, like myself, who grew and transformed personally and professionally through their association with it.

Book Review

Michael Hayes: The life of a 1798 Wexford Rebel in Sydney

Author: Vivienne Keely
Publisher: Anchor Books, 2019
ISBN: 9780648061656
Paperback: price: $30

Dixon of Botany Bay: The Convict Priest of Wexford

Author: Vivienne Keely
Publisher: Strathfield, N.S.W. St Pauls Publications, 2003
ISBN: 9781876295639
Paperback: 96 pages Illustrated, price: $24.50

Reviewed by Michael Sternbeck*

May 1803 is an auspicious date in the history of the Catholic Faith in Australia, since it was then that the first public Mass was authorised to be celebrated in the Colony of New South Wales. It was certainly not the first occasion that Catholics resident in the Colony had gathered for prayer, publicly or privately. It might not have been the first Catholic Mass to be celebrated on the continent of Australia—a point that is debated. For those present on that day, however, it was most certainly a moment of the greatest importance, both in terms of its signifying the freedom of the Catholic Faith from official prohibition,

---

* Michael Sternbeck is a liturgiologist and editor of the Catholic History blog *In diebus illis*, https://inthosedayes.blogspot.com/

and the sense for Irish-born residents of the Colony that a vital part of the life they had left behind in the Old World could now be enjoyed in the New.

In May 1803 it is estimated that just over 7000 men, women and children of English and Irish extraction were resident in the Colony of New South Wales. Of this number, between 25% and 40% were Catholics, many of whom were Irish and most of whom were convicts. They lived around Sydney-town, Parramatta and the Hawkesbury. Very little is known about those earliest of our ancestors in the Faith. We do know—for the most part—their names; in some cases, how they were occupied; we know the reasons they came to be in NSW. But, for most of those Catholics, very little else is known. Several hundred of that number had only arrived in the Colony over the previous three years (from 1800 onward) and had been transported to 'Botany Bay' as a consequence of their being caught-up in the Rebellion against British Rule in Ireland (June-July 1798). The administration of justice in the aftermath of that Rebellion was arbitrary, unsafe and severe by modern legal standards.

It so happens that three Catholic priests and several respectable Catholic men and women were caught up in those horrible conspiracies and found themselves on the far side of the world in the Penal Colony of New South Wales. Over the past century, historians have uncovered more details about the lives of these convict Catholics, some of whose names remain familiar to us. In this review, we discuss just two of them, Father James Dixon and Michael Hayes. These men are the subject of two compact, fine biographies by Sister Vivienne Keely of the Irish-based *Congregation of the Sisters of the Holy Faith*. Sister Keely is herself Irish, but for many years studied, worked and taught in Australia.

The story of Michael Hayes is detailed in often fascinating detail by Sister Keely in *Michael Hayes: The Life of a 1798 Wexford Rebel in Sydney*. Michael Hayes came from a comfortable family of merchants in the city of Wexford on the south-east coast of Ireland. In the Uprising of 1798, he was alleged to have participated in a massacre of British Loyalists but, even though credible witnesses placed him elsewhere at the time of the outrage, perjured evidence was sufficient to have him convicted and sentenced to be transported to the Colony of NSW. Like so many others, Michael Hayes' guilt was by association with the Rebellion, and he paid dearly for it. He arrived as a convict in NSW early in 1800, but was treated fairly both on the voyage to Australia and within the Colony itself. He was able to earn his own income and eventually was Pardoned in 1809. We would know very little of Michael Hayes, except for a number of invaluable letters which he wrote to members of his family in Ireland and elsewhere. The various business dealings of Hayes—mainly unsuccessful—and the sad circumstances of his death in 1825 are carefully examined in Sister Keely's study. The colonial tale of Michael Hayes would be the same story as many of the Exiles of 1798, except for something most important: after 1810, he was in no small measure responsible for procuring the ministry of a Catholic priest for the Colony. His strategy was to ask his family to petition influential people to secure such an appointment. His efforts were rewarded with the short-lived and unofficial ministry of Father O'Flynn from 1817–1818 and subsequently, the appointments of Fathers Therry and Conolly in 1820. One deficiency in this study, however, is that it makes no attempt to describe to readers the (very different) Faith life of early nineteenth century Catholics. Consequently, Michael Hayes' work to build-up the Church in NSW is presented more as activism, rather than the product of a deep religious Faith.

Like Michael Hayes, Father James Dixon was wrongfully accused of involvement in the Wexford Rebellion; various affidavits protesting his innocence were ignored. Along with Michael Hayes and a few hundred other Irish men and women, he was transported to the Colony of NSW, arriving in 1800. His story is told in an earlier monograph of Sister Keely's *Dixon of Botany Bay: The Convict Priest of Wexford.* Two other Irish priests were transported along with Father Dixon: Fathers James Harold and Peter O'Neil. Although Father Dixon came to NSW as a convict, he was treated with respect by the Colonial Government and it is thought that he had a private ministry amongst Catholics. Two particular episodes, however, assure the place of Father Dixon in Australian history. The first, mentioned above, was that he was the first priest to be authorised to offer Mass publicly in the Colony of NSW. How this came about is as fully described in Sister Keely's study as surviving records will permit. The second is his dramatic appeal to the Irish rebels at Castle Hill to put aside their arms and give themselves up to the Authorities. Fr Dixon is depicted in a famous contemporary drawing of the battle, March 1804. For Catholics, the ill-starred rebellion resulted in the

Governor withdrawing permission for Masses to be publicly offered, since he came to regard such gatherings as occasions where seditious acts were fermented. Father Dixon continued with a private ministry in Sydney until, having received a Pardon, he returned to Ireland in October 1809. There, he resumed a Parish ministry until his death at the age of 82.

This review cannot be anymore than a brief summary of these informative and readable monographs. The volume on Father Dixon includes several important documents to do with his ministry in the Colony. It is regrettable, however, that none of Michael Hayes' two-dozen-or-so letters was reproduced, so that readers could make their own judgements. Both volumes are recommended.

Book Review

Not Forgotten: Australian Catholic Educators 1820–2020

Editors: Anne Benjamin and Seamus O'Grady
Publisher: Melbourne, Coventry Press, 2020
ISBN: 9780648725152
Paperback: 278 pages
Price $34.95

Reviewed by Michael Bezzina*

Not Forgotten: Australian Catholic Educators 1820–2020 is the first hard copy publication of the *Biographical Dictionary of Australian Catholic Educators* project, and demonstrates the value of this ambitious project in a most timely and effective manner as we celebrate 200 years of Catholic education in Australia. It begins to address the gap in charting the history of Catholic education in Australia which has remained unfilled since the seminal work *Catholic Education in Australia 1806–1950* was published by Brother Ronald Fogarty in 1959.

Not Forgotten treats the two centuries of its compass in four periods: the Colonial era to 1880; 1880 to1960; 1960 to 2000; and

* Dr Michael Bezzina currently works in Catholic education through his own consultancy business. He has been a classroom teacher and school leader in Catholic schools, and has held senior roles in two diocesan systems and the Australian Catholic University, where he is an Adjunct Professor.

2000 to 2020. Each era begins with a chapter which sets the context, followed by a series of from five to ten biographies—a total of thirty word pictures overall. Each section concludes with a reflection which synthesises insights and often raises questions for the future.

The selected biographies are not meant to be lengthy treatises. They are typically between one thousand and fifteen hundred words. From all over Australia, they include the stories of lay, clerical and religious; men and women; native born and immigrant; and school and non school educators. They tell of sacrifice and success, hardscrabble local efforts and high level politicking—and of the delicate (and sometimes not so delicate) dances between Church and state, and within the Church itself. Through the thirty stories run the threads of devotion to the Good News and the struggle to keep the doors of Catholic schools open. And in the first three periods of our history it is impossible to ignore the profound influence of the Irish.

Just a few of the people who figure in *Not Forgotten* are George Marley, Australia's first teacher in a Catholic school; Brigid Dwyer, Australia's first native born teacher in a Catholic school; Sister Mary Gabriel, the founder of an Australian education for the Catholic deaf; Brother Aloysius Meldan fsc, national and international leader of the De La Salle brothers; Father Frank Martin, architect of the Catholic education system in Victoria; and Ann Clark the visionary first Director of Catholic Education in Parramatta.

At a time when new forms of governance seem to be displacing educators who have travelled parts of the journey described by this book from Boards and executive roles, its contents should become a key element of leadership formation. The context chapters tell the story with crystal clarity. The biographies put flesh on the bones of historical fact—and the reflections raise questions which those with senior roles would do well to consider. From the point of view of those working in schools, the four context chapters would prove an invaluable resource in the induction of teachers who know nothing of the story of which they are becoming an important part, and whose connections with Church may, at times, be somewhat tenuous. Schools could use the various biographies as a periodic reminder of the shoulders on which they stand, and the reflection sections could stimulate useful conversations as part of ongoing staff formation.

The authors of the various biographies are to be congratulated for the scholarship and insight they have displayed in capturing whole lives in such a short span of words. Those who wrote the contexts and reflections have provided a powerful lens through which both to view each educator's contribution and the story of a growing system of education to which these have contributed. The editors, Anne Benjamin and Seamus O'Grady can take much pride in this first of what we hope will be many volumes which capture the tales of triumph and adversity in Catholic education in this country, and of the people who made it possible through their faith, their effort and their wisdom.

It would be remiss of this reviewer were he not to note that there are a number of educators who have been most significant contributors to the evolution of Catholic education during the period covered by this volume who are not included in it. Fortunately for us all, they are still alive. While we look forward to their inclusion in subsequent volumes, we pray it is not too soon!

Book Review

A Bridge Between: Spanish Benedictine Missionary Women in Australia

---

Author: Katharine Massam
Publisher: (ANU Press: Acton, ACT) 2020
ISBN: 9781760463519
Hardback: 390 pages
Price: $65 (pdf free at https://press.anu.edu.au/publications/series/anu-lives-series-biography/bridge-between)

Reviewed by Kym Harris*

"Don't praise anyone" was the feisty injunction given to the author by Sr Teresa, one of the Spanish Benedictine Missionary Sisters who had lived and served at New Norcia for many decades and it is a refrain that she, Katherine Massam, often used to guide her research. I was knocked sideways by it, as there *was* much to praise in their work, as my sister saw, when she was a relief nurse at Kalumburu in the 1980s. And not only what she saw, but also heard in the stories about the sisters shared by the local indigenous people. Still, Sr Teresa was insistent.

This book is primarily an account of the years the Spanish Benedictine Sisters spent in Western Australia, but it also includes

* Sr Kym Harris has been a Benedictine Nun since 1975. She resides at Tanby, Yeppoon, Central Queensland.

the story of the Carmelite Sisters who preceded them at New Norcia in the first decade of last century. They had come to New Norcia to run St Joseph's Orphanage and School at New Norcia, originally founded by Abbot Salvado in the nineteenth century for indigenous girls. Interestingly, he did not want religious sisters to run it, rather local Aboriginal Matrons. The second Abbot of New Norcia, Torres, not having the same faith in the Aborigines, nor in women, had a different idea. He recruited Carmelite Sisters from Spain, a new congregation, trained in modern educational techniques and living in a convent designed by Gaudi, to come to his dry, isolated monastic town. From the outset, there were problems, largely centred around authority and workload. They had come to teach, yet were expected to do, with the indigenous girls in their care, the laundry work of the monastery, boys' school and orphanage as well as care for their own institution and basic teaching of the girls. When they withdrew after a few years one of their number, Sr Maria Harispe, remained, convinced her vocation was to be identified with the local 'natives' *(sic)*. Around her, over time, the Benedictine Missionary Sisters formed. It was a long and troubled birth: nearly twenty-five years till Constitutions were drawn up, over a decade till they were confirmed. Eventually, they elected their own superior and, in 1962, opened their own bank account. Clearly the Abbot of New Norcia determined much of their lives, from recruitment of members in Spain to the opening of new houses in Australia, to where and how they worked. But the core of their story was their faith in God and the relationships between the sisters and the residents of St Joseph's.

Even though she had begun her research some years before, Massam opens this history with the extraordinary Reunion in 2001. Over twenty years after most of the sisters had left Australia (three had chosen to remain at Kalumburu), indigenous women who had been former students organised and financed a reunion at New Norcia of the sisters who had cared for them in St Joseph's. They came from three continents, and included Sr Veronica Willaway, a local Yued woman, who has lived in Nebraska, USA for some decades. (She provides the Foreword to this history). Over three days, in story, ceremony and silence, the mystery of their lives together was honoured. It was in this context that Sr Teresa gave her injunction, not to praise. While there was much love and laughter, there was also the telling and acknowledgement of pain, some of which could only be shared in silence. I found the final pages amazing in an academic history. After describing the final confused departure of the sisters in 1975, she invites the reader to imagine reconciliation through a sustained reflection on the concluding Mass of the Reunion. Not since Salvado's times had so many indigenous people congregated at New Norcia. Both their lives and the sisters were honoured in the symbols presented at the Eucharist. In that celebration, they looked beyond the past, and even the present, to affirm in God the unity that God desires for us. It is that faith Massam sees as giving the vision and courage to bring about reconciliation in our present.

The history of these women in Australia covers nearly seventy five years and is complex. The sisters stood on the margins in so many ways. Not-monks in a monastic town, women in a man's world, Spaniards in an Anglo-Irish church, Catholics in a Protestant society. Their marginality is tellingly highlighted by language. No effort was made for decades to ensure they learnt English. Indeed, the early sisters picked up their English from the Aboriginal girls in their care. Only in 1950 was one of their number given the opportunity to learn the language of the country they were living in. Massam sees their marginality as the basis of opportunity for them to build bridges. I can see her point but wished she had drawn out this image more clearly.

This book is presented as the first account of the history of St Joseph's, with the sisters as the focus but Massam recognises the need for another history from the perspective of the indigenous women and girls who had passed through St Joseph's, preferably written by an indigenous historian. This close and detailed history, built on a diversity of resources, opens us to the complexity of the Spanish-Indigenous Encounter. Massam's research took over twenty years, across three continents: there is an extraordinary wealth of material. It repays close reading. Many times, I had to stop, think and reconsider. Having taken seriously the injunction, not to praise, Massam has an edge in what she draws out. As much as she does not praise, she does not condemn and, in the vexed arena of the history between Indigenous and European peoples, this has much to commend it. It underscores how much time, listening, reflection and patience is needed to come to an understanding of what was happening in situations that are largely foreign to our own. In that understanding we may gain some wisdom in how to act in our time.

Book Review

The Catholic Church in Colonial Queensland: 1859–1918

Author: Chris Hanlon:
Publisher: Brisbane Archdiocesan Archives, 2020
ISBN 9780646821160
Paperback: 200 +xxii pages
Price $40

Reviewed by: John Carmody*

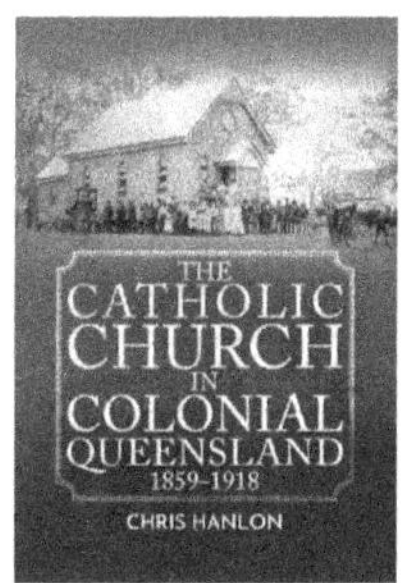

This is a rather homely book—Queensland people *do* tend to see themselves in that way—though it does have some social and episcopal insights which, regrettably, it tends to understate. Dr Hanlon refers to 'our Queensland way of doing things' and laments that the state's history has often been 'heavily circumscribed by the perspective and interests of people from the South', though I remain perplexed about what he means. (There is, however, *some* justification for his view: despite a thirty five year tenure as Bishop in Brisbane, Robert Dunne has no entry in the *Australian Dictionary of Biography.*)

Like the past, Queensland is, effectively a 'different country' (a truth about which they are almost aggressively proud) and perhaps the *Journal* Editor felt, in asking me to assess this book, that having been born and educated there, I might understand the place. Yet (apart from having, decades ago, crossed the Tweed in a southerly direction), I am scarcely even a 'former Queenslander', being a native of Brisbane, which is in the farthest south-east of the state: when

* John Carmody is President of the Australian Catholic Historical Society

people from the far-north refer to 'Southerners' they usually mean the people from that very capital city, while for Brisbane-ites the term refers to everyone south of the border, the 'Mexicans' as the former Premier, Wayne Goss, used to say. That attitude, a form of xenophobia as it is, was also shared by the early clergy, after Queensland was legally constituted as an independent colony (or state) in 1859 and left a mere 10½ pence by the government in Sydney.

Repeatedly, this little history reminds us how much Cardinal Patrick Moran and Robert Dunne (the second Bishop of Brisbane) despised each other, hostile attitudes which *do* reflect an enduring Queensland disposition about 'foreigners' and which flowed not just from their personalities or from Moran's constant white-anting of Dunne to the Vatican (or even because he marginalised the Queenslander at the Australian bishops' 'National Plenary Councils'), but importantly from Dunne's conviction that Moran was ignorant of Queensland conditions. Dunne opposed Moran's 'bricks and mortar' Catholicism: instead, he encouraged his flock to become property-owners because only then could they gain the vote and become integral members of Queensland society. That status inevitably directed them to politics and the public service.

Hanlon has, therefore, opted for a thematic rather than a chronological approach ('Community life in colonial Queensland', 'Immigration, Land Settlement, Buildings', 'Church and State' and 'Education'), though his rather scattershot method can blur their boundaries disconcertingly and it makes a degree of criss-crossing of his terrain inevitable. Accordingly, the astonishing lack of an index is all the more disabling for the reader. Furthermore, his butterfly-like treatment of people and themes is, at times (notwithstanding that he has been diligent in visiting several archives), almost perfunctory and, too often, seems to lack concern for context and depth. Could it be that the vastness of the geography which confronted the early clergy (which encouraged those pioneer bishops to take to foot, horse, and dray in their determination to get to know their diocese. initially the *entire* state, and its people) has misled him to prefer scope to depth?

In fact (apart from some wry acknowledgements that solely the ordained attended those 'National' Councils), it is only at the opening of his chapter on education—about the Catholic quiddity of which the bishops were notably hard-line—that Dr Hanlon asks any quasi-philosophical questions; indeed, it is the most substantial and thorough section of his history, with the fewest distracting divagations. After that, the book seems simply to dry up and disappear like an outback creek, leaving the reader to yearn for the diverse threads to be woven into something integrated.

It may seem harsh, but I wonder how much better even Queenslanders' understanding of their collage of a state will be when they have read this well-intentioned book.

Book Review

Religious Education and the Anglo-World: The Impact of Empire, Britishness, and Decolonisation in Australia, Canada, and New Zealand

---

Author: Stephen Jackson
Publisher: Brill, Leiden, Netherlands, 2020
ISBN: 978-90-04-43216-1
Paperback, 98 pages
Price: $146.97

Reviewed by Jeff Kildea*

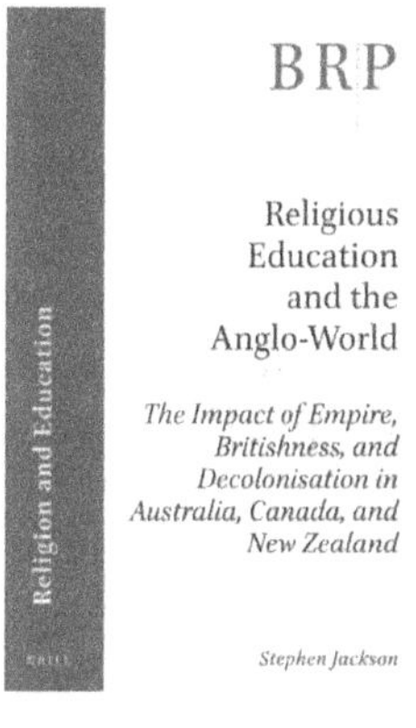

Across a number of areas of historical inquiry the focus is increasingly becoming transnational. By moving away from national studies and comparing the development of subjects across a number of countries, it is hoped to uncover deeper truths concerning those areas of study.

Such exploration of the similarities and differences between experiences in different jurisdictions is thought to help distil essential features and better discern underlying dynamics. By removing the blinkers of a national perspective we are led to see there were other ways to solve the problems of the past and we are thus emboldened to canvass a wider range of solutions to the problems of the present.

---

* Dr Jeff Kildea is an adjunct professor in Irish Studies at the University of New South Wales. In 2014 he held the Keith Cameron Chair of Australian History at University College Dublin. He is the author of many books and articles on the Irish in Australia. His latest work is *Hugh Mahon: Patriot, Pressman, Politician* Volume 1 (2017) and Volume 2 (2020).

Colin Barr's *Ireland's Empire: The Roman Catholic Church in the English-Speaking World*, separately reviewed in this issue, is one example of this trend towards transnational history. Another is Stephen Jackson's *Religious Education and the Anglo-World*. Its subtitle, 'The Impact of Empire, Britishness, and Decolonisation in Australia, Canada, and New Zealand' sets its parameters less ambitiously than *Ireland's Empire*.

Religious Education and the Anglo-World at seventy six pages of text and twenty two pages of bibliography is essentially an extended historiographical essay that, with regard to the three countries under review, brings the 'disparate national literatures into conversation with one another' with the aim of promoting 'a greater transnational approach to the study of religious education in the Anglo-World' (page 1).

Jackson's essay is a recent addition to Brill Research Perspectives, a series which Netherlands-based publisher Brill describes as 'the authoritative source for the state of scholarship' across a number of subjects in the humanities. Under that rubric *Religious Education and the Anglo-World* is certainly a worthy contribution.

Jackson's basic thesis is: 'Local circumstances, historical contingencies, and human agency provided each national or state-level system with unique features, but all of them experienced the transnational formative influence of empire' (page 4). That influence, which Jackson says, 'profoundly shaped religious education' in the three countries in the nineteenth and twentieth centuries, derived from the common experience of 'settler colonialism and the Anglo-World system'.

His analysis centres on three formative eras: the foundations of religious education systems in the mid- to late nineteenth century; the consolidation of religious education systems from 1880 to 1960; and the widespread reform movements in religious education as the attachment to Britishness weakened in the 1960s and 1970s.

According to Jackson, 'educators across the Anglo-World looked to each other for ideas, educational materials, and systems to emulate as they all addressed common challenges of public education.' (page 6). One of the common challenges for the three countries in their early development was how to teach religion to children while promoting a unifying transnational identity in an empire which was dominated by a virulently anti-Catholic Protestantism but which had large Catholic minorities. Furthermore, during the decolonisation phase of their development, 'The loss of an identity centred on the British Empire generated a great deal of soul searching on the topic of religious education' (page 7).

Jackson argues that the Anglo-World system moulded religious education in four primary ways: it promoted a transnational identity called 'Britishness' that embraced Protestantism as an important ideal; in the settler colonies it used migrant selection processes (example the White Australia policy) to ensure only migrants of the 'right type' were allowed to enter; it navigated the complication of the 'extraordinary levels of Irish Roman Catholic migration and the explosively tendentious relationship between Britain and Ireland'; and it transmitted 'quotidian practices of imitation, borrowing, and modelling'.

Nevertheless, the large Irish Catholic presence in the settler colonies challenged Protestant assumptions of Britishness, while fears of radical Irish nationalism led to discrimination against Catholics, making it difficult to settle the issue of religious education for more than a century. In this regard Jackson regards as particularly important the struggle of Irish Catholics for state funding of their schools.

For those interested in the history of religious education in Australia, or more generally across the empire, *Religious Education and the Anglo-World* is a valuable resource, both as a source of bibliographical information as well as a wellspring of highly developed ideas on the subject. But with a recommended retail price of ninety six euros, many potential readers will be discouraged unless they can persuade their school, college or local library to acquire a copy.

Book Review

Ireland's Empire: The Roman Catholic Church in the English-Speaking World, 1829–1914

Author: Colin Barr
Publisher: Cambridge University Press, Cambridge, 2020
ISBN: 9781108764131
Paperback, 580 pages
Price: $146.97

Reviewed by Jeff Kildea*

Colin Barr's dedication at the start of *Ireland's Empire: The Roman Catholic Church in the English-Speaking World, 1829–1914* states simply: 'For the archivists.' And reading through his bibliography that lists 104 archives in twelve countries on five continents—a veritable Cook's tour of the Catholic world—one can see why. American historian Barbara Tuchman once wrote that she used material from primary sources only, seeing secondary sources as but guides at the start of a project. 'I do not want to end up simply rewriting someone else's book,' she proclaimed.[1] Judging by the extensive list of secondary sources,

* Dr Jeff Kildea is an adjunct professor in Irish Studies at the University of New South Wales. In 2014 he held the Keith Cameron Chair of Australian History at University College Dublin. He is the author of many books and articles on the Irish in Australia. His latest work is *Hugh Mahon: Patriot, Pressman, Politician*, Volume 1 (2017) and Volume 2 (2020).

1. Barbara W Tuchman, *Practising History: Selected Essays* (London: Macmillan, 1983), 18–19.

Barr is not as puritanical as Ms Tuchman. Yet *Ireland's Empire*, which Barr explains was inspired by a visit to Australia and grew out of 'an archival odyssey that . . . lasted well over a decade' (page viii), is certainly not someone else's book. It is a *tour de force* of transnational ecclesiastical history by an author well versed in his subject that is both enlightening and rewarding.

The text includes chapters on the United States and the British dominions of Newfoundland, India, South Africa, Canada, Australia, and New Zealand, with reference throughout to other places such as Scotland, Gibraltar, Trinidad, and the Falkland Islands. England is not included, explains Barr, because '[Cardinal Paul] Cullen and his successors never challenged the powerful English church on its own terrain' (20).

In his introduction Barr observes that in the period under review a transnational Irish empire emerged throughout the English-speaking world: '[B]y 1914, Irish Catholics across the English-speaking world largely worshipped in the same way, read the same books, were educated by the same religious orders, observed the same social and sexual disciplines (especially surrounding marriage), and shared the same heroes, villains, and martyrs' (21). He contends that this was due to the fact that wherever the Catholic Irish settled they maintained their Irish Catholic identity, unlike Irish Protestants who blended with the dominant British culture. While some historians might question the latter contention,[2] Barr's concern, of course, is Irish Catholics, who, he persuasively argues, maintained their identity through an organised campaign conducted by Propaganda Fide under Cullen's influence to ensure Hiberno-Roman dominance of the Catholic Church in those various places. According to Barr, 'Ireland's empire was planned. . . . It was also largely the work of one man: Paul Cullen' (7).

The focus of the book, he explains, is 'the ecclesiastical politics associated with the Hiberno-Roman takeover of each national Church and its immediate aftermath . . . how Ireland's spiritual empire was built and not how it was then governed' (21). So, for the most part the book is an examination of high politics as practised by bishops in Rome and in each of the selected countries rather than a

2. *Cf* Dianne Hall, 'Defending the Faith: Orangeism and Ulster Protestant Identities in Colonial New South Wales', in *Journal of Religious History*, 38/2 (2014): 207–223.

comparative study of the Irish Catholic people across the English-speaking world. Nevertheless, in the concluding chapter Barr does provide an overview of attitudes and practices that were common to the Irish Catholic faithful living in those countries.

Australian readers will be pleased to know that the book's longest chapter is the one devoted to Australia. At 122 pages, it fully occupies a quarter of the book's text, well in excess of any of the other chapters. It begins with a survey of the historiography of nineteenth-century Australian Catholicism and the division between those who have praised and those who have disparaged the contribution of the Benedictines. Barr describes John Moloney's failed attempt to shift the debate by emphasising the power of Rome rather than Ireland in shaping Australian Catholicism and how Patrick O'Farrell's counter-interpretation overwhelmingly prevailed: 'O'Farrell accepted that the two "were blended, but it was an Irish blend"' (284). According to Barr, more recent scholarship has dispensed with the 'goodies versus baddies' approach in favour of an attitude he supports that acknowledges both the hibernianism of the Irish bishops and the influence of Rome.

The chapter then describes the church's development in Australia through the nineteenth century, beginning with the early years of the colony, when 'neither the English nor the Irish bishops had much interest in Australia: at every stage it was Rome that took the initiative' (page 289). Barr details Polding's struggle to forge a national church that was neither Irish nor English but Australian, an endeavour in which he failed. According to Barr, by 1868 the Irish had won: 'The appointments of Murray, Quinn, Murphy, Lanigan, and O'Mahony, together with James Quinn in Brisbane, introduced undiluted Hiberno-Roman Catholicism to Australia' (349).

The next section of the chapter, 'Building the Irish Church', covers the period from 1867 to 1883. Its complex narrative of ecclesiastical feuding in Australia and Rome suggests Barr's declaration of Irish victory may have been premature. The appointment of the wily English Benedictine Roger Vaughan to Sydney and of the Anglophile Robert Dunne to Brisbane along with the eccentric resistance of James Goold in Melbourne delayed the Cullenite takeover. But as Barr observes, 'Vaughan's death changed everything.' The appointment of Cullen's 'literal and ecclesiastical heir', Patrick Francis Moran to replace him 'set the course of Australian Catholicism as a whole well into the twentieth century' (376). Somewhat controversially, Barr argues that 'Moran rejected the assimilationist hopes of Polding and Vaughan', calling into question the view, which he attributes to Peter Cunich and John Luttrell, that Moran accepted 'an Australian church neither Irish nor Roman' (379).

The final section of the chapter dispenses with high politics, devoting itself to a description of Moran's 'transformative' rule when the Australian church became almost completely Hiberno-Roman, with Brisbane under Dunne holding out until his death in 1917. According to Barr, 'the church now followed almost without exception a distinctively Hiberno-Roman pattern of rapid growth, institutional consolidation, and social, sexual, and educational separation overseen by Irish priests, nuns, and bishops' (382). Devotional uniformity and social conformity were imposed on Australia's Catholics, while their 'institutions and community identity were saturated in Irish imagery even as they took their place in Australian life and defined themselves as Australians'. From Barr's 'top-down' perspective his conclusion in this regard is supportable, yet some historians who have adopted a 'grass-roots' perspective have argued that only a small proportion of the Irish population took an active interest in the promotion and retention of Irish identity and culture.[3]

For those with an interest in the ecclesiastical politics of the Irish diaspora throughout the English-speaking world, Barr's book is essential reading. Yet, even those whose interest is normally confined to Australia will find the book's extensive coverage of the local church enlightening, while its transnational coverage provides insights into the history of the church in Australia that national histories struggle to convey.

3. See, for example, Louise Ann Mazzaroli, 'The Irish in New South Wales, 1884 to 1914: Some Aspects of the Irish Sub-Culture' (PhD Thesis, University of New South Wales, 1979).

Book Review

Wearing the Green: The Daltons and the Irish Cause

Author: Elisabeth Edwards
Publisher: Orange & District Historical Society, Orange, NSW, 2019
ISBN: 9780995443013
Paperback, xii, 308 pages
Price: $60

Reviewed by Jeff Kildea*

Although one is not supposed to judge a book by its cover, Elisabeth Edwards' *Wearing the Green: The Daltons and the Irish Cause* is the exception that makes the rule. The production quality of this particular book is outstanding, matched by the quality of the research and writing. The subject matter of the book, the Daltons of Orange, will appeal to anyone interested in the development of Irish Catholicism in New South Wales from the 1850s to 1920.

The history of the Daltons is a quintessential 'rags to riches' story, one that almost ended before it started. Transported to New South Wales in 1835 for his role in the abduction of a widow (a not uncommon crime in nineteenth-century

* Dr Jeff Kildea is an adjunct professor in Irish Studies at the University of New South Wales. In 2014 he held the Keith Cameron Chair of Australian History at University College Dublin. He is the author of many books and articles on the Irish in Australia. His latest work is *Hugh Mahon: Patriot, Pressman, Politician,* Volume 1 (2017) and Volume 2 (2020).

Ireland), James Dalton was fortunate to survive the voyage. His ship, the *Hive*, ran aground on a sandbank 120 miles south of Sydney at what is now called Wreck Bay, near Sussex Inlet. Dalton and his fellow passengers were forced to scramble ashore onto a desolate stretch of beach backed by scrubby dunes. Lying exhausted on the sand, his left elbow dislocated, the young man must have felt his life would soon end in obscurity. Instead, he survived the ordeal and went on to found one of the colony's wealthiest dynasties.

In very readable prose, Edwards tells in meticulous detail how that dynasty came about and prospered. After receiving his ticket of leave and then his certificate of freedom, James set up a store in 1847 at Summerhill, near present-day Orange. After gold was discovered nearby, the business grew rapidly, supplying the influx of miners with their essential needs. Soon James was able to open a store in Orange and then an inn, which he named the O'Connell in honour of the Liberator.

When James departed Ireland in 1835 he had left behind in County Limerick a wife, Ellen, and three children: Thomas, Margaret and James Junior. In 1849, with the famine ravaging Ireland, James Junior, then aged fifteen years, emigrated to Australia, while Thomas, aged twenty, and Margaret, aged eighteen, went to America. By then Ellen had died.

After landing in Sydney, James Junior made his way to Orange where he joined his father in the business. He was followed in 1854 by Thomas and then in 1866 by Margaret, who had married in America. Meanwhile, James Senior remarried in 1851 and, over the next decade, he and Johanna Hogan had six children, three dying in infancy.

While James Senior concentrated on running the inn until his death in 1865, his sons managed the stores, forming a partnership in 1858 known as Dalton Brothers. In time the firm expanded into other fields: buying and selling land, flour milling, shipping agents, warehousing, slaughterhousing, and pastoralism. It had its own wharf and warehouse in Sydney.

Apart from their business interests, the brothers became heavily involved in the community and the church. James became a magistrate and mayor of Orange, while Thomas, after also serving as mayor, entered the Legislative Assembly and later the Legislative Council. The Daltons were generous donors to worthy causes and major benefactors of the church. Each had his service recognised by being appointed a Knight Commander of the Order of St Gregory the Great (KCSG). The altar in the Chapel of the Irish Saints at St Mary's Cathedral was erected in memory of Thomas by his son Thomas Joseph, also a KCSG.

Wearing the Green reads well as genealogy, biography and history. Woven seamlessly into the story is background information that a lesser writer might have placed in sidebars. Without disrupting the narrative, Edwards tells us about conditions in Ireland, including the famine, landlordism, the O'Connell repeal movement, and Parnellism, about the sea journey from Ireland to Australia, and about life in colonial New South Wales, including the convict system, the discovery of gold, the development of road and rail transport, and the support of Irish home rule.

Such information is not perfunctory detail, for the lives of the Daltons are inextricably bound up with those events. For instance, Johanna Dalton (James Senior's daughter by his second marriage) married the Irish nationalist leader John Redmond during his ten-month fundraising tour of Australia in 1883, while Eleanor Dalton (James Junior's daughter) married Redmond's brother William. James Junior's son, James Joseph, was elected to the British Parliament in 1890 representing Parnell's Irish National Party. Thus, the politics of the home rule movement both in Ireland and Australia is integral to the Dalton family history.

Wearing the Green tells the story of the Dalton family up to the death of James Junior on St Patrick's Day 1919. An epilogue extends the story further into the twentieth century with brief details of some Dalton descendants as well as of the fate of buildings and businesses connected with the family. A series of genealogical charts helps the reader untangle the complex web of family relationships. Scattered throughout the text are numerous colour, sepia and black-and-white photographs of amazing clarity. At 250 mm high, 200 mm wide and 16 mm thick, *Wearing the Green* is small enough to read in bed, yet, with its visually attractive cover, large enough to lay on a coffee table.

Book Review

To Foster an Irish Spirit—The Irish National Association of Australasia 1915–2015

Authors: Richard Reid, Jeff Kildea, Perry McIntyre
Publisher: Anchor Books Australia, 2020
ISBN: 9780646804309
Paperback, 360 pages
Price: $39.95

Reviewed by: Chris Geraghty*

In November 1926, my father landed in Sydney with his younger brother John. They had spent three months on board the P & O Steamer *Barrabool*, travelling steerage from London and were walking the gangplank with their sparse belongings to find their land legs on foreign soil. They knew no one. No job. No qualifications or degrees. No shelter. A few English pounds in their pocket which their father had given them before they had left home. A strange world for two teenagers from Ballinasloe in County Galway.

James Geraghty never saw his mother or father again, or ever spoke to them by phone (they were not blessed in Ireland with a telephone—nor were we, in the days before his parents' death), and since he was to all intents and purposes illiterate, he never wrote to tell them of his life in Sydney, of his Australian family, his brother, his children. He was to live his adult life far from his roots in the bogs of Ireland.

---

* Chris Geraghty is the author of *The Priest Factory, Dancing with the Devil* and other books.

Fortunately, the Irish National Association of Australasia had commenced its life in Sydney ten or so years before his arrival in a sun-burnt country and it would prove to be a comforting contact with all things Irish. Until his death over seventy years later, he remained a loyal native of Ireland. He never lost his pride in his fellow countrymen and their struggle. He never wavered in his support for the unification of his homeland. He never tempered his contempt for the invading Black and Tans or his disregard for England and its monarchy. The Irish National Association and the Irish clergy were responsible for the preservation of my father's lost world.

When it turned one hundred in 2015, a trinity of well-known Irish scholars agreed to tell the story of the Association.

Jeff Kildea opens with an account of the foundation of the INA during the First World War, and continues the narrative with a somewhat turbulent history, including the internment of the 'Irish Seven" and the troubles which beset the founder, Albert Dryer—and he concludes his part of the story just before the Second World War.

Richard Reid then grabs the baton and traces the story, up and down, crises, arguments, struggles and triumphs, from 1936 to the centenary year in 2015, focusing particularly on its twenty-odd golden years from 1956.

Perry McIntyre concludes the work with her two entertaining and substantial chapters—one on the annual Saint Patrick's Day Parade from 1979 to 1998, and the other on the Memorial of the 1798 Irish Martyrs located in Waverley Cemetery.

The reader is well served with an impressive (perhaps in part over-zealous) battery of endnotes to each of the eight chapters, a helpful index and a selected bibliography of archival material, major newspapers, of books and relevant articles. *To Foster an Irish Spirit* is a work of true scholarship, full of interesting details for a son or daughter of an Irish-born parent, for those with Irish forebears, for lovers of Irish culture and those interested in Australian history. The authors address a litany of items of interest—conscription, the IRA and Sinn Féin, religious bigotry on both sides of the aisle, Eamon de Valera, England, the monarchy, republicanism, hurling, Irish dancing, Gaelic football, the Irish clergy, our eccentric family doctor, Dr Michael Fitzpatrick gets a long mention, Archbishop Daniel Mannix of course, Dan Minogue, the Albert Dryer Memorial Library—heroes, characters, villains, celebrations, fights, intrigue, lost causes and social events—euchre parties with several hundred participants, raucous Saturday night dances, picnics, moonlight harbour excursions, poetry recitals, concerts, lectures, Gaelic language classes and the establishment of a fife and drum band.

The Association was founded in a distant land to keep alive the spirit of Ireland. From the beginning and throughout its life, it was determined to promote a national spirit separate and distinct from England and the Crown. It set out to foster the study of the history of Ireland, her literature, music, art and dancing, and the dominant part played in the history of the world by Ireland's saints and scholars. It organized annual events like the St Patrick's Day Sports and the St Patrick's Day Concert to showcase Irish music and dancing. Since the 1920s the Association arranged the Easter Sunday Oration in the Waverley Cemetery at the Memorial of the Irish Martyrs of 1798 and where for years, up until 2015, the Rosary was recited in Gaelic.

From the beginning the elite and the Establishment believed that the real aim of the founders of the Association involved intrigue, secrecy, conspiracy, disloyalty, treachery and treason, sending money overseas to support the Sinn Fein in Ireland and the Irish Republican Brotherhood in the USA. The story of these initial turbulent years is fascinating. However, as the Association settled into its traces, it became clear that the aims were a little more benign—to foster Ireland's national destiny and to provide a club for its members to celebrate their Irishness.

In the end the Association proved to be a Sydney-sited organisation. The founder's initial plan to go national, and later attempts in the 40s and 50s to reignite a national organization with branches in Brisbane, Melbourne, Adelaide and Canberra, eventually failed by the end of the 60s. The Padraig Pearse Branch in Devonshire Street, Surry Hills remains the only witness to the dreams of Albert Dryer and others.

As he turns the pages of this book the reader revisits the high points and low points of the recent history of Ireland and the Irish people's struggle against oppression and enslavement. The story is told of a significant ethnic migrant group coming to terms with sharing a land, far from home, with strangers whose forebears entertained hostile loyalties and unorthodox articles of faith.

As a schoolboy, I participated in the St Patrick's Day Sport Carnival where Cardinal Norman Gilroy used to confer the medals. I was forced by my father to sit, fidgeting for hours without end, in the Town Hall, listening to Gaelic music, Irish rebel songs and watching Irish dancing—the St Patrick's Day Concert put on by the Association. An occasional visit to the martyrs' shrine at Waverley. Regular Sunday afternoons at the Domain listening to Irishmen and shouting down Orangemen. The Association was supporting people far from home, people like the Geraghtys who were made to feel inferior in the colony, Catholics making their way in a hostile world and keeping alive memories of a distant land.

Book Review

Federation's Man of Letters—Patrick McMahon Glynn

Author: Anne Henderson
Publisher: The Kapunda Press (an imprint of Connor Court Publishing)
ISBN 9781925826487
Paperback: 156 pages
Price: $29.95

Reviewed by: Tony Abbott*

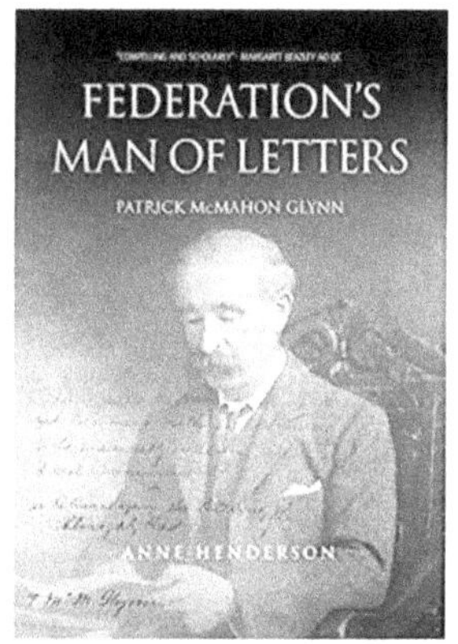

Biographies are worth writing and reading because they open a window into the lives of our distinguished forebears; remembering how they grappled with their problems helps us to better handle our own. The best teacher, after all, is experience; and biography is a way of turning other people's experience to our own benefit and bringing the wisdom of the ages to bear on our own time.

So what's there to learn from the life of Patrick McMahon Glynn, a South Australian state MP prior to federation, a delegate to the federation conventions, a member of our first parliament, and a minister in Australian governments on and off until 1919? Quite a lot, as it turns out, in Anne Henderson's lively essay; in particular, how much stays the same, even while almost everything seems to have changed.

---

* Tony Abbott was the 28th Prime Minister of Australia.

So much from 100 years ago is almost unrecognisable—except human nature and how it plays out in the rarely-fair world of politics.

Glynn was one of those MPs of high ability, strong character, and great industry who never made it past middling rank; in part because he did not revel in the rough and tumble aspect to public life. Unsuccessful as a barrister in his native Ireland, he arrived in Australia in 1880 to make his fortune in a land where connections meant less; yet he still hoped to make the most of the connections he had. Here too, he struggled initially, despite letters of introduction to a judge and a colonial premier. Eventually, thanks to a Catholic connection that did pay-off, he secured a position as a solicitor in Kapunda, about eighty kilometres north of Adelaide.

Fired up, as many were back then, by Henry George's dream of better government with lesser burdens on the common man, via replacing existing taxes with a tax on land, he narrowly won a state seat in 1887. Despite much-more-than-average diligence in attending to his constituents, he narrowly lost at the next election; in part because his opponent misrepresented his ideas. He tried several times to get back; eventually-but-briefly succeeding for a different seat. In his time, as in ours it seems, for a democratic electorate, a candidate's intrinsic merit was but one consideration only: alongside 'is he one of us', and 'for whom and for what will he fight?'

Still, Glynn became a regular and well-regarded contributor to public debates, was chosen as a delegate to the 1897 constitutional convention, and when South Australia elected members for the first federal parliament (initially on a list basis), came in third and eventually sat as the Member for Angas. But he retained his aversion to 'them and us' politicking which meant he was respected by most but embraced by few. In that more politically fluid era, he was apparently considered for attorney-general in the first federal Labor government, despite never being a party member. He did become attorney-general in the fusion Liberal government of Alfred Deakin, and then Minister for Home and Territories in Billy Hughes Nationalist government after the Labor split over conscription.

Glynn was essentially a 'small government conservative', telling the parliament in 1904 that the 'true province' of the state was to 'destroy monopoly, to afford to all equal opportunity, and to leave to private enterprise, to individual intelligence and guidance, the task of perfecting and sustaining what is best'. His one-time account of Edmund Burke, his political hero, as 'above' the House of Commons 'forgetful of idle clamours of party and of the little views of little men' in order to appeal 'to his country and the enlightened judgment of mankind' was probably how he also saw himself.

A cause célèbre from those days was the case of Father Charles Jerger, a German born Catholic priest who reportedly deprecated the war effort from the pulpit and was detained as an enemy alien before being finally deported in 1920. It's telling that Glynn argued the case for leniency within the government, unsuccessfully, perhaps because his colleagues sensed that he'd only go so far to make his point. Then, as now, if you don't fight, you rarely win.

Pre-federation, Glynn stood out on two issues. At first, his move to acknowledge God in the constitution failed, as too 'preachy'—even though Glynn sometimes seems to have struggled with his faith. But after numerous church leaders demurred, and some 150,000 people petitioned the convention, his fellow delegates changed their minds and 'humbly relying on the blessing of almighty God' became enshrined in the preamble. And he was an early advocate for federal control of Murray-Darling water, culminating in the first federal water act of 1915. The moral from these is that persistence pays off and that there are some issues worth losing for. A believer in Crown and Empire, Glynn was also responsible for the lapidary description of Australia, under the constitution, as 'a crowned republic'.

Glynn was not the first prominent Catholic in Australia's public life but he was perhaps Australian Catholicism's first public intellectual, hence is justly commemorated in the Australian Catholic University's PM Glynn Institute.

Henderson's essay, in the style of Lytton Strachey's *Eminent Victorians*, is nicely pitched to the contemporary reader, who's unlikely to be interested in all the minutiae of earlier times. Another fine touch is the brief closing reflections from other authorities: such as constitutional lawyer Anne Twomey's thoughts on Glynn's place as an early 'liberal conservative' and the late former NSW Premier John Fahey's comparison of the role of religion in politics, then versus now. This Glynn essay is a cousin to Connor Court Publishing's series of biographical monographs (so far covering Neville Wran, Joh Bjelke-Petersen, and Lindsay Thompson, as well as Robert Menzies, Harold Holt and Joe Lyons). They do not substitute for full length biography (such as the celebrated Jesuit theologian Gerald Glynn O'Collins' 1965 life of his kinsman, or indeed Henderson's own fine treatment of Lyons) but are a very accessible way of bringing the past to life. May there be many more of them!

Book Review

Dorothy Day in Australia

Author: Val Noone
Publisher: Mary Doyle & Val Noone, Fitzroy, Vic., 2020
ISBN: 9780646820880
Paperback: 132 pages
Price: $30 posted anywhere in Australia. Email: valnoone@iinet.net.au or by post to Val Noone, PO Box 51, Fitzroy, Vic 3065

Reviewed by Michael Costigan*

The Melbourne historian and writer Dr Val Noone has recorded much of value and interest in the 132 pages of this book marking the 50th anniversary in August 2020 of the legendary Dorothy Day's only visit to Australia.

Helped in a special way by the memories of his wife, Mary Doyle, and his own diligence as a researcher, Noone covers the following areas in an Introduction and four Chapters crammed with information.

First is his reflection on why Day, a radical supporter of, among other things, trade unions and anti-war activism, was an exceptional American Catholic, whom Pope Francis, addressing the United States Congress on

---

* Michael Costigan was Associate Editor (as a priest) of *The Advocate* (Melbourne); founding Director of the Literature Board of the Australia Council; first Executive Secretary of the Australian Bishops Committee for Justice, Development, Ecology and Peace; and, after retirement, an Adjunct Professor of Australian Catholic University.

24th September 2015, had singled out for high praise, along with Abraham Lincoln, Martin Luther King and the Cistercian monk Thomas Merton.

Secondly, the author provides a summary of her earlier Australian links and influences, some deserving of more recognition.

Thirdly he provides an account of the three eventful weeks spent by Dorothy Day in NSW and Victoria in August 1970, accepting an invitation from a well known Sydney priest, Roger Pryke, with the cooperation of Melbourne's Father John Heffey, who, with Pryke, a young Father Guilford Young and other Australian clerics or seminarians returning home from Rome's Propaganda Fide College early in the Second World War, had on their way visited Dorothy in New York.

Finally, Val Noone offers his own challenging thoughts on her enduring legacy. He writes: "From within the nooks and crannies of a disintegrating Catholicism, Dorothy's basic insights and her witness continue to intrigue and inspire many."

Referring to the priority to be given to social concerns, while thinking above all of people 'who are trapped in a cycle of poverty', Pope Francis in his memorable speech to Congress had explained his choice of Dorothy Day as one of his American icons in these words: 'I cannot fail to mention the Servant of God Dorothy Day, who founded the Catholic Worker Movement. Her social activism, her passion for justice and for the cause of the oppressed, were inspired by the Gospel, her faith and the example of the saints.'

In spite of its title, what distinguishes this book is that it is so much more than a simple description of what were a hectic three weeks spent by Day and her friend and companion, the peace activist, writer and lecturer Eileen Egan, addressing capacity audiences, conducting seminars, visiting urban and country communes in or not too far from Sydney and Melbourne and giving multiple media interviews. The report of the tour in Chapter Three, fascinating as it is, occupies only about one quarter of the book's pages. The rest offers the reader hugely informative if in some cases previously unpublished details about the visit's historical context and an explanation for why the life of this American woman and her biblical and liturgically motivated actions had such an impact on many people in and beyond the USA, at least one Pope among them.

Through his footnotes, lists of references and of Day biographies, ad hoc mentions and in other ways, Val Noone points the way to resources for anyone wishing to learn more about any of the characters, organisations, places and events he names, some of them needing to be better known. I am thinking of personalities like Pryke and Heffey, Sydney's Tony Newman, Tom Dunlea, Ted Kennedy, Gai Smith, Brian Johns, Mum Shirl, Meg Gilchrist, Little Sisters of Jesus and Dick Buchhorn, as well as Melbourne's Ray and Betty Triado, Geoff Lacey, Max Charlesworth, Margaret Coffey, Paul and Marie Ormonde, Michael McGirr, Bruce Duncan, Brian Noone and Dally Messenger. The names of a host of others could be drawn from the book's comprehensive Index.

Significant too in Dorothy Day's Australian story as related in this book are publications headed by Australia's own *Catholic Worker*, edited initially in 1936 by Bartholomew ('Bob') Santamaria and later promoted for a long time by John Ryan, who, like Tony Newman and a few others, quickly became a good friend of Dorothy Day after meeting her. Other relevant journals had briefer but in their own ways momentous lives, such as Val Noone's and Garry McLoughlin's *Priest Forum*, Roger Pryke's *Nonviolent Power* and Edmund Campion's *Report*. The mainstream media, Catholic and secular, also gave the 1970 visit due attention.

Of considerable interest are Val Noone's summaries of the history of a number of Catholic communes that came into existence during and after the 1930s and thrived in Australian cities and more usually in the country, often consciously or unconsciously inspired by Dorothy Day's and Peter Maurin's American Catholic Worker Movement. Four well remembered back-to-the land settlements were at San Isidore near Wagga Wagga, Whitlands in northern Victoria, Maryknoll in Gippsland and Gladysdale in the Yarra Ranges, where Dorothy stayed happily for four days as Father Heffey's guest during her wintry Victorian visit. A city open house, where the homeless were given hospitality, was created in 1969 by Mary Doyle and Brian Noone in Fitzroy—and maintained for a few more years, close by in that same Melbourne suburb by Mary, with Brian's older brother, Val. In Sydney, Fathers Ted Kennedy, John Butcher and Fergus Breslan launched the popular St Vincent's house of hospitality in the Redfern area early in the 1970s.

Substantial variations existed in the ways in which all this activity was performed in different places or from time to time in the one place—and even in attitudes to global events like the Spanish Civil War and the Vietnam War (Dorothy Day herself opposed the Second World War). It is unquestionable, however, that the power of Dorothy's spirit played some part everywhere, with its stress on peace-making, non-violence, hospitality and Christ-like compassion for the poor and disadvantaged, who were at best seen as teachers rather than recipients of largesse.

A hint of the enigmatic side to Day's own personality is neatly expressed in words that Noone quotes from Edmund Campion: 'Dorothy Day stood for a radical Catholicism that was earthed in the experience of being poor. Her Catholicism managed to keep together in one whole non-violence, personalism, opposition to state power, traditional religious devotions, orthodox theology and deference to Church authority'.

Searchers for a better understanding of what Dorothy was truly like are well served by her autobiographical books (she was from early youth a skilled journalist and wordsmith) and by her numerous biographies. Notable among them are those by Jim Forest, Nancy Roberts and, more recently, her granddaughter Kate Hennessy as well as John Loughery with Blythe Randolph.

That picture is verified on virtually every page of Val Noone's book. He does well, for example, to quote at length from his wife's account of two months spent in 1976 in an ageing Dorothy's company by the two of them, with their baby son Michael, on the Catholic Worker farm at Tivoli, 100 miles north of New York city.

Unable to travel any more because of the serious heart condition that was to end her life four years later, Dorothy had invited the Noone family to join her and other residents. It might have had the tone of a command rather than an invitation. In one revealing quote, Mary wrote: 'My experience at Tivoli was that the Catholic Worker people in general and Dorothy Day in particular went to extraordinary lengths to accept and make welcome and just let be the most difficult people you could ever wish not to meet'. She adds that healing was often managed 'just by loving' those people 'who might be on drugs and behaving really strangely'. Mary quotes Dorothy's comment on efforts made to have more 'structure' at Tivoli Farm: 'We have the meals, we sweep the dining room, and we have Compline; that's enough structure for me'.

Written under pressure during the covid-19 pandemic, *Dorothy Day in Australia* successfully met the author's anniversary deadline by appearing early in August 2020. It has also proved to be a well timed contribution to the Catholic Church's Just War debate, reawakened by papal statements on and attitudes to war and peace. It is recommended for serious attention and discussion. It can be seen as complementing and updating some of what Val Noone wrote on complex issues like pacifism, conscientious objection, conscription, nuclear weapons, civil disobedience and the whole peace movement in his longer (333-page) book *Disturbing the War* (Spectrum, 1993).

Book Review

Consider the Crows: Centenary of the Catholic Diocese of Wagga Wagga, 1917–2017: General Diocesan History

---

Author: Justin Darlow
Publisher: Triple D Books for the Catholic Diocese of Wagga Wagga 2020
ISBN: 9780648535812
Paperback: 283 pages
Price: $34.99

Reviewed by Anthony Robbie*

The proliferation of dioceses across rural Australia was caused to no small extent both by the vast distances involved, which must have seemed intimidating on a map in a Roman office and equally by the fatigue of weary Australian bishops and their agents, called upon to travel across them in disobliging circumstances. That doesn't seem to have been the case with the Diocese of Wagga Wagga, created in 1918 from territory taken from Goulburn Diocese as it then was. The Vatican mercifully (and rather unusually) looked to the aboriginal meaning of the name Wagga and Christened it with the charming Latin title of Corvopolitana when it erected the new Diocese. There was always

---

* Father Anthony Robbie is a priest of the Archdiocese of Sydney. He has degrees in Law, Theology and Church History and has lectured in Theology and Ecclesiastical History in Australia and overseas. He is currently the postulator of the Cause of Eileen O'Connor.

something a bit different about Wagga Wagga. It covered an area both manageable and somehow logical. This was no mere arbitrary line on a map, or a diocese left with the bits that hadn't been parceled off elsewhere. A former bishop of the diocese used to boast of having attended a Roman conference where he was asked to give an account of the agricultural and industrial products of his diocese. The list was so impressive that an admiring Cardinal replied 'You should declare independence!'

That independence of the diocese is one of the themes of Father Justin Darlow's impressive new history, which is lavishly illustrated and finely produced. It follows the interests and careers of the bishops of Wagga Wagga in turn and dwells not a little on their characters as it lists their achievements. It is a story familiar to many rural communities across the country and indeed the anglophone world over the last century. The Church at the height of her confidence planning resolutely for the pastoral needs of a future which seemed so sure and predictable. The parishes and churches, the schools and convents expand year by year, a great work of sacrifice and devotion until in the sixties a new world appears and everything turns around. Wagga Wagga diocese has always ridden the crest of the wave and in the hopeful post-conciliar years it was a trail-blazing test ground for the new theories of how to live the Church's life. Promoted by the much loved Bishop Henschke and then by his chosen successor the young and highly motivated Bishop Frank Carroll, Wagga developed quite a reputation as the ecclesiastical *avant garde* capital of Australia.

A rather different path began in 1984 when Bishop William Brennan succeeded the now Archbishop Carroll. A renewed attention to the content of the Faith and to the formation of children as well as clergy drove the new bishop, an education enthusiast, culminating in a new education curriculum and famously a new seminary. Both were controversial decisions. Some saw this as a betrayal of the hopes and the promise of the conciliar Church. Brennan and his supporters countered that the Council itself called for a close eye to the "signs of the times" and that progressive elements may have misread what those signs were saying. Father Darlow's book is particularly useful in covering the controversies and makes a valuable and much needed contribution to this important field. His use of interviews with former bishops, clergy and laity is helpful and enlightening. An expanded edition might profit from an examination of the contribution of the religious orders to the story of the diocese and there are many interesting episodes like the settlement of San Isidore, an attempt at a Catholic rural community based on Catholic cooperative social principles and founded just outside Wagga in 1957. What happened to it? Nonetheless, Father Darlow is to be highly commended for producing such a valuable and helpful history. One hopes that it will be widely read in the Diocese and beyond.

Book Review

Screen Priests: Depictions of Catholic Priests in Cinema, 1900–1918

Author: Peter Malone
Publisher: ATF Press, Adelaide, 2019
ISBN: 9781925872897
Paperback: xiii and 701 pages
Price: $54.90

Reviewed by Richard Leonard*

The second line in Peter's excellent and large book is a relief: '. . . [This book is] not intended to be read from cover to cover . . .' though it does go on '. . . although it could be, since it takes the reader through the history of cinema'.

Given the prominence of films about priests—for good and for ill—it is incredible to think that that this is only the third major book on this subject. It is, however the most comprehensive.

Peter quickly draws our attention to what he considers to be three of the best portrayals of priests in more recent years: the story of the French Cistercian martyrs of Algeria in *Of Gods and Men* (2010); the Irish film, *Calvary*, 2014; and Martin Scorsese's 2016 *Silence*, the portrait of Jesuit missionaries in seventeenth century Japan, the lay Catholics, persecution, torture and execution and ultimate challenges for belief (and disbelief).

After a masterful summary of the complex history of the priesthood and religious life in the Catholic Church, he goes straight to the silent

* Rev Dr Richard Leonard SJ is the director of the Australian Catholic Office for Film & Broadcasting and the author of *Movies That Matter: Reading Film Through the Lens of Faith*; and *The Mystical Gaze of the Cinema: the Films of Peter Weir.*

era and he works through each decade from the 1930's on. Rather than leaving it at the summary and synopsis of films of each period, Peter chooses a film that he argues typifies the portrayal of the priest in that period. Most of them a wide audience will know: *Going My Way*, *On the Waterfront*, *The Cardinal*, *M*A*S*H* (the movie), *The Mission*, *Priest*, *Keeping the Faith*, *Of Gods and Men*, and *Calvary*.

The only film given this special attention by him that I have not seen is '*The Fighting 69*th' from 1939, with an *Angels with Dirty Faces* plot, James Cagney as a brash and self-centred soldier who encounters the ministrations of the most regularly cast priest, Pat O'Brien as a sympathetic army chaplain. What's not to like about any of that?

Added to this wonderful walk through the cinematic museum of screen priests, Peter also looks at films with religious themes or characters. *Entertaining Angels*: *The Dorothy Day Story*; *The Postman Always Rings Twice*; *The End of the Affair*; *Grace of Monaco*; *Chocolat*; *Heaven Help Us*; *Cinema Paradiso* and *The Magdalene Sisters*, just to name a few.

But just when we think our vast and meticulous chronological journey is complete, Peter is only warming up. The last third of the book looks at thematic developments of the portrayal of the priests firstly within two national cinemas, who are case studies for different reasons: Ireland and Australia; and then the priest as an exorcist and devil hunter; and, of course, and much to our eternal shame, as a sexual predator against children.

A book like this is always hard to bring to a conclusion because, just when the author thinks he or she is good to go to press, another, potentially important, film is released. Peter says, A book on Screen Priests has to end at some time even when the film priests continue to appear on the screen. For this book, there is something of a providence in the 2016 appearance of Martin Scorsese's *Silence* and the 2017 screening of the BBC series, *Broken*. Here are serious probings of priests and priesthood when the cinema going public and the television audience least expected it. These are the appropriate images and themes to bring this book to a close.

Let me give two tastes of this important work:

> . . . *Broken* (d Ashley Pearce, Noreen Kershaw) was written by Jimmy McGovern, a follow-up to his 1995 film, *Priest*, already considered as a key film of the 1990s. At the time

> of *Priest*, McGovern was reconsidering his belonging to the church, a recovering Catholic. Michael Kerrigan is a hardworking Liverpool parish priest in a working-class parish. He is in his later 40s . . . We get a good idea of the strength of Michael's faith and commitment as a priest, his taking for granted his pastoral role and the need for listening and for personal presence. Faith and commitment are a journey, not quickly achieved. His life can be lonely, alone in the presbytery—prayer and some support in a drink. He is a committed celibate. . . . He is propositioned by a desperate woman planning suicide. He is challenged by a gay man as to whether he ever wondered about his sexual orientation . . . Michael respects the authorities in the church but they do not impinge very directly on his day-to-day life. . . . Considering the worldwide loss of respect for the Church, especially in the Western world, the seeming lack of credibility in stances on sexual morality, the scandals of clerical sexual abuse, Jimmy McGovern offers a convincing portrait of a good priest . . .
>
> . . . *Silence* is Martin Scorsese's version of Shusaku Endo's novel, *Silence*, which had become an award-winning, Cannes-screened, Japanese film in 1971. Scorsese wanted to make his version for 25 years but, until now, had failed in raising sufficient finance. His film now is a fine Scorsese achievement . . . the first two hours of *Silence* play as an appeal to the Catholic ethos of the 1940s and 50s . . . the final forty minutes that the film moves its audience, faithful as well as non-Christian, sympathetic or not, to consider questions about priesthood that have arisen since the Vatican Council. . . . Does the film suggest that the no greater love is not necessarily laying down life in death but in sacrificing one's own life in living so that others may live? *Silence* raises the issue of commitment to vocation, challenge to vocation, mental and emotional pressure, the experience of feeling 'forsaken' intellectual arguments, and the crisis of conscience of renunciation to save others' lives . . .

Peter has done so many of us a great service—from Catholics/interested co-religionists/and to cinema scholars and film buffs—I may be biased for obvious reasons but his prism is as fascinating as any other in analysing the many key developments throughout the history of the cinema.

Whether it's priests as champions of the poor and the moral good, the conflicted confessor, paying the price for celibacy or leaving for love; heroic missionaries, social justice campaigners, naughty and funny and runaway popes, driving evil away, perpetrating despicable evil acts with innocents, or as saints, sinners and mystics, this volume has them all.

Peter produced this work in his eightieth year which is as astounding as I hope it has been satisfying. The traditional symbol of the eightieth anniversary used to be the oak, but now it's the pearl. The work and passion behind a lifetime of film watching in *Screen Priests* is as solid and strong as an oak and this book is a pearl of great price.

Book Review

Dear Movies

Author: Peter Malone
Publisher: Coventry Press,
ISBN: 9781925872897
Paperback: xiii and 701 pages
Price: $44.95

Reviewed by Richard Leonard*

Full disclosure: Peter Malone has been my friend and colleague since 1994. I succeeded him as the Director of the Catholic Film Office in 1998 when he moved to the UK to become the President of SIGNIS (World Catholic Association for Communication). Upon his return to Australia in 2006 he became an associate of the newly titled Australian Catholic Office for Film & Broadcasting.

In 2018 when the Australian Catholic Bishops Conference (ACBC) marked his 50th anniversary as a Catholic film reviewer, the ACBC President, Archbishop Mark Coleridge, noted that, beginning with the To Sir With Love in 1968, "Fr Malone has seen some 6,000 films, and his reviews have been published in every major Australian Catholic newspaper, as well as *Compass* and *Annals*,

* Rev Dr Richard Leonard SJ is the director of the Australian Catholic Office for Film & Broadcasting and the author of *Movies That Matter: Reading Film Through the Lens of Faith*; and *The Mystical Gaze of the Cinema: the Films of Peter Weir.*

among several other journals. He combined his love of the cinema with an active academic career, lecturing at Yarra Theological Union for twenty five years, editing *Compass Theological Journal* from 1972–1998 and authoring over sixteen books, including *Screen Jesus* and *Screen Priests*. In 2008 the Melbourne College of Divinity conferred on him the Degree of Doctor of Sacred Theology (Honoris Causa) recognising Peter's 'outstanding contribution to theological learning and education, especially for his significant contribution to bringing a critical Christian perspective to the study, interpretation and enjoyment of the visual media.'

Dear Movies starts twenty years earlier than his first film review, with his introduction to the cinema: *Anna Karenina* in 1948. What follows is not only a letter to 102 films, but the whole volume is a love-letter to the cinema as a window on the world.

The letter device works well, each one approximately 1,000 words. It is not a book recommending films that Christians should watch. There are some titles here that some people would baulk at: *Bad Lieutenant*; *Salo*; *Django Unchained*; *Life of Brian*; *Godfather*; and *The Devils*; while there other films we might expect a priest reviewer to include: *Jesus*; *The Nun's Story*; *The Mission*; *Of Gods and Men*; *Babette's Feast*; *Bruce Almighty*; *Jesus of Montreal*; *Priest*; *Calvary*; and *Sister Act*. The rest of the films are as individual and idiosyncratic as any personal selection is going to be. The choice has been made because of what they have evoked in Peter, meant to him at the time, or how they charted a shift in his take on the world.

I have seen fifty five of the films Peter presents in *Dear Movies*. While he often fills in enough of the details of the films I had not seen for me to enjoy his engagement with them, I wonder if a very short synopsis of each film would have enhanced the work even more. Even so, the capsules are easy to read, insightful and engaging. Appropriate for the device, the tone is conversational. I read the work from cover to cover, but it is also a book one can dip into and out of or one could refer to time and again.

On a deeper level this work establishing a dialogue between faith and culture in an increasingly secular world. *Dear Movies* is a bridge between implicit and profound faith and the work of visual artists over the last 72 years.

Riffing on Jeremiah 20:7 it's clear from this work that the cinema has seduced Peter and he has let himself be seduced; for it was too strong for him, and it has prevailed; even, and often, finding God there. But in saying that *Dear Movies* is a love letter from Peter to the cinema, it's clear the affection has been reciprocal and so this mystical marriage has been mutually patient, generous, trusting, respectful and faithful.

Book Reviews

Paul Stenhouse MSC: A Life of Rare Wisdom, Compassion and Inspiration

---

Author: Wanda Skowronska
Publisher: Connor Court
ISB9781922449443
Paperback: 307 pages
Price: $35

Paul Stenhouse: A Distinctive and Distinguished Missionary of the Sacred Heart
Editor: Peter Malone MSC
ISBN: 9781922454034
Publisher: Australian Scholarly Publishing
Paperback, $20 (plus $9.00 p&p)

Reviewed by Irene Franklin*

Father Paul Stenhouse MSC was such an exceptional person that two books have been written about him in the year since he died. Many more could be written in order to do justice to what he achieved. He was best known as the long-term editor of the journal of Catholic culture, *Annals Australasia,* but as Skowronska's biography shows, that was just the tip of the iceberg of an extraordinarily diverse life of service.

Skowronska's book is a very well researched, readable biography. The Introduction alone is a must read section, especially for those who did not have the good fortune to meet this man but something to treasure for those of us who were fortunate to be among his multitude of friends.

---

* Irene Franklin is an ACHS member.

Paul was born on 9 December 1935. His father died before Paul turned one. His mother with her two very young sons moved to Camden close to her family. Times were tough. Paul loved learning and was home schooled by his mother in the early years because of illness. His mother was a convert from Anglicanism and kept in contact with her Anglican friends and relations. She was obviously an intelligent woman who was a good role model for her sons to learn from. Paul did get some schooling in the local Catholic school. He needed to leave at fifteen for financial reasons and got a job with the local newspaper.

He saw an advertisement in *Annals* by the Missionaries of the Sacred Heart and joined their novitiate, being ordained in 1963. He went on to study Ancient History and Hebrew at Sydney University, later specialising in Samaritan studies. He was invited to be secretary to the Father General in Rome. During that time he was working on his PhD and ended up going to Communist Dubrovnik to finish it.

When Paul returned to Australia he returned to being editor of *Annals*, which became the centre of his life's work. With his education, wide reading of many subjects, travel experiences and innumerable friends and acquaintances he was able to put together a journal of Catholic Culture with wide appeal of great educational value which I always found uplifting. Its diversity of Catholic ideas and stories from history was legendary.

Of the themes he wrote on himself, one that recurred was reminding Australian people of the war in Lebanon and its effect on the people. He conducted secret mercy missions taking pharmaceuticals to Lebanon via Malta and wrote from first-hand experience of Lebanon. His long study of Islam—Arabic was one of the many languages he mastered—convinced him that Islam was a dangerous ideology which the West did not understand.

Other ministries included many decades of reaching out to Asian students from a number of countries studying in Australia to help them solve their social and other problems. He was also a principal force behind the Aid to the Church in Need, the charity that supports persecuted Christians worldwide.

Father Paul Stenhouse was always courteous, kind, thoughtful, helpful and generous with his time, advice and gifts. He made many people feel special, truly a friend. I have read a number of times how a priest should emulate Christ. A very tall order for any human creature. He, more than anyone else, showed me the face of Jesus. To be treated as though one is special naturally causes a person to want to respond in kind.

Paul suffered the attacks of five cancers; four disappeared but the fifth one ended his life. I often wonder if his trip to out-of-bounds Chernobyl was the cause.

I was fortunate to welcome him to the home I share with my husband, Jim, on a number of precious occasions so I will treasure the book Wanda Skowronska has written with such satisfying and pleasing thoroughness.

Malone's book is a collection of memoirs divided into sections. The first is about Paul the person by a few of his confreres, his cousin Tricia and others. The second section is by people who knew him as a priest scholar then another concentrating on his various ministries and finally a section of tributes. Some notable contributions included those by Tony Abbott and Piers Paul Read on Paul's opposition to Islam, that by Joseph Assaf on his deep connection with Lebanon, various recollections of the editing of *Annals,* and a brief tribute by Cardinal Pell (who was also interviewed for Skowronska's book).

Book Review

The Write Stuff—Voices of Unity on Labor's Future

Edited by Nick Dyrenfurth and Misha Zelinsky
Publisher: Connor Court Publishing, 2020
ISBN: 9781922449429
Paperback: 304 pages
Price: $29.95

Reviewed by David Cragg*

This anthology brings together views on the Federal ALP—a group post mortem on the May 2019 federal election loss as well as some speculation on Labor's post Covid electoral prospects. It's a gathering of the ALP's Right—moderate or social democratic—group in deep reflection, and providing in particular a platform for Federal MHRs and Senators.

After a Foreword by former Senator Steve Loosley and an Introduction by the coeditors, there are thirty chapters of an average 8 pages apiece. The coeditors each contribute a fine essay—of the remaining twenty eight, no less than nineteen are from current or former members of ALP Federal Caucus (but surprisingly, not including the current pot stirrer Joel Fitzgibbon). Of the balance, four essays are from party activist thinkers, three from trade unionists and strangely only two contributions from successful regional Labor politicians—Michelle Roberts MLA of WA and Selena Uibo MLA of the NT. A State and Territory anthology is hopefully in the pipeline!

Former Shadow Treasurer Chris Bowen (Chapter 8) comes as close as any politician might to giving an apology for his part in the 2019 election policy train wreck. His subtle and positive take on what

---

* David Cragg is a Life Member of the ALP.

opportunities might present themselves in a post Covid political environment doesn't mention the Federal Election at all, but it's not hard to read between the lines. The lesson he draws from Covid—the need for 'focus and prioritisation' in ranking policies, 'as ambitious and impatient as Labor can be'—really dates from May 2019. Don't run on new taxes from Opposition—the post John Hewson principle of politics! Bowen's upbeat future focus makes the best of what must be pretty painful for him. His successor as Shadow Treasurer, Jim Chalmers (7) discusses post Covid in more detail, thinking how Labor might 'manage change thrust upon us'. The two chapters are a neat contrast and complement each other. Bowen's audience is an internal party one, Chalmers is talking to the broader Australian community about tough times ahead. He shows a rare talent to talk economics in understandable everyday terms, something John Howard mastered to great effect. His staid title 'The Future of Labor' should be changed to something more like 'The Coming Recession'. . . .

Perhaps the most unexpected essay is 'Faithful and Labor—What Labor Ignores at its Peril' by party veteran Michael Easson (22). He point-blank argues that Labor must consciously make a place at its table for people with conservative values. Labor today risks being locked inside an intolerant identity box, cutting itself off from people of personal faith who are interested in community justice. Easson raises fascinating questions about the limit of politics and the role of the state just as a facilitator rather than as the solution to all life's problems. Because Labor feels uncomfortable with questions of faith, we vacate the field and leave fertile ground for other political parties. Research after May 2019 suggests that we damaged ourselves most with newly arrived migrant communities for whom religion provides a core cultural affirmation and sense of well-being.

Sam Crosby, now of the St Vincent de Paul Society, backs this in his essay 'True Believers' (27), and coeditor Nick Dyrenfurth makes the same plea that Labor treat people of faith with respect in his opening essay (1). Easson wonders whether Australia's general enthusiasm for multiculturalism may help the ALP to talk with respect to other non Christian religions—and then learn to apply the principle to all faiths equitably. He says you can't be serious about multiculturalism without respecting religious diversity. These important essays deserve to be spun off into a separate collection on faith in politics. (Senator Deborah O'Neill (21) writes on the importance for Labor to reconnect with small business in Australia, one of the party's historic bases. This could be easily rejigged to fit in with a discussion of faith, or a discussion of how unions need to rethink their business model.)

The need for Labor to talk to non-metropolitan Australians deserves a volume of its own. A great starting point is provided by five essays in this collection—Jenny Hill (13), Robbie Dalton (15), Senator Anthony Chisholm (23), Senator Raff Ciccone (25) and Selena Uibo (30)—which open up the indigenous issue as part of a broader agrarian economic debate including regional development and migration. Labor was once trusted to reflect the values of rural & regional Australia—can this relationship ever be restored? These essays too are worth the price of the whole volume.

Ros Kelly (19) provides a fragment of memoir about her years in Canberra 1980–1995—which could be a starting point for a collection of pointed vignettes from former MPs who don't feel the need to write full volumes. And two of the unionist contributions—Josh Peak (17) and Diana Asmar (20)—could seed another useful collection of essays centred on the harsh realities of working life experienced by too many in our community today. Coeditor Misha Zelinsky (4) and Clare O'Neil (10) could also be included here. The security of work achieved by Australian Labor a century ago has flown out the windows, to Labor's shame.

Only a few essays seem like they may have been pro forma written by the Parliamentary Library, and in a volume of this size that is truly impressive. I hope that any second edition might include some formatting gestures to help the reader—an Index at the back, a List of Contributors at the front, and maybe some attempt to group the essays into a few themed sections.

Book Review

Faith's Place: Democracy in a Religious World

Editors: Bryan S Turner and Damien T Freeman
Publisher: The Kapunda Press/Connor Court.
ISBN: 9781922449337
Paperback: 242 pages
Price: $32.95

Reviewed by Michael Easson*

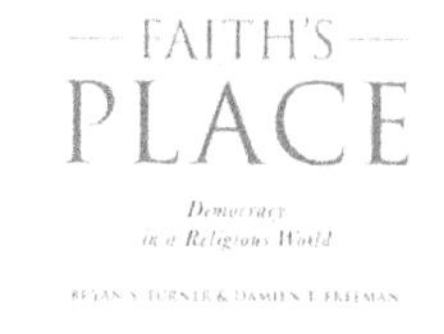

Australia's political culture, as with western ruling elites generally, with the partial exception of the United States, is becoming more secular. Yet the world is becoming more religious. Faith still registers strongly in western societies. (Even in Australia, though the trend is clear, a clear majority still identify as Christian, though this is dropping.)

Is the interaction of the religious, the agnostics, and atheists, a dialogue of the deaf, or is something richer and more interesting possible? This is a question that has preoccupied thinkers of all stripes from The Enlightenment onwards.

Turner and Freeman's book gathers two main essays (theirs) and various responses to the topic at hand—faith's place in the land and in a world increasingly religious. The issues are both localised (Australia) and international (including Australia's engagement with the rest of the world.)

---

* Michael Easson is Executive Chair of EG Funds Management and has an interest in public policy and philosophy.

The book opens with a Foreword by Brisbane's Catholic Archbishop Mark Coleridge who argues 'faith speaks not just of God and the things of heaven but also of human beings and the things of earth', suggesting that the earthly and heavenly cannot be neatly compartmentalised.

The editors' joint introduction opens with a reference to the early 1990s thesis by the late Professor Samuel Huntington (1927–2008) on democracy's 'third wave' and the need for researchers to discern global trends, such as the Catholic Church's more benign attitudes to democracy in the twentieth century, and the sweeping appeal of democracy post the collapse of the Soviet empire. The reference to Huntington, who wrote widely, is interesting. He is perhaps best known for his thesis on 'the clash of civilisations' which he developed a few years after his *The Third Wave: Democratization in the Late Twentieth Century* (1991) book (based on an article published the same year) and its relatively optimistic argument about the spread-of-democracy and realistic assessment of major stumbling blocks. In his essay 'The Clash of Civilizations?' (1993) for the journal *Foreign Affairs*, which he turned into a book (without the question mark), *The Clash of Civilizations and the Remaking of World Order* (1996), Huntington posited that Western, Orthodox, and Islamic civilisations would clash, with potential for comparable civilisational rivalries from Hindu, Sinic, Japanese, Latin American, and possibly African cultures. What some of these hazy nomenclatures might mean was controversial, debatable, and interesting. Without discussing the later development of Huntington's ideas (unnecessary in a volume like this), the editors wonder how 'might he have evaluated our current situation'.

A key component of that 'situation' is highlighted by reference to the Pew Research Center's 2015 report on *The Future of World Religions: Population Growth Projections 2010–2050*, which they consider authoritative. Islam and Christianity are likely to grow strongly (with Africa's population growth, increases in longevity, and improved health care, contributing strongly to the overall story.) The editors say: 'The challenges presented for democracy in a religious world are the subject of this volume'.

Turner kicks off the debate with a wide-ranging essay on 'Liberal Societies in a Religious World'. Unfortunately, rambling might be a better description of what he writes. Though his summation of

Pentecostalism as a modern-day version of Methodism is very interesting, this is not explored deeply. Statements about 'the wars in the Middle East under the presidency of Donald Trump' (hmmm, were there any?), the 'slow death of the Great Barrier Reef' (Are there not signs of life?), the 'most interesting development' in the recent history of the United States with 'the rise of groups such as InCel—involuntary celibacy' (surely a small, fringe group), support for Trump 'from increased numbers of Jews' (in the recent presidential election at least 70% voted against him; the Jewish vote, despite Trump's commendable progress on Arab-Israel relations, went backwards for him in percentage terms. The 2017 Charlottesville far-right, Nazi-flag heralded rally and its violence, together with Trump's characterisation of 'some very fine people on both sides', rocked and frightened that community and they voted accordingly), and a few other bloops, mar the discussion. Unconvincingly, Turner writes: '. . . the forces that are changing and eroding citizenship and democracy are the same forces that are changing and undermining religion'. There was potentially a good essay here, but this contribution needed firmer editing.

Of considerable merit is Freeman's Chapter on 'Democratic Leaders in a Religious World'. He quotes Burke: 'The temper of the people amongst whom he presides ought . . . to be the first study of a statesman'. From this plank, Freeman seeks to construct the argument that understanding the people requires empathy and intellectual engagement (unless the purpose is to better suppress them!) In a liberal democracy, however, 'the liberty of the entire population matters'. From there, he discusses what might be incomprehensible to certain secular politicians: the beliefs of the religious. He suggests five key elements: belief in the transcendent; commitment that metaphysics 'dictates ethics' (in marked contrast to relativism); the conviction that there are certain obligations we cannot renounce; the anti-individualist idea that life is led through a community; and, finally, that human flourishing requires discovering meaning inherent in the world and obliges adherents to act accordingly. There is a useful discourse on what all this means in the context of the shared Abrahamic faiths' beliefs in all five principles, though noting variety and shifting perspectives on them. This reviewer believes the claim that religion dictates the actions a believer must follow is debatable. What Sandel and Freeman mean is that a metaphysical world view, a religion for example, prescribes what a person should do. If ethics is the study, interpretation, and elucidation of good actions, and the grounds for adhering to them, then the point is that for some people it is entirely decided by their beliefs. But as Saperstein points out (and as further discussed below), every day you make choices; it is not like people are automatically programmed robots.

Freeman refers to Dyson Heydon's description of modern, anti-clerical, 'elites' who do not understand or appreciate various religious creeds, who desire 'unconditional surrender' to the dictates of the secular state. (This is a reference to Heydon's essay/inaugural 2017 PM Glynn lecture, 'Religious 'Toleration' in Modern Australia: The Tyranny of Relativism'.) But there are grounds to suggest competing and contrasting views need not be impenetrable, from one to the other. Freeman suggests: 'The levels of mutual suspicion, misunderstanding, and ambivalence that attend this rapprochement will . . . likely be determined by self-interest and any amicable relationship may well entail its own peculiar contradictions'. Then he becomes absorbing, discussing the political theorist Michael Sandel's ideas about the 'encumbered self' and the desirability of understanding religious freedom as 'freedom of conscience, not freedom of choice'. The former suggests freedom to follow a duty, based on the this-is-who-I-am argument. Freeman argues that the 'encumbered self is a richer concept than the duty to adhere to conscience' position, on the principle that verisimilitude matters, though Freeman's argument would benefit from greater elucidation. (Perhaps this is a subject for a future book.)

But what is the meaning of the encumbered and the unencumbered self? This is not more than sketched, though it lies at the heart of Freeman's analysis and his development of Sandel's thinking.

In brief, Sandel charges that the liberal embrace of an unencumbered, individualist self, is unsustainable. Freeman quotes Sandel: 'where conscience dictates, choice decides'. This fits with the idea that my personhood is decided by who I am. It is not so much that a person chooses what to believe, it is that intrinsic identity decides what are their beliefs. This is a difficult and tricky territory to negotiate.

Freeman sees a possible bridge from secular to religious perspectives, suggesting that just as gay and transgender persons are what they are, and can only be that, then it is irrational to criticise them for not 'choosing' to be otherwise. He argues for the need for protection of 'some aspect of the encumbered self' and references the thinking of Rabbi Jonathan Sachs (1948–2020) about 'the dignity of difference' and proposes 'we need to understand ourselves as part of communities of meaning'. Freeman goes on to conclude: 'That religious conscience gives rise to an encumbered self should not be incomprehensible to leaders if they reflect on other senses of the encumbered self that are more immediately comprehensible to them'.

This suggests that difference in society needs empathy, sympathy, an open mind, and the imagination to link apparently incompatible positions into a more nuanced appreciation of the world as it is.

Freeman's analysis is partly contested by the most interesting (and longest) response in the book, David Saperstein's essay 'Religious Freedom in the Twenty-First Century'. Before returning to this—the most important and subversive aspect of the book—it is commendable of the editors to have drawn a rich array of responders.

A former Labor Senator for NSW, now CEO of Catholic Social Services Australia, Ursula Stephens, references her experiences including in the all-party Parliamentary Christian Fellowship where, in an atmosphere of trust and confidence, policymaking was influenced. Luke Gosling, a Federal Labor MP in the Northern Territory writes on 'Amen to the Holy Land in Australia'. He links the beliefs of Aboriginal cultures and the 'introduced faiths', saying:

> If we have leaders who help others to see the constructive intuitions in these traditions—including in the Indigenous connection with land, sea, sky, and all creatures great and small—then we've got a chance of upholding the holiness of life, the dignity of every person, and of living more sustainably on this planet.

Current Liberal Senator for Western Australia, Dean Smith, writes on religious diversity, commenting that the incomprehension of religious attitudes exists not only between secular and religious, but is also 'alive between religious people'. Comparative religions anthropologist Robert Hefner's piece on 'Faith's Place in an Age of Democratic Trial' addresses the book's themes (affirming 'the importance of an encumbered and democratic selfhood even within the circumstance of only modestly overlapping truth claims'), as does religion scholar Jocelyne Cesari's 'Democracy in a Religious World or Religion in a Democratic World?', who regrets, unpromisingly, 'the analysis of the never-ending interactions between religion and politics is challenging, if not impossible, within existing political theories'. She tries to repair the gap, careful about widening it. Australian Emeritus Professor Riaz Hassan's account of Islamophobia and secularism in liberal democracies draws parallels between the suspicion of liberal elites towards Islam, and what he sees as the: 'Pressing need for . . . consideration of how to develop appropriate public policies to manage religious and ethnic diversity and to promote inter-religious harmony'. The alternative is localised, small-pond style clashes of civilisation with other religious viewpoints and secular modernity.

James Franklin's essay, 'Incomprehension of Religion in Australian Society', neatly responds to the themes of Freeman's argument, including the arrogant and wilful dismissal by some prominent secularists about the logic and coherence of Christian, especially Catholic, beliefs on life, sanctity of the person, etc. He characterises this as the 'elected ignorance of religion', playing on the idea of the 'elected' as the guardians of liberal elitism as well as their political cousins. In the teaching of history to school children, accounts of the motivating religious convictions of Australian historical figures is mostly ignored. He calls this 'a human rights abuse perpetuated on children'. But there is hope in the centrist voters, who decide elections under Australia's compulsory voting system, where 'there remains a strong commitment to the sort of tolerance that is shocked by 'cancel culture'. Conservative philosopher and public policy intellectual Michael Casey, the Director of the PM Glynn Institute, provides an overarching, thoughtful piece: 'Conclusion: Rethinking Religion in a Secular World.' He asks: 'What happens, however, if religion refuses to be over?' And goes on to address the Freeman challenge, which he describes in part as referring to 'those whose attachments to place, attributes of identity, and special relationships of obligation decisively mark who they are, beyond any choosing'. He notes: 'Sexuality and gender identification are also seen as attributes of identity which are not chosen'. But this is a rabbit hole to be warily entered. Casey insists that 'the encumbered self of religious conviction remains set apart' and argues why this is so.

It is now appropriate to return to an earlier point: Rabbi Saperstein's grappling with the matters raised by Freeman, which is the highlight of the book. He strongly contests Sandel's and Freeman's characterisations of conscience and choice: 'the difference between conscience claims and choice claims is not always clear'. In this reviewer's opinion, Sandel draws a longer than necessary bow to argue that encumbered selves are unable to choose freely. The formation of citizens, in the cultivation of civic virtues, requires a place in community. That the community constitutes us rather than vice versa is not to exhaust meaning, however. Some questions are begged. Ironically, identity politics can enact the Sandelian premise that we are not primarily individuals but members of certain communities. This is a complex field, and it is enough in this work that the right questions are asked. Saperstein posits the question: '. . . is not the religious conscience approach to religious freedom as likely to result in moral relativism as the rights approach?' This is indeed a rich area of focus which this book can claim as its primary achievement.

Read the book is my strong recommendation to anyone even slightly interested in these matters. This volume draws on local and international authors, with depth and breadth in philosophy, practical affairs, and scholarship in Catholic, Christian, Islamic, Jewish, and other traditions.

In sum, this is another impressive volume in the Kapunda Press series commenced in 2018 (in association with Connor Court, publishers) for the PM Glynn Institute of the Australian Catholic University. The series' general editor, Damien Freeman, is an entrepreneur of ideas, with nine books (including this one) and another in the pipeline.

Book Review

The Persecution of George Pell

Author: Keith Windschuttle
Publisher: Quadrant Books, 2020, Sydney
ISBN: 978-0-6489961-1-8
Paperback, 408 pages
Price: $39.95

Reviewed by Damian Grace[*]

This remarkable book examines Cardinal Pell's appearances before the Royal Commission and his trials, raising important questions about the climate of prejudice in which both were conducted. Allegations that Pell sexually assaulted two boys in St Patrick's Cathedral were widely believed, and persuaded a jury to convict at his second trial. A Royal Commission made findings against him based on questionable inferences. How was this possible? Why was Pell a target? These are the questions addressed by Keith Windschuttle in *The Persecution of George Pell*, a work whose title and themes evoke *Marat/Sade.*[1]

Windschuttle's interpretation of the role of social causes, such as sexual liberation, and politicised institutions, such as Victoria Police, lead to plausible but contestable conclusions about the treatment of Pell. His analysis of evidence presented against the Cardinal is, however, accurate, thorough, and forensic. Whether critics engage with it or choose to play the man remains to be seen.

---

* Damian Grace is co-author of *Reckoning: The Catholic Church and Child Sexual Abuse* (2014).

1. The full title of Peter Weiss's play is *The Persecution and Assassination of Jean-Paul Marat as Performed by the Inmates of the Asylum of Charenton Under the Direction of the Marquis de Sade.*

'A wise man proportions his belief to the evidence', wrote David Hume, and this is exactly what Windschuttle does. The law allows acceptance of guilt on the uncorroborated evidence of one complainant. Nevertheless, the alleged events have to be possible and the allegations plausible, neither of which conditions was satisfied by the evidence against Pell. Witnesses placed him at the front of the cathedral greeting parishioners at the time the complainant said he and his friend were being assaulted. Where were the concelebrating priests if not in the priest's sacristy at the time the assaults allegedly occurred? Then there is the matter of an Archbishop wearing layer upon layer of vestments and always being accompanied by the Master of Ceremonies or a substitute. These obstacles did not stop Pell's conviction or a decision by the Court of Appeal to uphold it. Two Appeal justices found Pell's jury was entitled to discount evidence that would weaken the complainant's testimony. The High Court did not agree. It held that the Appeal Court should not have found that the jury had assessed the evidence to the required standard, and quashed Pell's conviction.

The problems of getting reliable testimony from victims of historical child abuse are well known. This partly explains why Victoria Police trawled for evidence against Pell. Evidence, however, must be tested to ensure accused persons are treated justly. The evidence of Pell's complainant fails this scrutiny. It does not follow that the falsity of his testimony makes him a liar. Nor does it follow that because he was a compelling witness, he should be believed. His evidence changed many times, and this should have weakened the case against Pell. Criticism of his testimony was diffident in the major news outlets, its shortcomings dismissed because the complainant 'survived' cross examination by Robert Richter QC. A jury believed him, but that does not mean his evidence was sound.

Could Pell get a fair trial? Don Aitkin described the 'visceral hatred' directed at Pell as unprecedented. Windschuttle agrees. The early chapters of his book examine the creation of a climate of hostility to Pell and the Catholic Church. In this context inconsistent allegations were believed by Victoria Police, whose fumbling investigation was matched by a determination to prosecute a weak case. This climate did not change with Pell's acquittal. Premier Andrews declared that he still believed the complainant. Believing the complainant had become, quite unfairly, the test of whether one took the crime of child abuse seriously. When Catholics, like Fr Frank Brennan, tried sympathetically to introduce rationality into the discussion they were accused of being deniers or worse.

After the High Court's decision, Pell's adversaries still hoped unreleased material in the report of the Royal Commission into Institutional Responses to Child Sexual Abuse would incriminate him. It did not, but it did make findings against him. The ABC website proclaimed, 'History will not be kind to George Pell'.[2] This shameless attempt at self-vindication shrivels in the light of Windschuttle's arguments. He points to flaws in the Commission's findings that should have been noticed, for example that it was 'inconceivable' that Pell did not know about Gerard Ridsdale's offending. Windschuttle points out that the use of the term, 'inconceivable', violates the Royal Commission's own Briginshaw standard that requires findings to be grounded not only in the 'satisfaction' of the commissioners, but also in the facts. It was the absence of facts that led the Commission to use the persuasive term, 'inconceivable'. The Royal Commission was also inconsistent in its findings. It accepted Father Madden's evidence that he did not know of Ridsdale's offending, but rejected the very same testimony when it supported Pell's denial that he knew about it.

Many matters in the report of the Royal Commission deserve re-examination in the light of Windschuttle's arguments. These arguments rest on evidence and logic, not on the credibility of allegations or witnesses. His method as well as his conclusions challenge the standard versions of Pell's trial and appeals, and the Royal Commission's findings. Those who have read transcripts of these proceedings will find their knowledge enriched by Windschuttle's book. For those who have relied only on the media for information about the saga of Pell, reading this book is a duty.

2. Retrieved at https://www.abc.net.au/news/2020-05-08/george-pell-royal-commission-findings-revealed/12225690/

Book Review

Prison Journal, Volume One: The Cardinal Makes His Appeal
27 February–13 July 2019

Author: George Cardinal Pell
Publisher: Ignatius Press, San Francisco, 2020
ISBN: 9781621644484
Price: $39.95
Paperback: 348 pages, no index

Reviewed by Edmund Campion*

When Cardinal George Pell went to jail, he knew he must set up a daily routine to stop himself going mad. With a Jerusalem Bible he planned serious biblical study, first of the Book of Job, next Revelation. Also he had his breviary, from which the Office psalms and readings would afford him rich material for meditation. As well there were some challenging books to stretch his mind, *War and Peace* for bedside reading, a few magazines, a 'prison rosary' and Sudoku puzzles. For exercise he could expect two half-hours alone in a small prison yard; and for relaxation Australian Rules football games on TV in his cell . . . Would these be enough? So, to maintain his mental balance, he decided to write a journal, starting with his first day in solitary confinement and kept it up daily, thus averaging two or three printed pages in this first volume.

Pell is a man of faith, which means that secularists will dislike this book while Christians may see it as spiritual reading. Seminary life was a good preparation for prison, he says. He draws strength from the redemptive sufferings of Jesus—'offering it up' in Catholic parlance. Jailtime humiliations, such as strip searches, remind him that Jesus too was humiliated (*cf.* MT 26:67–68, Mk 14:65, Lk 26:63–65,

---

* Edmund Campion taught church history at the Catholic Institute of Sydney.

Jn.19:1–3). There are telling images of him washing his socks or sweeping his cell and the exercise yard. When asked by jail officers how he was, he always replied, 'No complaints'. Once, asked whether he was in danger of self-harm or suicide, he barked (his word), 'Don't be bloody silly'. No, jail did not break him.

Daily meditation gives him material for early pages of the journal, suggesting that he intended it to be a book of spirituality. Sister Mary O'Shannassy SGS, jail chaplain, brings Holy Communion twice a week and prompts him to watch Sunday Mass on his cell TV, where he sometimes follows this with the Hillsong program and, later in the day, *Songs of Praise*. Quite soon, shoals of letters arrive from sympathisers and even prisoners (these he answers quickly, knowing the joy of mail when you're locked up).

The piles of letters open the journal to problems in the church, changing the focus of the book. There are few surprises: in this church the bishop is still the boss; and he dodges criticism of 'the Vatican' by writing about the Pope, although he allows himself to criticise Papa Ratzinger for hanging round the Vatican in his retirement. He considers Trump a barbarian 'but our (Christian) barbarian' and reckons him an argument against popular election of the president in a republic.

Throughout, his legal team has access to him to prepare an appeal against his sentence. Twice a week friends and family can make short visits; and he can telephone them from the exercise yard. On Holy Saturday (20 April) he receives a *Quadrant* article that reveals suspicious parallels between his case and maybe made-up accusations in USA. A fortnight later the appeal opens, closing the next day. Pell's legal team and his friends are jubilant, sure that he will be acquitted. He tries to rein in his optimism but it is hard going when people learned in the law keep telling him he will surely win, 3–0. So the days drag on, with no result and this volume ends on 13 July, Cardinal Pell still in the dark.

Writing to his collaborators in last century's *Bicentennial History of Australia*, KS Inglis told them to write about people who did not know what happened next—that is, Cardinal Pell's situation at the close of this volume of his prison journal. We know, but he does not, that 39 days later, on 21 August, the court will reject his appeal, 2–1. To learn how the Cardinal endures this disappointment, we must await his Volume Two.